Transformative Change and Real Utopias in Early Childhood Education

D0070975

WITHDRAWAL

Early childhood education and care is a major policy issue for national governments and international organisations. This book contests two stories, both infused by neoliberal thinking, that dominate early childhood policy making today – 'the story of quality and high returns' and 'the story of markets', stories that promise high returns on investment if only the right technologies are applied to children and the perfection of a system based on competition and individual choice.

But there are alternative stories and this book tells one: a 'story of democracy, experimentation and potentiality' in which early childhood centres are public spaces and public resources, places where democracy and experimentation are fundamental values, community workshops for realising the potentiality of citizens. This story calls for transformative change but offers a *real* utopia, both viable and achievable. The book discusses some of the conditions needed for the story's enactment and shows what it means in practice in a chapter about project work contributed by a Swedish preschool teacher.

Critical but hopeful, this book is an important contribution to resisting the dictatorship of no alternative and renewing a democratic politics of early childhood education. It is essential reading for students and teachers, researchers and other academics, and for all other concerned citizens.

Peter Moss is Emeritus Professor of Early Childhood Provision at the Institute of Education University of London, UK.

Contesting Early Childhood series
Series Editors: Gunilla Dahlberg and Peter Moss

This groundbreaking series questions the current dominant discourses surrounding early childhood, and offers instead alternative narratives of an area that is now made up of a multitude of perspectives and debates.

The series examines the possibilities and risks arising from the accelerated development of early childhood services and policies, and illustrates how it has become increasingly steeped in regulation and control. Insightfully, this collection of books shows how early childhood services can in fact contribute to ethical and democratic practices. The authors explore new ideas taken from alternative working practices in both the western and developing world, and from other academic disciplines such as developmental psychology. Current theories and best practice are placed in relation to the major processes of political, social, economic, cultural and technological change occurring in the world today.

Titles in the *Contesting Early Childhood* series include:

Moss (2014) *Transformative Change and Real Utopias in Early Childhood Education*

Sellers (2013) *Young Children becoming Curriculum*

Taylor (2013) *Reconfiguring the Natures of Childhood*

Moss (2013) *Early Childhood and Compulsory Education*

Vecchi (2010) *Art and Creativity in Reggio Emilia*

Taguchi (2009) *Going Beyond the Theory/Practice Divide*

Olsson (2009) *Movement and Experimentation in Young Children's Learning*

Edmiston (2007) *Forming Ethical Identities in Early Childhood Play*

Rinaldi (2005) *In Dialogue with Reggio Emilia*

MacNaughton (2005) *Doing Foucault in Early Childhood Studies*

Penn (2005) *Unequal Childhoods*

Dahlberg and Moss (2005) *Ethics and Politics in Early Childhood*

HARVARD UNIVERSITY
GRADUATE SCHOOL OF EDUCATION
MONROE C. GUTMAN LIBRARY

Transformative Change and Real Utopias in Early Childhood Education

A story of democracy, experimentation and potentiality

Peter Moss

Routledge
Taylor & Francis Group

LONDON AND NEW YORK

HARVARD UNIVERSITY
GRADUATE SCHOOL OF EDUCATION
MONROE C. GUTMAN LIBRARY

First published 2014
by Routledge
2 Park Square, Milton Park, Abingdon, Oxon OX14 4RN

and by Routledge
711 Third Avenue, New York, NY 10017

Routledge is an imprint of the Taylor & Francis Group, an informa business

© 2014 Peter Moss

The right of Peter Moss to be identified as author of this work has
been asserted by him in accordance with sections 77 and 78 of the
Copyright, Designs and Patents Act 1988.

All rights reserved. No part of this book may be reprinted or reproduced
or utilised in any form or by any electronic, mechanical, or other means,
now known or hereafter invented, including photocopying and recording,
or in any information storage or retrieval system, without permission in
writing from the publishers.

Trademark notice: Product or corporate names may be trademarks or
registered trademarks, and are used only for identification and
explanation without intent to infringe.

British Library Cataloguing in Publication Data
A catalogue record for this book is available from the British Library

Library of Congress Cataloging-in-Publication Data
Moss, Peter.
    Transformative change and real utopias in early childhood education : a story of
    democracy, experimentation and potentiality / Peter Moss.
        pages cm
    Includes bibliographical references and index.
    ISBN 978-0-415-65600-9 (hardback)—ISBN 978-0-415-65601-6 (paperback)—
    ISBN 978-1-315-77990-4 (ebook) 1. Early childhood education. 2. Early childhood
    education—Social aspects. 3. Democracy and education. 4. Education and state.
    5. Educational change. I. Title.
    LB1139.23.M676 2014
    372.21—dc23
                                    2013040781

ISBN: 978-0-415-65600-9 (hbk)
ISBN: 978-0-415-65601-6 (pbk)
ISBN: 978-1-315-77990-4 (ebk)

Typeset in Bembo
by Swales & Willis Ltd, Exeter, Devon

Printed and bound in the United States of America by Publishers Graphics,
LLC on sustainably sourced paper.

Contents

Acknowledgements

A book such as this, which draws on many years of work, is only made possible by inspirational encounters with many other people, all of whom have shown in one way or another that there are alternatives. Too numerous to name each individual, I would single out four people whose work has been particularly influential: Jack Tizard, Gunilla Dahlberg, Michael Fielding and John Bennett. I would also like to mention the members of the European Commission Childcare Network; partners in the multinational magazine *Children in Europe*; other authors in the *Contesting Early Childhood* series; and the educators in Reggio Emilia.

I have benefited greatly from the astute but sympathetic comments of three readers of an earlier draft of the book: Rianne Mahon, Ann Phoenix and Rosemary Moss. I take total responsibility for the final text as it appears here. Finally, my thanks to Alison Foyle, my editor at Routledge, who has been unfailingly supportive.

Chapter 1

Telling stories, transformative change and real utopias

> We believe that the roots of [the converging crises of our times] lie in the stories we have been telling ourselves . . . We will reassert the role of story-telling as more than mere entertainment. It is through stories that we weave reality.
>
> (Dark Mountain Project, 2009a)

The Dark Mountain Project is a network of writers, artists and thinkers 'who have stopped believing the stories our civilisation tells itself . . . [as the world enters] an age of ecological collapse, material contraction and social and political unraveling'. These once potent but now unbelievable stories, they contend:

> tell us that humanity is separate from all other life and destined to control it; that the ecological and economic crises we face are mere technical glitches; that anything which cannot be measured cannot matter. But these stories are losing their power. We see them falling apart before our eyes.
>
> (Dark Mountain Project, 2009b)

Like the Dark Mountain Project, I believe the stories we tell ourselves are important. It is through stories – with their images and assumptions, their hopes and fears – that 'we weave reality', giving meaning to the world, making sense of our experiences. Stories are highly productive in other ways, too. Not only do they shape what we think of as problems, but also how we respond to these problems, including the policies, the provisions, the practices we adopt and work with; 'they determine our direction and destination'.

This book appears in a series that recognises the importance of story-telling for an approach to early childhood education that adopts a critical stance and values plurality; *Contesting Early Childhood* 'questions the current dominant discourses in early childhood, and offers alternative narratives of an area that is now made up of a multitude of perspectives and debates'. In such a spirit, this book is about the stories – both dominant and alternative – that we do tell or that we could tell about 'early childhood education', by which I mean those formal services whose stated intention is care and/or learning for children under compulsory school age, both under and over 3 years of age. These services, in the English-speaking world, go under many different names – nurseries, crèches, kindergartens, long-day care centres, nursery schools and classes, children's centres, playgroups, preschools, and more besides – and in other languages have many, many other names. Early childhood education so defined encompasses much variation, not only in names used but also in how services define themselves and their purposes. It includes services that adopt a narrowly educational remit and those described, equally narrowly, as 'childcare services', as well as those that openly acknowledge combining education and care or, indeed, consider education and care to be inseparable.

I also recognise that these services have the potentiality for doing much more besides education and care. They are capable of many other projects and purposes, an important point to which I will return. So in choosing the term 'early childhood education', I realise its meaning is contestable; and that later on in this book I must examine further my own understanding of 'education', an understanding that embraces a holistic and inclusive concept – 'education-in-its-broadest sense'.

But the book is not just about early childhood education. For early childhood education cannot, any more than any other sector of education, be abstracted and isolated from the world: it is a child of its times and was ever so. Stories about early childhood education are necessarily framed and shaped by other and more epic stories, meta-narratives about the political economy, the social condition, the environment – in short, stories about the state we are in. Like the Dark Mountain Project, I believe the world has entered into 'an age of ecological collapse, material contraction and social and political unraveling': a story about early childhood education that has nothing to say about this, a story that takes more of the same for granted, a story that blithely speaks of investing in the future or preparing children to succeed in the global race without interrogating what that future might be or the sustainability of that global race, that story just will not do. Like the Dark Mountain Project, also, I reject stories, whether about the environment or early childhood education, that are about control, calculation and technical practice; they are 'losing their power' and 'falling apart before our eyes'. And like the Dark Mountain Project, I believe '[n]ew stories are needed for darker, more uncertain times'.

This book is a contribution to telling new stories about early childhood education, those alternative narratives that this series celebrates. But though the times are dark and uncertain, and the new stories need be under no illusions, neither need they be stories of unmitigated doom and gloom. They can offer hope that another world is possible, a world that is more equal, democratic and sustainable, a world where surprise and wonder, diversity and complexity find their rightful place in early childhood education, indeed all education. They can offer faith in people, of all ages, and their potentialities. They can offer us cause to believe in the world again.

From the start I must admit a certain ambivalence towards my subject. I am a long-term enthusiast for early childhood education, who finds that today it has gained a high profile among the movers and shakers of contemporary life. It is, seemingly, the favourite, must-have policy of every think tank, every national government and every international organisation! Yet rather than feeling unalloyed pleasure at this turn of events, I am left with a feeling of deep unease. Like all education, early childhood education should and can be an important public service and public resource for children and their families, for communities and for wider society; it has great potential for emancipation, for bringing something new to life, for fostering important values such as equality, democracy and sustainability. But the spirit of Michel Foucault (1926–1984) whispers in my ears, 'everything is dangerous' (1983, p. 232). So I recognise that early childhood education, like all education, has another potential: for governing children and adults alike, for reproducing the already known, for inculcating belief in necessity and essentialism, and for fostering the values of and the subjectivity required by a rapacious, technocratic and harmful economic regime.

Early childhood education, like all education, is at issue. It is not self-evidently a good thing, but an institution and practice to be critiqued and contested. Which leads back to stories, since that is one way in which the contest can take place: contrasting stories confronting each other, offering listeners conflicting alternatives.

I will start by telling a story about early childhood education that is today much heard around the world, what I will call 'the story of quality and high returns'. It is a story of control and calculation, technology and measurement that, in a nutshell, goes like this. Find, invest in and apply the correct human technologies – aka 'quality' – during early childhood and you will get high returns on investment including improved education, employment and earnings and reduced social problems. A simple equation beckons and beguiles: 'early intervention' + 'quality' = increased 'human capital' + national success (or at least survival) in a cut-throat global economy. Invest early and invest smartly and we will all live happily ever after in a world of more of the same – only more so. Reassured by this story of early childhood education as a technical solution to some of our most immediate problems and anxieties, it is tempting to sign up to it rather than ask difficult questions about what sort of world we want or embark on the hard, messy and political task of clearing the deepening slough of inequality and injustice that breeds so many of the social problems that early childhood education is supposed to solve.

Familiar as it is, I find the story of quality and high returns both troubling and unsatisfying. It seems to have forgotten it is a story, one way of making sense of the world, one of many narratives that can be told. Instead, it projects itself as a factual documentary that gives a true account of how the world really is. It strives to become, to use a Foucauldian term, a 'dominant discourse', seeking to apply a decisive influence on a particular subject, in this case early childhood education. It does so by projecting and imposing a 'regime of truth' that exercises power over our thoughts and actions, directing or governing what we see as the 'truth' and how we construct the world: it makes 'assumptions and values invisible, turn[s] subjective perspectives and understandings into apparently objective truths, and determine[s] that some things are self-evident and realistic while others are dubious and impractical' (Dahlberg and Moss, 2005, p. 17). Such dominant discourses provide the mechanism for rendering reality amenable to certain kinds of actions (Miller and Rose, 1993) – and by so doing, they also exclude other ways of understanding and interpreting the world, marginalising other stories that could be told.

From local beginnings, emerging from a particular spatial and temporal context, to be precise from the English-speaking world in the 1980s, the story of quality and high returns has been borne far and wide by the economic *zeitgeist*, positivistic science[1] and the English language. It has crossed borders and gained international credibility in a process of hegemonic globalisation, 'the successful globalisation of a particular local and culturally-specific discourse to the point that it makes universal truth claims and "localises" all rival discourses' (Santos, 2004, p. 149). A local story has gone viral, become an international best seller. Now all sorts of people, from politicians to practitioners, academics to media commentators, talk the same talk around the world, telling themselves and others the same story over and over and over again.

So this discourse, this story of quality and high returns, has abandoned its local roots, forgotten it is just another local tale, claiming instead to tell a universal truth as if its way of talking about things is natural, neutral and necessary. In so doing, the story drowns out other stories about early childhood education, alternative ways of making meaning of the world, rendering them unimaginable and unspeakable, limiting what it is possible to think. Whether in high profile research reviews, official reports or conference presentations, certain privileged voices are heard time and again re-iterating the story, while other voices telling other stories are heard not at all or only faintly. This much-told story has made some things familiar and others strange, whilst stifling critical thinking and questioning by its pretensions to being self-evident, proven and undeniable.

I am troubled, therefore, by the way this story, of quality and high returns, marginalises other story-telling about early childhood education, striving to impose DONA – a 'dictatorship of no alternatives' (Unger, 2005a, p. 1) – on early childhood education. (DONA is the first cousin of TINA – 'there is no alternative' – much beloved of Margaret Thatcher and other politicians when seeking to impose their views, rubbish those of others and head off democratic debate.) But I am troubled in other ways. The story seems to me incredible: which would not matter since magic realism has its place in story-telling, only the story tellers insist they tell objective truth, that they really do have the one right answer, and others act on this claim. Nor do I like the politics that pervades the story, expressed in the answers it assumes or espouses to the political questions that define education. Last but not least, I fear its consequences, arising from the will to control and govern children and adults alike that is inscribed in the story.

But I am not only troubled. I am left deeply unsatisfied by the story itself and the way it is told: by its lack of curiosity, imagination and originality; by its instrumental rationality and reductionist logic that eschews complexity and context; and by the banality and dullness of its language. Told repeatedly, the story of quality and high returns has drained education of its potential to amaze and surprise, to invoke wonder and passion, to emancipate and experiment, leaving instead a lifeless husk of facile repetition and clichéd vocabulary: 'evidence-based' . . . 'programmes' . . . 'quality' . . .'investment' . . . 'outcomes' . . . 'returns' . . . 'assessment scales' . . . 'human capital'. This is a story told in the desiccated language of the managerial memo, the technical manual and the financial balance sheet. Not to put too fine a point on it, the story of quality and high returns dulls and deadens the spirit, reducing the potentially exciting and vibrant subject of early childhood education to 'a one-dimensional linear reductive thinking that *excludes and closes off* all other ways of thinking and doing' (Lenz Taguchi, 2010a, p. 17; original emphasis).

I go into this story, and my problems with it, in more detail in the next chapter. I also introduce there another story that is spreading in early childhood education, and that likewise troubles me deeply: the story of markets. This is a story about commodification, competition and (individual) choice, and (like the story of quality and high returns) the reduction of early childhood education to a set of economic relationships and quantitative variables. In Chapter 3, I put forward one reason why these two stories have such a powerful hold today, demonstrating how both stories relate to a much larger story about competition and choice, calculation and contracts: the meta-narrative of neoliberalism. It is this story, I will contend, that has provided a favourable context for the spread in early childhood education of the stories of quality and high returns and of markets, whilst cautioning against adopting too simplistic a view of neoliberalism and too reductive a notion of causation.

In Chapter 4 I will tell *an* other – not *the* other – story about early childhood education, what I call the story of democracy, experimentation and potentiality, an education built upon and inscribed with two fundamental values – democracy and experimentation – and a belief in the endless and unknowable potentialities of people and the institutions they create. This is a story that I like, that I find attractive and satisfying. It is a story that attaches the utmost importance to early childhood education, but for reasons quite different from the story of quality and high returns. Nor does it have any sympathy with the story of markets, and its fetish of commodification, competition and choice. My story contests these stories and resists DONA, insisting there are alternatives, with different rationales and rationalities – and that all should be heard and debated.

For just as my aim is not to undermine the case for early childhood education, neither is it to impose a new censorship, to replace one DONA with another. There are many stories to be told about early childhood education, and about education more generally, and others may certainly choose the story of quality and high returns, the story of markets, or any other story – if they find that story to their liking, if it makes meaning for them of the world *and* if they acknowledge and welcome the presence of other stories and have, at the very least, taken the trouble to listen to some of them. You may not agree with other stories: but you should be aware they exist and know what some of them say, and only then decide which story you like and wish to tell.

I not only tell the story of democracy, experimentation and potentiality in Chapter 4, but explore its origins. Where has this story come from? The origins are to be found in answers, my answers, to political questions, treating early childhood education (like all education) as first and foremost a political practice involving choices that need to be made between conflicting alternatives. Democracy and experimentation are part of the answer I offer to one of these questions: what are the fundamental values of education? Given the particularly important part they have in my story, Chapter 5 is devoted to considering these values in greater detail, as well as the relationship between them. While Chapter 6 gives an example of the story of democracy, experimentation and potentiality being enacted in practice in the Crow Project, an account of a year's work in a Swedish preschool[2] narrated by Ann Åberg, a Swedish educator.

At a time when the stories of quality and high returns and of markets hog the sound waves and hold such sway over policy and practice, the story of democracy, experimentation and potentiality calls for transformative change through a real utopian project, a project that not only holds out hope of a better future but also pays careful attention to what is needed to attain that future. This is the subject of Chapter 7. Here I ask: how might the institution of early childhood education be re-designed, what conditions might be needed to enable the story of democracy, experimentation and possibility to establish and flourish?

I conclude with a chapter about why transformative change is possible and why we should not subside into acquiescence and despond in the shadows cast by DONA and the juggernaut of neoliberalism. I urge readers to think historically, to see the present as but a moment in time, and to remember that what may seem self-evident, incontrovertible and inevitable today, may have seemed inconceivable but a few decades ago – and could seem so again in a few decades time. Crises create fertile ground for change and there can be little doubt that we are living in a time of deepening and converging crises, which will see today's dominant stories 'losing their power', making room for others more attuned to humankind's condition and hopes. Indeed, we should not forget that some of these other stories are already to be heard by those who listen carefully, and that such stories are not just being told: they are being put to work in early childhood centres, by educators and others. In such instances, some of which appear in this book, a transformed future is already emerging through a prefigurative practice, a practice of possibility.

This is my plan and these are my hopes for the book. But before moving on to Chapter 2, I want to devote some space to considering the meaning of the two terms I have just introduced and that figure so prominently in this book: 'transformative change' and 'real utopias'.

Transformative change

This is a book about change, or the possibility of change, and about the change that might be wrought by telling ourselves a different story about early childhood education. But not just about any change, for this is a book about *transformative* change. To counsel the need for change is hardly original. 'Change' is one of those words, like 'quality', that is everywhere, indeed the *zeitgeist* is about the imperative of change as a necessary condition for survival in a ruthless world: change or be a loser, we are constantly admonished. But the ubiquity of change, even 'transformative change', does not mean it has a universally agreed meaning so I need to discuss what meaning I attach to the concept. To clear the decks, I can say first what I don't mean.

'Transformative change' is not what Foucault terms 'superficial transformation': that is 'transformation that remains within the same mode of thought, a transformation that is only a way of adjusting the same thought more closely to the reality of things' (1988, p. 154). This is change that does not open up new perspectives, new understandings, new ways of seeing and relating to the world. This is change that, in the words of social theorist Roberto Unger, is 'reformist tinkering with the established system . . . [consisting] simply in the accumulation of practical solutions to practical problems' (Unger, 2004, p. lviii). Such change represents much of today's policy and organisational change, constantly introducing new procedures, new techniques and new structures but retaining the same mode of thought and the same direction of travel: for example, in early childhood education, better technologies to improve quality and increase returns on investment or steps taken to improve the workings of markets.

But neither is 'transformative change' revolution, if by that is meant the replacement of one dominant regime, one indivisible totality by another through a sudden rupture. One DONA swept away, another taking its place. So transformative change is definitely not 'big, systemic alternatives, like capitalism and socialism, overcome or inaugurated in great moments of sweeping change' (ibid.).

'Transformative change' is not a neoliberal understanding of change as so-called 'creative destruction', a ceaseless and restless search for new, improved or cheaper products or services driven by the need to create new demand and increase profit, discarding the past and the present in the process as a drag on future growth, indifferent to the suffering caused by destruction as an unavoidable price to be paid. Such febrile change is deeply implicated in the crisis enveloping our species for, as ecological economist Tim Jackson describes in his report *Prosperity without Growth*:

> [t]he relentless pursuit of novelty creates an anxiety that can undermine
> social wellbeing. Individuals are at the mercy of social comparison. Firms
> must innovate or die. Institutions are skewed towards the pursuit of a mate-
> rialistic consumerism. The economy itself is dependent on consumption
> growth for its very survival. The 'iron cage of consumerism' is a system in
> which no one is free. It's an anxious, and ultimately a pathological system.
>
> (Jackson, 2009, p. 9)

In education and other public services, this anxious, restless change takes the
form of incessant reviews, rushed reforms and hurried evaluations.

Nor do I understand transformative change as the description of a transitory
episode, a moment of movement from one static position to another. This
common understanding of change draws on a 'Parmenidean[3] intellectual legacy
which implicitly elevates permanence over change, discreteness over immanent
interconnectedness, linear progress over heterogeneous becoming, and equi-
librium over flux and transformation' (Chia, 1999, pp. 225–6). I agree with
Liselott Mariett Olsson, writing in this series, that '[m]oving from one position
to another is just shadow movement; it is a change of position and not continuous movement. Movement and experimentation in subjectivity and learning
are subordinated to the outcome and to position' (Olsson, 2009, p. 6).

What then do I consider to be transformative change? It starts by telling
a new story, or put another way adopting a new mode of thought, thinking
differently, which, in Foucault's terms, occurs when 'one can no longer think
things as one formerly thought them'. With this new story, we weave a new
reality, viewing the world in a different light from a different perspective – the
familiar is made strange, what was formerly self-evident no longer seems so.
Then, once we can no longer think things as we formerly thought them, 'transformation becomes both very urgent, very difficult and quite possible'.

Transformative change is the antithesis of 'creative destruction'. The past
and the present are not simply to be discarded and disowned, left behind in
an endless, restless search for productivity, performance and profit. They are
instead to be valued for the important contributions they can make to the
future, especially when thinking differently helps us see the past and present in
a new light, enabling new connections to be made to experiences and traditions
that we might not have seen before or previously saw in a different way. We
can then rediscover the importance of historical or contemporary figures and
movements to the alternative stories that contest the dominant stories that have
overlooked or spurned such figures and movements. The future is immanent in
the present, which has itself emerged from the potentiality of the past. Creative
destruction may make sense where the preeminent goals are creating new consumer demand, clearing-out inefficient businesses and driving sales and return
on investment; but not where reviving long-standing goals such as democracy,
social justice or sustainability is concerned, and where past traditions and experiences still speak to present struggles and future possibilities.

Transformative change, too, is about opening up to a continuous state of movement, not just a short burst of movement whilst traversing from one static position to another. This idea of the world in a constant state of flux and emergence is especially important. French philosopher Felix Guattari (1930–1992) writes that '[l]ife is a work in progress, with no goal in sight, only the tireless endeavour to explore new possibilities, to respond to the chance event – the singular point – that takes us off in a new direction' (2000, p. 13). Such an idea is found in pre-Socratic Greek philosophy[4] and re-emerges in the work of Leibniz (1646–1716), Bergson (1859–1941) and Whitehead (1861–1947). It is, argues Chia:

> this resurrecting of the primacy of movement and change over that of stabilised entities and end-states which provides a radically alternative view for understanding movement and change in general . . . According to the revised perspective, our experience of the world around us, particularly of what we call 'living systems' is one of inherent becoming and perishing.
>
> (1999, p. 217)

Or, to bring matters closer to our subject of early childhood education, we can look to the pedagogical thinking and practice of Loris Malaguzzi (1920–1994), the first director of early childhood education in the Italian city of Reggio Emilia, an educational experience of great importance to which much reference is made throughout this book. As Alfredo Hoyuelos writes, in his study of Malaguzzi's ethical stance:

> According to Loris Malaguzzi's ethical conception, variability or change is an invariable element of life. Change should be understood not as the transition from one state to another, but rather as the permanent state of human existence – not the permanency of pre-established ideas, but the permanent capacity to modify and change behaviours as a function of the essential variability of the human being. One of Malaguzzi's teachings is to avoid getting caught in any cage, even if it is made of gold.
>
> (2013, p. 329)

Or we can draw on Olsson's study of pedagogical work in Swedish preschools, inspired by the theoretical ideas of philosophers Gilles Deleuze (1925–1995) and Felix Guattari:

> [W]hat has been looked for both in practice and theory are ways of working with *change as something continuously ongoing and as something more than effecting a move from one predefined position to another*. Questions have been asked about how to work, practically and theoretically, with the driving forces at stake before everything has settled again into new patterns. In short, what has become the latest challenge to practice and research is finding ways of *regaining movement and experimentation in subjectivity and learning*.
>
> (2009, p. 8; emphasis added)

Following this line of thought, with the importance it attaches to continuous movement and to emergence, possibilities and becoming, and drawing also on Deleuzian theoretical perspectives, Chia argues for a '"rhizomic" model of organisational change', which views change as complex, continuous and unpredictable:

> Change takes place by variations, restless expansion, opportunistic con-quests, sudden captures and offshoots. Rhizomic change is anti-genealogical in the sense that it resists the linear retracing of a definite locatable originary point of initiation . . . Change, renewal and transformation develop along locally identifiable lines of least resistance rather than according to any pre-designed template.
>
> (1999, pp. 222–3)

Change, in this sense, is not predictable, either in process or outcome. It is not a planned progress from A to B, a straight line from one known position to another taken without deviation. Rather, change is a constant process with no starting or ending point, in which wonder and surprise are important elements. Philippa Bennett (2009) suggests that the most fundamental and radical aspect of wonder is 'revolutionary potential', while for Chia the:

> element of surprise, and hence creativity and novelty, is necessarily built into the very core of change and transformation . . . [O]utcomes of change can, in principle, be always 'other than' that which is expected . . . Change always implies 'surprise' and otherness because of its essentially indeter-minate character . . . [W]hat actually does happen is always a unique and never-to-be-repeated coalescence of a multiplicity of potentialities.
>
> (ibid., pp. 223, 224, 226)

Transformative change, then, begets a state of continuous movement: not the closure that comes from achieving a new and desired but static state of being, but the open-endedness of constant becoming. This is transformational change as a long-term project, capable of taking unexpected directions and of being a con-tinual source of surprise. This is transformational change not as creative destruc-tion but as constant creative construction, working with the past and the present to enable the emergence of something new, the realisation of potentiality.

Can such transformational change accommodate the element of intention-ality, that is if we intend and want transformative change to move in a par-ticular direction? For example, if we want early childhood education to turn away from the story of quality and high returns and move towards the story of democracy, experimentation and potentiality, a story that welcomes wonder and amazement, unpredictability and surprise, the chance event and the unex-pected line of flight. In which case we do need to get from here to there, from one story to another, and that means a sense of direction matters.

For Unger, direction does matters; it is vital to the process of transformative change, a process that consists of continuous movement. For him, the central question is 'where to?' Change is a sequence of steps, piecemeal but incremental and cumulative, setting in train not a sudden rupture, but a gradual curving away from where we are now towards where we want to be. An essential component of this type of change is experimentation, or more specifically 'democratic experimentalism', 'the organisation of a collective experimental practice from below' providing opportunities to try out different ways of doing things – 'different forms of life, as well as experiments in the lives of people and in the activities of groups' (Unger, 2004, p. civ).

This process of change Unger calls 'radical reform'. It is 'the piecemeal but *motivated and directed* reconstruction of the institutional arrangements and the enacted beliefs we ordinarily take for granted' (ibid., p. xxi; emphasis added). And it is the:

> combination of parts and the succession of steps, reaching far beyond the starting point, and changing along the way our understanding of our interests, ideals, and identities, that makes a reform project relatively more radical. [While] it is the direction in which the steps take us that make it more or less democratic.
>
> (1998, p. 19)

'Radical reform', as envisaged by Unger, seems full of movement, yet movement constrained to some extent, or rather channelled by political purpose defined by answers to the question 'where to?' How that purpose is decided can be 'more or less democratic'.

As I understand the term, transformative change means the telling of a new story about early childhood education. It offers one answer to the question 'where to?' But more than just telling. Transformative change involves very different ways of thinking about education, but also very different ways of doing education – 'motivated and directed reconstruction'. I want the new story to be put to work, shaping policy, provision and practice in early childhood education. Not because this story claims to be the truth, the one and only answer, and not because it seeks to drown out or banish other stories. I want the story to be put to work because, hopefully, it resonates with the values and hopes of many listeners and convinces politically and ethically. Moreover, I want other stories about early childhood education to be not only told, but listened to, in a democratic politics of education, with the possibility acknowledged that they may prove more appealing than mine. My story must take its chances along with others.

Telling a new story, and putting it to work, will require much and continuous movement, productive of gradual cumulative change in the process of 'radical reform' described by Unger. But I also want my own preferred story to be capable of constant evolution, to generate revised versions and

sequels – in response to new conditions, new perspectives, new understandings. It sets a direction, but that direction can be altered over time, it is not
fixed for ever. And I want the education in this story to be an education of
movement and experimentation, capable of taking off in unexpected ways and
different directions, generating new thought and new perspectives, provoking
surprise and amazement. So I am arguing the case for movement to a story that
is itself about movement.

Just as a desire for surprise and amazement does not mean abandoning all
intentionality, nor does it mean discarding all common intent. A public education of democracy, experimentation and potentiality can and should, I believe,
have certain shared, agreed values, purposes and goals, a common predetermined core. But it will also aim – in this story – to keep a large space open for
that which is not predetermined, for what we do not yet know, for the emergence of new knowledge, for movement and experimentation, for thought. In
the words of Reggio Emilia *atelierista*[5] Vea Vecchi, '[i]t is important to society
that schools and we as teachers are clearly aware how much space we leave
children for original thinking, without rushing to restrict it with predetermined
schemes that define what is *correct* according to a school culture' (Vecchi, 2010,
p. 138; original emphasis).

There is a tension here, in my thinking about transformative change and in
the story I will tell of democracy, experimentation and potentiality: between
what is held in common and what is open to diversity, between movement
and intentionality, between the reproduction of what is currently valued and
the construction of the not-yet known and valued. There is no neat formula
or solution to remove that tension. All we can do is acknowledge its existence
and work the tension, making it the subject of research, experimentation and
democratic deliberation.

Real utopias

Utopias do not always get a good press. For some they are just irrelevant and
unattainable abstractions, mere dreams or pie in the sky, of no use whatever to
those who live in the 'real' world. To others, they seem dangerous: this is especially true of 'classical "blueprint" utopianism [that] has been at best eliminative
of difference and at worst authoritarian' (Anderson, 2006, p. 691), leading all
too readily to totalitarianism (Gray, 2007). This totalitarian idea of utopia is,
researcher on utopia Ruth Levitas observes, 'implicit in most lay usage of the
term [and] is of a perfect society which is impossible and unattainable. It is
either an idle dream or, if attempts are made to create that society, a dangerous
illusion' (2003, p. 3). Such utopias readily become dystopias.

But it need not be like this. Carefully and critically handled, utopian thinking can be a constructive force, both emancipatory and pragmatic. Emancipatory because it helps us escape the clutches of DONA, creating 'space for challenging what is, for disrupting dominant assumptions about social and spatial

organisation, and for imagining other possibilities and desires' (Pinder, 2002, p. 238). It is an urgent reminder, if needed, that there are alternatives. It requires us to think about where we are now and where we want to be, and if what we have now is really inevitable and the only life possible. As sociologist Boaventura de Sousa Santos puts it, 'by utopia I mean the exploration by imagination of new modes of human possibility and styles of will, and the confrontation by imagination of the necessity of whatever exists – just because it exists – on behalf of something radically better that is worth fighting for' (Santos, 1995, p. 479). Utopian thinking leads us, therefore, to an awareness that another world is possible – that early childhood education, for instance, could be thought and done differently. By so doing, it gives vent to our longings and desires for a better way of living and being.

Such utopian thinking calls for certain qualities of mind. A critical attitude 'towards those things that are given to our present experience as if they were timeless, natural, unquestionable' (Rose, 1999, p. 20), and capable therefore of resisting the claims to necessity of what already exists just because it does exist. The curiosity and imagination of the border crosser, willing to transgress in search of new perspectives, eager to explore alternatives. The desire to innovate and experiment, to see what might be possible. The capacity for wonder, 'the willingness to be perceptive and receptive to the opportunities for wonder that present themselves to us on a daily basis . . . [and] to allow those opportunities to affect, and perhaps transform us' (Bennett, 2009, p. 13). The courage to hope that a better world is conceivable and possible. Not to mention a facility with self-criticism and self-deprecation that keeps utopian thought under continuous sceptical questioning and acknowledges the existence and validity of other perspectives.

Utopian thinking, so understood, has much in common with some forms of story-telling, both exploring alternate ways of thinking and being. But as Levitas reminds us, utopian thinking is not just about an imaginative search for alternatives, a 'quest for the substance of human flourishing . . . a process of the imaginary reconstitution of society, which involves looking holistically at alternative modes of livelihood and social organisation'. It is also about practicalities: a 'quest for its conditions' *and* considering 'means of transition' (2008, p. 90). It should be pragmatic as well as emancipatory. This calls for practical qualities, in particular a capacity to analyse, design and build that goes beyond simply envisioning utopian alternatives to working out how they might be realised: what might make a better world not only conceivable but possible. This is what philosopher Ernst Bloch called 'concrete utopia', as opposed to the 'abstract utopia' of wishful thinking that is merely fantastic (Levitas, 2010). This, too, is Unger's radical reform, working pragmatically and steadily towards the desired direction; and it is what sociologist Erik Olin Wright has termed 'real utopias', a mixture of imagination and what is pragmatically possible.

It is to Wright's work that I now turn, since there is much here that resonates with what I am trying to do, not least the attention given later in the book to the design of and conditions for a transformed early childhood educa-tion. Wright's work on 'real utopias' is grounded on three principles or values – equality, democracy, sustainability – and a claim and a thesis:

> Many forms of human suffering and many deficits in human flourishing are the result of existing institutions and social structures.
>
> Transforming those institutions and structures has the potential to sub-stantially reduce human suffering and expand the possibilities for human flourishing.
>
> (Wright, 2012)

Public education might be counted as one of these institutions, with a potential already acknowledged both for harm and for good. Wright suggests there are two approaches to be taken to such institutions: ameliorative reforms, which seek to identify institutional flaws and propose improvements; and real uto-pias, which involve envisioning an alternative world, then looking at ways to re-design and hence transform institutions that will move us towards that des-tination. In this concept of 'real utopias', Wright seeks to embrace the tension between dreams and practice, arguing their complementarity:

> '[U]topia' implies developing visions of alternatives to existing institutions that embody our deepest aspirations for a world in which all people have access to the conditions to live flourishing lives; 'real' means taking seri-ously the problem of the viability of the institutions that could move us in the direction of that world. The goal is to elaborate utopian ideals that are grounded in the real potentials of humanity, utopian destinations that have accessible way stations, utopian designs of viable institutions that can inform our practical tasks of navigating a world of imperfect conditions for social change.
>
> (Wright, 2013)

Practical considerations lie at the heart of Wright's approach: institutional design; accessible way stations – 'intermediate institutional innovations that move us in the right direction but only partially embody those values' (Wright, 2007, p. 38); attention to navigating imperfect conditions; and criteria for elab-orating and evaluating real utopias. He proposes three such criteria – desir-ability, viability and achievability. Desirability is about laying out values, ethics and goals:

> [O]ne asks the question: what are the moral principles that a given alterna-tive is supposed to serve? This is the domain of pure utopian social theory and much normative political philosophy. Typically such discussions are institutionally very thin, the emphasis being on the enunciation of abstract principles rather than actual institutional designs
>
> (ibid., p. 27)

Viability is about designing new policies and institutions based on desirable principles. It is:

> a response to the perpetual objection to radical egalitarian proposals 'it sounds good on paper, but it will never work' . . . [The exploration of viability focuses] on the likely dynamics and unintended consequences of the proposal if it were to be implemented. Two kinds of analysis are especially pertinent here: systematic theoretical models of how particular social structures and institutions would work, and empirical studies of cases, both historical and contemporary, where at least some aspects of the proposal have been tried.
>
> (ibid.)

Achievability is about the process of transformation and the practical political work of strategies for social change: 'It asks of proposals for social change that have passed the test of desirability and viability, what it would take to actually implement them' (ibid., p. 27). Wright argues that these three criteria are 'nested in a kind of hierarchy: Not all desirable alternatives are viable, and not all viable alternatives are achievable' (Wright, 2006, p. 96).

Wright, like Unger, seeks transformative change; and, like Unger, he sees this as involving a gradual and intensely practical process of design, experimentation, study, learning, taking stock. But always with a desirable end in mind, an answer to the question 'where to?', which in Wright's case is 'a world in which all people have access to the conditions to live flourishing lives'. No quick fixes or magic potions here, only a long, hard slog; steady movement sustained by the vision of a better life. Visionary alternatives that take viability seriously, and have achievability always in mind. Visionary alternatives, also, that are not fixed and dogmatically pursued, but are provisional, subject to reflection and deliberation, with direction open to amendment, not an imperative to be relentlessly pursued come what may.

It is in this spirit of real utopian thinking that I offer an other story of early childhood education – the story of democracy, experimentation and potentiality with its narrative of a flourishing future – and consider not only the transformative change it could bring about, its desirability, but also the conditions for its realisation: how it might be brought about, the viability and achievability of this desirable future, what could make it a *real* utopia. Knowing the direction of travel, what steps would we take? How would we re-design the institution of early childhood education? What conditions might be needed to sustain the re-designed institution, an early childhood education inscribed with values of democracy and experimentation? How can it retain movement, a capacity for taking new lines of flight? How can it avoid closure, remaining instead emergent, becoming, welcoming of wonder, surprise and the new? Why, in the face of the neoliberal juggernaut, might we think that it could be achievable?

I return to these questions later in the book, in Chapters 7 and 8 – though they are big questions and I don't claim to have all or even most of the answers. Indeed this real utopia is only partially designed, more a series of sketches than a set of detailed propositions. For now though I turn to look in more detail at the two stories that are much heard in today's early childhood education: the story of quality and high returns and the story of markets. It is away from the dominance of these stories and their damaging consequences that I want to see early childhood education move, towards a richer and more diverse narrative anthology including (but not only) the story of democracy, experimentation and potentiality.

Notes

1 By 'positivistic' I refer to research that believes in the possibility of gaining true or valid knowledge of a real world through the application of scientific method; searches for natural laws or generalisable conclusions; and places a strong emphasis on quantitative methods and statistical analyses. The researcher is assumed to be objective, observing the world from a position outside of it to gain a true representation.
2 Preschools (forskolen) are centres for children from 12 months to 6 years of age, and are the main form of early childhood provision in Sweden; the great majority of Swedish children will attend a preschool for at least 3 years.
3 After Parmenides of Elea, a Greek philosopher of the early fifth century BCE, who privileged reality and considered change impossible and existence timeless.
4 Heraclitus of Ephesus, a Greek philosopher of the late sixth century BCE, is an important precursor of this thinking, emphasising 'the primacy of a changeable and emergent world, whilst Parmenides, his successor, insisted upon the permanent and unchangeable nature of reality' (Chia, 1999, p. 214). One of the best known aphorisms of Heraclitus, encapsulating his ideas of flow and flux, is that 'You cannot step into the same river twice, for fresh waters are ever flowing in upon you'. The Parmenidean view has, however, 'decisively prevailed over Heraclitean thinking in the West and has led to impressive achievements in the sciences' (ibid.).
5 An educator with a background in visual arts working alongside teachers in early childhood education in Reggio Emilia and in some other places.

Two early childhood education stories

Quality and high returns and markets

In this chapter I delve further into two stories much-heard in early childhood education today: what I term the 'story of quality and high returns' and the 'story of markets'. I consider each story line in more detail. But I also take a critical perspective. I explain why I don't find either story appealing, indeed why I don't like them at all.

In the next chapter I consider how the stories relate to each other and to a third story, much larger in scope and ambition: the 'story of neoliberalism'. I shall recount this story in some detail in that chapter: but for now it can be summarised as being about a world built on relationships of competition, contract and calculation; inhabited by a breed of autonomous, flexible and utility maximising individuals; and actualised through markets, individual choice and technical practice. As this all-encompassing story of neoliberalism – a truly meta-narrative – has emerged and gained increasing dominance, it has provided a favourable context in which the story of quality and high returns and the story of markets have readily acquired listeners and adherents.

The story of quality and high returns

> There is a substantial body of evidence that participation in high-quality pre-primary education has long-lasting benefits in terms of achievement and socialisation during individuals' schooling and careers because it facilitates later learning . . . European and U.S. experience shows that early intervention programmes, especially those targeted at disadvantaged children, can produce large positive socio-economic returns, and that these persist well into adulthood. Effects include better school achievement, grade retention, employment rates, earnings, crime prevention, family relationships and health.
>
> (European Commission, 2006, p. 5)

There is a growing body of evidence that some of the greatest returns on taxpayers' investments are those targeted to Canada's youngest citizens. Every dollar spent in ensuring a healthy start in the early years will reduce the long-term costs associated with health care, addictions, crime, unemployment and welfare. As well, it will ensure Canadian children become better educated, well adjusted and more productive adults.

(Butler-Jones, 2008, p. 69)

Convergence in the results of substantial international evidence, based on well-designed longitudinal research studies and cost-benefit analyses, reveals positive long-term effects for individuals who have experienced high-quality early childhood education compared to individuals who have not . . . [Long-term cost-benefit analyses of effects] show that for every dollar invested, the resulting returns fell within the range of $3 to $16

(Early Childhood Education Taskforce (New Zealand), 2011, p. 21)

Looking at ECEC [early childhood education and care] as an investment makes sense because the costs today generate many benefits in the future. And the benefits are not only economic: benefits can be in the form of social well-being for individuals and society as a whole. Economists such as Nobel prize-winner, James Heckman have shown how early learning is a good investment because it provides the foundation for later learning. The big insight from these economists is that a dollar, euro or yen spent on preschool programmes generates a higher return on investment than the same spending on schooling . . . [But] early childhood education and care needs to be of sufficient quality to achieve beneficial child-outcomes and yield longer term social and economic gains . . . The OECD is now developing an Online Policy Toolbox for identifying how to improve quality . . . The toolbox will include checklists, self-assessment sheets, research briefs, lists of strategy options etc.

(OECD, 2011a, pp. 1, 7, 8)

The beginning years of a child's life are critical for building the early foundation needed for success later in school and in life. Leading economists agree that high-quality early learning programs can help level the playing field for children from lower-income families on vocabulary, social and emotional development, while helping students to stay on track and stay engaged in the early elementary grades. Children who attend these programs are more likely to do well in school, find good jobs, and succeed in their careers than those who don't. And research has shown that taxpayers receive a high average return on investments in high-quality early childhood education, with savings in areas like improved educational outcomes, increased labor productivity, and a reduction in crime.

(White House, 2013)

Early childhood education is not new. Formal services such as nurseries and kindergartens have been around for two centuries, and some countries have had well developed systems of provision for decades. It has been, too, a subject of research and theory for many years. But today, interest has spread far and wide, attracting the attention of international organisations and nation states, the political classes and policy wonks, and a range of academics from disciplines that have not previously shown interest in the subject – in particular economists. Countries that have previously neglected early childhood education are now putting money into developing services, which are growing in many places; worldwide between 1999 and 2010, the number of children enrolled in preschool (for children from 3 years of age) rose by 46 per cent to a total of 164 million, though there continues to be large differences between attendance in affluent and poorer countries (UNESCO, 2012, p. 50). What has attracted this attention and motivated this action is, I would argue, the growing appeal of a story, a story already introduced in Chapter 1 as the 'story of quality and high returns'.

The story is about the high returns to be gained from many forms of early intervention, including parent education and support, and sometimes involving home visiting. I will, however, focus my attention on early childhood education in early childhood centres, and the high and long-term returns it is argued to bring, both by the reduction of negative outcomes associated with poverty and inequality (teenage pregnancies, addiction, unemployment, crime, etc.) and by improving positive educational and economic outcomes through the cultivation of 'human capital'. Human Capital Theory (HCT) – with its concern for realising the skills, knowledge, competences, attitudes and other characteristics of an individual that can contribute to his or her productivity – has a big part in the story of quality and high returns, as it does in economics in general. In recent years HCT 'has developed into one of the most powerful theories in modern economics . . . [and] lays considerable stress on the education of individuals as the key means by which both the individual accrues material advantage and by which the economy as a whole progresses' (Gillies, 2011, pp. 224–5). As well as shaping thinking about education, forcing it increasingly into a purely economic mould, HCT shapes how individuals think about themselves and hence their self-identity: '[t]he theory positions actors in a particular way, understanding themselves and acting on themselves, and others, as "human capital". This is central to neoliberal governmentality and the notion of the self as enterprise' (ibid., pp. 228–9). We become entrepreneurs of the self, seeking to enhance and invest our 'human capital' for best return.

HCT goes hand in hand with the concept of 'social investment', which has its origins as far back as the 1930s, in the ideas developed by Alva (1902–1986) and Gunnar Myrdal (1898–1987) in Sweden, but which has re-emerged in the 1990s as an important perspective on social welfare and policy, taken up and circulated widely by international organisations. Central to social investment is the idea of national resources being targeted on human capital development and the efficient use of that capital, and on preparation rather than repair

(Morel *et al.*, 2012). Central, too, is the role of early childhood education as a particularly good investment. The development of publicly funded child care and education programmes, says one report:

> constitutes an essential dimension of the social investment approach. Such services express the goals of this perspective in two ways: they invest in the human capital of mothers by helping them remain in paid work; and they invest in the human capital of children by providing them with quality educational stimulation at an early age.
>
> (ibid., p. 9)

The European Commission is typical of many international organisations in its enthusiasm for social investment and the high returns it predicts from investing in early childhood education. In a document titled 'Towards Social Investment for Growth and Cohesion', the Commission urges the case:

> Future economic growth and competitiveness require investing in human capital . . . The need for investment in human capital starts at very early age [*sic*] and continues throughout life . . . [Member states should] further develop the potential of early childhood education and care (ECEC), using it as a social investment to address inequality and challenges faced by children through early intervention . . . Access to early childhood education and care (ECEC) has positive effects throughout life, for instance in terms of preventing early school leaving, improving employment outcomes, and facilitating social mobility.
>
> (European Commission, 2013a, pp. 3, 6, 20–1)

I recognise that the concept of social investment is more complex than this initial introduction might suggest, for example with 'thin' and 'thick' versions, and I will go further into this complexity in Chapter 4, when considering whether 'social investment' has a place in the vocabulary of my alternative story. For the moment, though, I confine myself to introducing the concept, establishing its link with human capital, observing the shared economistic language, and noting its influence on the story of quality and high returns.

At a time when the welfare state has come under political attack and financial pressure, and former rationales such as citizenship, social security and entitlement carry far less weight, 'social investment' provides a contemporary rationale for public funding of new services: putting money into early childhood education and other early interventions in the evidence-based expectation of being repaid many times over. This rationale is summed up succinctly in the title of a report for the UK government – 'Early Intervention: Smart Investment, Massive Savings' (Allen, 2011a), a report that holds out the prospect of extraordinarily high returns, starting with the picture of a stack of gold ingots on its front cover and followed by a text full of tempting offers:

Early Intervention investment has the potential to make massive savings in public expenditure, reduce the costs of educational underachievement, drink and drug abuse, teenage pregnancy, vandalism and criminality, court and police costs, academic underachievement, lack of aspiration to work and the bills from lifetimes wasted while claiming benefits.

(ibid., p. xiv)

Smart investment, which will secure such high returns and massive savings, has a number of conditions. First, the need to invest *early*, in education and other interventions. The economists, who figure prominently in this story, especially the much cited Nobel Prize-winner James Heckman, have had a 'big insight': that early education is the best educational investment to be had. Their insight comes both from selected early intervention research studies, to which I will return, and from the work of another group of scientists in neuroscience:

Why does this [high return on investment in early childhood education and care] happen? Brain researchers have shown that the brain develops at an astonishing rate in the earliest years of life. But the brain's capacity to adapt and develop slows with age. A process of 'use it or lose it' comes into play.

(OECD, 2011a, p. 1)

A short digression seems in order here. The above statement is typical of the over-simplified and over-determined claims often made about neuroscience and young children in the story of quality and high returns, a symptom of what has been variously termed 'neuromania', 'neuro-determinism' (Tallis, 2011) and 'neuroessentialism' (Rose and Rose, 2012) to describe 'the rise and rise of brain science as the apparent explanation of every aspect of human life' (Tallis, 2011, p. 5). Without denying the value of neuroscience or the importance of the first few years of life, more critical and nuanced readings are needed by the new converts to early childhood education, whose judgement can at times seem blinded by their epiphany.

Seeking to put matters in more perspective, John Bruer concludes that 'it is not the case that birth to three is the critical period for brain development': 'most learning is not subject to critical (or sensitive) period constraints', and experience-dependent brain plasticity, which accounts for most of our learning, 'is retained throughout our lifetime'. He adds that 'the evidentiary base for claims about early brain development does not seem to be expanding, the interpretations are not improving, and the same examples, phrases, and images constantly recur' (Bruer, 2011, pp. 6, 11). Such cautious comments are supported by Sarah-Jayne Blakemore and Uta Frith who, while welcoming the debate about early education, conclude that:

[research] does not support the argument for a selective educational focus only on children's earliest years. Rather, learning needs to be available at all ages. To put it simply, deprived environments are never good for your brain; on the other hand, enrichment may not be necessarily good for the brain . . . The research tells us that sensitive periods exist at least for vision, and also encourages us in the optimistic belief that missed opportunities can to some extent be reversed.

(Blakemore and Frith, 2005, pp. 35–6)

So yes, the earliest years do matter – as many early childhood educators have known for many years. But let's remember that 'claims that the window of opportunity for brain development closes on a child's third birthday are completely unfounded' (National Scientific Council on the Developing Child, 2007, p. 5). And yes, let's bring neuroscience into the story. But let's not go entirely overboard, as if it provides the answer to life, the universe and everything, as if we are our brains so that 'peering into the intracranial darkness is the best way of advancing our knowledge of humankind' (Tallis, 2013).

Back to the conditions needed for high returns and massive savings. Second, the necessity of *predefined goals*, outcomes that are knowable, definable and measurable, outcomes that are prescribed before any early interventions begin; for without such given goals, the likely return on investment is not calculable. At the heart of the story of quality and high returns is a logic 'that always begins with formulating preset goals and universal values for our educational practices. *We start with the end* – what is to be achieved and assessed' (Lenz Taguchi, 2010a, p. 16; original emphasis). And because of this logic, we are drawn to strive and look only for these prescribed goals, to ask only if Johnny or Jemima have met these goals according to our measures, to reduce their education and learning to the sum of these measures. One consequence, into which I delve in later chapters, is that the full potentiality of early childhood education and children, what Johnny and Jemima actually can or might do, is overlooked in a fixation with narrowly prescribed and predetermined outcomes.

The third condition for high returns is *high quality*. 'Quality' is the most over-used and under-conceptualised of words in early childhood education, sprinkled liberally and indiscriminately throughout policy papers, journal and magazine articles and conference presentations, often to the extent of seeming meaningless.[1] But to the extent it does have meaning, it is this: quality describes assemblages of 'human technologies' believed to ensure delivery of predetermined outcomes. 'High quality' in this sense is the assurance of effective performance by the presence of these technologies, a promise of achieving conformity to desired norms.

Nikolas Rose has coined the term 'human technologies' to describe 'technologies of government . . . imbued with aspirations for the shaping of conduct in the hope of producing certain desired effects and averting certain undesired events' (1999, p. 52). Their purpose is to understand and act upon human capacities, so as 'to achieve certain forms of outcome on the part of the governed'. They cover numerous and varied technical means, some quite mundane others more sophisticated, some structural others processual: such as 'forms of practical knowledge, with modes of perception, practices of calculation, vocabularies, types of authority, forms of judgement, architectural forms, human capacities, non-human objects and devices'. Rose gives the nineteenth-century schoolroom as an example of one assemblage of such human technologies:

> This was an assemblage of pedagogic knowledges, moralizing aspirations, buildings of a certain design, classrooms organised to produce certain kinds of visibility, techniques such as the timetable for organizing bodies in space and in time, regimes of supervision, little mental exercises in the classroom, playgrounds to allow the observation and moralization of children in something more approaching their habitat and much more, assembled and infused with the aim of the government of capacities and habits.
>
> (ibid., p. 53)

Fast forward to today and to early childhood education, and another assemblage of technologies figures in the story of quality and high returns: child development concepts, knowledge and vocabularies; developmental and learning goals; early years curricula; pedagogical and other programmes, such as developmentally appropriate practice; the authority of various expert groups; the competencies and deployment of staff; child observation techniques and normative assessment methods; regulatory and inspection regimes; particular (though often implicit) social constructions or images (e.g. of the child, the parent, the educator); and selected research. None of these technologies, in isolation, may be particularly effective; but connect them up into an assemblage and you have a powerful machine. This is 'high quality' as shorthand for technologies that will effectively produce 'predefined goals' and is thought, therefore, to guarantee the high returns that justify initial investment. The OECD, as noted at the start of this section, now helpfully offers a 'Quality Policy Toolbox' containing technologies for policy-makers seeking to realise the many benefits from an investment in ECEC – for 'the magnitude of the benefits is conditional on "quality"' (OECD, 2012, p. 9).[2]

The fourth condition is *rigorous selection and application* of technologies to go in the Quality Toolbox. They must be carefully selected on the basis of proven track record: they must be 'evidence-based'. Then once selected, they must be precisely applied, with operatives following prescribed procedures. The importance of this condition in the story of quality and high returns is captured in oral evidence to a British Parliamentary Committee in 2009 by psychologist Edward Melhuish, in which he discusses some reasons for the perceived failure of the first phases of Sure Start, an early intervention 'programme' of the English government focused on children under 4 years in disadvantaged areas (for a fuller account of Sure Start, see Eisenstadt, 2011):

What was interesting about the way in which Sure Start was initially set up was that it emphasised community control to such an extent that communities that had a Sure Start programme could decide more or less for themselves what to put into place, without any particular model being offered to them as guidance. That was exactly the opposite of what the evidence was telling us, which was that *very tightly defined programmes produced good results.* In that sense, while there was some evidence that inspired this idea that early intervention works, the way that Sure Start was initially put in place did not pay too much attention to the detail of that evidence.

(House of Commons Children, Schools and Families Committee, 2010, Ev 14, 2 November 2009; emphasis added)

In short, Sure Start (or so the story went) failed because it thought it was a community resource, to be used by communities as they thought best, when it should have understood itself as a setting for the rigorous application of selected technologies of proven effectiveness in achieving predefined goals.

Perhaps the fullest account of the need for this condition is given in the UK report whose title and claims have already been mentioned, *Early Intervention: Smart Investment, Massive Savings.* Written by a Labour Party (centre-left) Member of Parliament, Graham Allen, at the request of a Conservative/Liberal Democrat (centre-right) coalition government, it illustrates how the same dominant story is now told and listened to across much of the political spectrum. The report argues that 'early intervention', wider than early childhood education, can bring high returns through reducing a range of child and adult problems. But to work, such intervention calls for the deployment of effective programmes, carefully selected and assiduously applied. This means a 'focus on evidence-based policies and programmes, measurable outcomes and associated cashable savings . . . to help set up outcome-based contracts' (Allen, 2011a, p. xxvi): in other words, the rigorous selection by experts of programmes to be linked via contracts to a system of payment by results, to ensure the delivery of predetermined outcomes that can be exactly measured.

Opportunities to invest in such 'outcome-based contracts' and share in the high returns from early intervention should, Allen proposes, not be confined to public funding. They should be open to private finance 'through the establishment of an Early Intervention Fund or Funds in close co-operation with the Big Society Bank, which over time can be developed to offer [private] investors a diverse range of Early Intervention products' (ibid., p. xxi). Financial capital investing in human capital.

So the story, in its fullest form, goes: invest in high-quality early childhood education or in other early interventions such as parenting programmes, apply proven technologies prescriptively and you will get predetermined outcomes, delivering high returns for the initial investment, anything up to 1,800 per cent. For looking at a broad range of early years interventions, a recent UK report concludes enthusiastically that '[t]he consensus among . . . American approaches and reviews, including even the most cautious and circumspect in its recommendations, have suggested returns on investment on well-designed early years interventions [that] significantly exceed both their costs and stock market returns', with rates of return for every dollar invested ranging from $1.26 to $17.92 (Wave Trust, 2013, p. 38).

But this is not told as a story. Rather, it is presented as objectively true knowledge supported by 'substantial international evidence, based on well-designed longitudinal research studies and cost-benefit analyses', and backed by leading economists and results from cutting-edge biosciences. It is a story of technical practice and management, economics and neuroscience, carrying no risks or dangers, no hint of down-side. Who would not be seduced by such a story? Well, myself for a start, though I am not alone.

Why I don't like the story of quality and high returns

Incredulity!

The story of quality and high returns promises substantial, wide-ranging and long-lasting benefits especially for disadvantaged children. Its grand claims raise great expectations in politicians and policy-makers, as illustrated by this policy statement from the New Labour administration that governed England between 1997 and 2010, setting out the many objectives that 'the availability of good quality, affordable childcare is key to achieving':

> Childcare can improve *educational outcomes* for children. Childcare enables parents, particularly mothers, to go out to *work*, or increase their hours in work, thereby lifting their families out of poverty. It also plays a key role in *extending choice for women* by enhancing their ability to compete in the labour market on more equal terms, helping them to overcome the glass ceiling, and by ensuring that they themselves may not face poverty in old age.
>
> Childcare can also play an important role in meeting other top level objectives, for example in *improving health, boosting productivity, improving public services, closing the gender pay gap* and *reducing crime*. The targets to achieve 70 per cent *employment amongst lone parents* by 2010 and to *eradicate child poverty* by 2020 are those that are most obviously related. Childcare is essential for these objectives to be met.
>
> (Department for Education and Skills *et al.*, 2002, p. 5; emphasis added)

As this wish list demonstrates, the story of quality and high returns makes early childhood education seem an obvious 'best buy' for policy-makers wondering what they can do to reduce social dysfunction and discontents today and to ensure survival tomorrow in the 'global race'. But its added appeal lies in its promise of technical problem-solving without needing to rock the boat, avoiding any political pain by focusing instead on young children and early intervention. Problems solved without spooking markets, without scaring off elites, without unsettling multinational corporations by proposing to pursue greater equality, democracy and sustainability; indeed, even appealing to these constituencies by offering them new opportunities for investment and profit, opening up new territory for capital to exploit. What's not to like about this story?

Quite a lot. I don't like its authoritarian tone, I don't like its stultifying aesthetic, and I don't like its politics. But, first, to adopt the story's economistic tone, I just don't buy it. I am incredulous that early childhood education, and other early interventions, can be such a lucrative investment. If something seems too good to be true, it probably is!

Let me begin by bringing a little scepticism to the evidence adduced to support the claims. I offer a small and a big example. First, the small example. The OECD document on 'investing in high-quality early childhood education and care', quoted from at the start of this section, offers as one justification for such investment its longer-term educational impact. In support, it cites the organisation's own highly influential Programme for International Student Assessment (PISA), a multinational programme for assessing 15-year-olds in reading, maths and science. Across OECD countries, in the 2009 PISA study, students who attended 'preschool' for one year or more scored over 30 points higher in reading at age 15 than those who did not (OECD, 2011a). But even more striking:

> [i]n Belgium, France and Israel, students who reported that they had attended pre-primary school for more than one year scored at least 100 points higher in reading than students who had not. Comparing students from similar backgrounds, the gap narrows but remains above 60 score points.
>
> (OECD, 2011b, p. 1)

Despite the fact that attending pre-primary education in some other countries – such as Estonia, Finland, Korea and the United States – shows little or no relationship to later performance among students of similar socioeconomic backgrounds, the results for Belgium and France seem very impressive. Yet, dig a little deeper and they seem less clear cut. For instance, the great majority of children in Belgium and France attend 'pre-primary school' (*kleuterschool* or *école maternelle*) for three years; European Commission statistics show that 98 and 95 per cent of all 3–6-year-old children in these two countries are receiving this education (European Commission, 2013b, Table 2.2.3). Put another way, in both countries children attending for one year or less are a very small and exceptional group, and have been for some time. Perhaps, then, the large differences in reading score at 15 say more about the particular composition and circumstances of this atypical and very small minority than the vast majority's experience of early childhood education. Sadly, this possibility is not raised in the OECD document.

Now for the big example. Many of the assertions of the long-term and widespread benefits of early childhood education, including James Heckman's much quoted conclusions that early childhood education gives the highest return on educational investment, are based on findings from three longitudinal studies of local interventions undertaken in the United States: Perry High/Scope (begun in 1962), Abecedarian (1972) and Chicago Child-Parent Centres (1983). It is worth, therefore, paying some attention to what have been referred to as 'iconic studies' (NESSE, 2009, p. 29), which have been, in Helen Penn's words, 'endlessly recycled in the literature' (2011, p. 39).

All three were situated in small areas of a very large country, with samples – 111, 123 and 1,539 children respectively – drawn mainly from one group, poor 'Afro-American' families. All three were commenced decades ago, since when much has altered, for example understandings of issues such as race and motherhood together with economic transformations that have led to huge changes in employment and family life and massive growth, as will be seen, in income and wealth inequality. At the same time, the three studies differed from each other in a variety of ways, for example in scope, in curriculum, in the length of time the intervention was offered, and in the effects measured and the instruments used to measure the effects. The results were also somewhat contradictory; for example, one study found 'no impact on crime ratings [in later life], which is the main source of cost savings in the other two studies' (Penn et al., 2006a, p. 3). Furthermore, the assessments of benefits are highly context-specific, depending on local school models and high US levels of imprisonment and victim compensation.

Given these circumstances, it is not surprising that a systematic review of the evidence on the 'long-term economic impact of centre-based early childhood interventions', conducted at the EPPI (Evidence for Policy and Practice Information and Coordinating) Centre of the Institute of Education University of London, arrived at distinctly agnostic conclusions. The EPPI reviewers found that these three studies were the only ones to meet their criteria for inclusion in the review, i.e. that studies should 'deal with the long-term economic outcomes of centre-based early childhood interventions'. Overall, they concluded that the studies 'provide evidence for the beneficial effects of centre-based early years interventions for very poor black children living in deprived inner city areas of the USA in the late 1960's [sic] and early 1970's [sic]' (Penn et al., 2006b, p. 1) – a time of heightened racial tension.

But the conclusion is highly qualified: the evidence provided by the three studies needs contextualising and interpreting with great care. While there appeared to be 'some positive financial returns', the authors of the review point out that 'the magnitude of the return is very sensitive to the assumptions made in the cost estimates' (Penn et al., 2006a, p. 24). Above all, the reviewers caution against generalising from research conducted in such very specific spatial and temporal contexts:

These findings cannot be assumed to be generalisable elsewhere. The findings from these studies should not be used as justification for investment in similar enterprises in different populations and locations and time periods . . . [T]he results of the three studies are not easily transferable to modern contexts in countries such as England. The results indicated should therefore all be read with the caveat of 'for the specific population in these studies'.

(Penn *et al.*, 2006b, p. 1)

In a later literature review, Penn again concludes that '[t]o make long-range predictions on the back of them is problematic' (NESSE, 2009, p. 29).

Yet despite this warning, not only have the results of these three studies been frequently generalised to other affluent countries, but the World Bank has 'extrapolated [the information] from the United States context without caveats, and applied [it] to Africa and other regions' (Penn, 2011, p. 55). Instead of being treated as quantitative case studies providing local knowledge and requiring careful interpretation that should take account of spatial and temporal context, they are treated as bearers of universal and timeless truths.

So one conclusion is not to accept things on face value: beware of generalisations, over-reliance on numerical data, and avoidance of complexity and context; and be sure to read all the small print. For complexity and context are not just irritants that can be ignored or controlled, but are profound and irreducible presences, which we ignore at our peril. Such neglect of context and its attendant complexities forms part of a scathing criticism by educationalist Robin Alexander (2012a) about the way the English government has made use of international comparisons of student performance, such as PISA, stripping 'a country of the complexities of culture, values, social structure, politics and demography . . . [though] these are the very features with which we must engage if we are to understand education elsewhere, explain why one country outperforms others' (p. 2). This leads, he argues, to policy advisers advocating 'policy borrowing on what I believe is a culturally reckless scale' (Alexander, 2012b, p. 5).

But a deeper cause of my incredulity with the story of quality and high returns is that, irrespective of the results from local studies, it is hard to detect any discrete impact of early childhood education on the big picture. Take the United States, the home not only of these three iconic (and endlessly recycled) studies, but of many other early childhood research studies and early intervention programmes, and whose influence is felt well beyond the country's borders due to the reach of the English-language and of American research and academic journals. The first and best known of these early intervention programmes, Head Start, was initiated in 1965 by President Lyndon Johnson as part of the so-called 'War on Poverty', since when more than 25 million children have used its services. Starting as an 8-week summer measure, Head Start has grown to become a major national programme, targeted at low income preschool children and their families, covering not only early education but also health, social services and parental involvement.

Stand back, though, and ask to what extent the massive research effort and Head Start and other targeted early childhood programmes have improved social problems in the United States, and the picture becomes less clear, the claims less solid. Despite all this research and intervention work and despite all the evidence-based programmes, the United States has a persistently poor record when it comes to the health and welfare of its citizens. And this despite being one of the richest countries on earth, measured by per capita GDP.[3]

Let me give some examples of this poor record. Poverty rates amongst American children were marginally higher in 2012, at nearly 22 per cent, than when Head Start began in 1965 (Denavas-Walt *et al.*, 2013, Table B-2). Out of 34 'economically advanced' countries in the late 2000s, the US had the second highest level of child poverty (UNICEF, 2012, Table 1b); while among 34 OECD member states, child poverty levels in 2008 were only higher in Turkey, Romania, Mexico and Israel (OECD Family data base: Chart CO2.2.A). The United States has far and away the worst score out of 21 affluent countries for an index constructed from indicators of nine social and health problems (Wilkinson and Pickett, 2009, pp. 19, 20). Social mobility is low, with a stronger link in the United States between parental education and children's economic and educational outcomes than in any of the other countries included in the Pew Trusts' Economic Mobility Project (Stiglitz, 2013b). A comparison with 16 other affluent countries on a range of health indices concludes that not only are American lives shorter, but they 'also have a long standing pattern of poorer health that is strikingly consistent and pervasive over the life course' – including faring worst on infant mortality and low birth weight (Institute of Medicine of the National Academies, 2013, pp. 1–2). To round off this litany of failure, the United States comes 26 out of 29 countries in UNICEF's review of child well-being in rich countries, managing to beat only Lithuania, Latvia and Rumania (UNICEF, 2013), and comes at the bottom of that same organisation's league table for inequality in child well-being (UNICEF, 2010).

What seems to lie at the heart of this poor performance is a nexus of social injustices and political failure, which over recent decades has harmed the well-being of many Americans, more than cancelling out any small benefits that might have accrued from early childhood interventions. At the heart of this nexus is high inequality, which has been growing in recent decades, leading to what Nobel Prize-winning economist Paul Krugman terms the 'Great Divergence' to describe the widening gap between the economic elite and the great majority of citizens. In a 2011 report titled 'Why inequality keeps rising', the OECD notes that the US 'has the fourth-highest inequality level [among 34 member states] in the OECD, after Chile, Mexico and Turkey. Inequality among working-age people has risen steadily since 1980, in total by 25%' (OECD, 2011c).

Inequality might be considered an evil in its own right. But its malign influence spreads far and wide. In their landmark book *The Spirit Level: Why More Equal Societies Almost Always Do Better*, epidemiologists Richard Wilkinson and Kate Pickett deploy a mass of evidence to support their argument that inequality 'seems to make countries socially dysfunctional across a wide range of outcomes' (2009, p. 174). This evidence is seemingly ignored by those who advocate the technical fix of evidence-based early interventions as the answer to social dysfunctionality, who usually make no reference to this well researched and carefully argued book! (For a further withering indictment of the toll taken by inequality, see Stiglitz, 2013b.)

James Heckman and his colleague Dimitry Masterov recognise that the condition of the United States is not good and, in some ways, has been getting worse: 'in the past few decades relatively more of all American children are born into adverse environments . . . [which includes] the absence of a father, low levels of financial resources, low parental education and ability, a lack of cognitive and emotional stimulation, and poor parenting skills' (2007, p. 14). They see this as adding force to their argument for greater investment in early interventions targeted at children from 'adverse environments' – technologies to rectify individual failings. But some might draw other conclusions, being struck by how the deteriorating situation of American families 'in the past few decades' corresponds with the rise of neoliberalism in the US (the subject of the next chapter), and the related emergence of what has been termed a 'winner-take-all' economy, augmenting income inequalities, in particular a hyperconcentration of income at the very top of society:

> The share of income earned by the top 1 percent has increased from around 8 percent in 1974 to more than 18 percent in 2007 . . . If you include capital gains like investment and dividend income, the share of the top 1 percent has gone from just over 9 to 23.5 percent. The only time since 1913 (the first year of the data) that this share was higher was in 1928 . . . The more closely we look at changes in the distribution of economic rewards, the more it becomes clear that the big gains have been concentrated at the very, very top.
>
> (Hacker and Pierson, 2011, pp. 15, 17)

There has been, as geographer and social theorist David Harvey puts it, 'thirty years of wage repression', with US household incomes generally stagnating since the 1970s against the backdrop of 'an immense accumulation of wealth by capitalist class interests' (Harvey, 2010, p. 12). America, as Nobel Prize-winning economist Joseph Stiglitz puts it, 'has been growing apart, at an increasingly rapid rate' (2013b, p. 3), with levels of inequality last seen in the years preceding the Great Depression of the 1930s. These shocking data on income distribution and inequality are just one part of a bigger picture of regressive change that has characterised recent decades: falling tax payments and increasing political influence by the individual and corporate rich; the decline of traditional industries and labour unions; and an inexorable but unsustainable growth of household debt as low and middle-income families have struggled to sustain their standard of living in the face of stagnant real earnings, culminating in the implosion of the sub-prime mortgage market, the near collapse of the financial system and a prolonged economic downturn (for a discussion of the relationship between increasing income inequality, growing debt and the post-2007 financial and economic crises, see Kumhof and Rancière, 2010).

Hardly surprising, one might think, that in these circumstances early childhood education in particular and early intervention more generally has made little discernible impression on the wider scene in the United States. But, it could be argued, the problem is that early childhood know-how has not been given a proper chance to show what it can do. The problem might be implementation; research has shown what works, but it has proven difficult to get successive American governments to act on this information.[4] It could be argued that had federal and state authorities in the United States only applied the proven human technologies in 'quality' early childhood programmes, then the USA today would today be reaping high returns such as lower poverty, higher social mobility and better health and social indicators.

This line of argument does, of course, beg the question. Why have US authorities *not* acted, or rather why have they not acted enough, faced by such apparently overwhelming evidence and such a plausible story? Any answer would have to delve into the country's political context, with its deeply divided (some would say dysfunctional) system of government, its growing political polarisation, its phobic attitude to taxes and government action (at least among a vociferous minority), and its increasing susceptibility to the influence of organised groups representing the interests of the rich and powerful (Hacker and Pierson, 2011; Stiglitz, 2013b). In short, it is possible that the problems that early childhood education is meant to address and the problems of implementation are connected: they share common roots that are mainly political and economic.

An examination of the Nordic countries would support this explanation, that there is not and cannot be a simple causal relationship between early childhood education and wider societal well-being. Like the United States, Nordic countries consistently score well on measures of economic competitiveness (World Economic Forum, 2013, Table 3; www3.Iforum.org/docs/CSI/2012–13/GCR_Rankings_2012–13.pdf). But unlike the United States they also score consistently well on comparative measures of child poverty as well as other indicators of well-being; and they also have exemplary systems of early childhood education. There are many other differences. Unlike the United States, Nordic countries also do well on measures of income and gender equality. Unlike the United States, they have strong and extensive welfare states, including universal free health care, generous financial benefits for families, and support for working parents including well-paid parental leave.[5] Unlike the United States, they have strong trade unions, with high levels of membership across the labour force. Unlike the United States, they have high levels of taxation reflecting widespread trust and confidence in the state.[6] And all these interdependent features are sustained by strong political and social values that favour solidarity, universalism and rights.

The conclusion is clear. If we step back from small-scale, local and highly positivistic studies and look instead at cross-national and wide-ranging comparisons, it becomes all too obvious that well-functioning societies, defined in terms of a variety of well-being and economic indicators, cannot be explained or produced by any one factor, such as early childhood education. Rather they are the product of complex, interrelated economic, social and political influences. Arguably, it is strong underlying democratic, solidaristic and egalitarian values that are the basis for societal well-being: both directly, because as Wilkinson and Pickett (2009) argue, more equal societies are more cohesive and cooperative; and indirectly, through enabling the creation of redistributive policies and a range of supportive services including but not only early childhood education. Early childhood education matters – but only as part of this bigger picture and only made possible by these underlying values. Everything connects in this complex web of relationships, from which it is invidious and impractical to extract and privilege any one part.

Recent events, sadly, add credence to this conclusion. Nothing is immutable and, under the malign influence of neoliberalism, Nordic societies have begun to show some disturbing signs of change for the worse. In Sweden, for example, in recent years taxes have been substantially cut, public services such as schools have been privatised and inequality has grown at the fastest rate among any OECD member states (OECD, 2011c). The country remains one of the most egalitarian in the world, but 'it is taking big steps in the wrong direction . . . [and] increasingly poor Swedes are getting pushed backwards' (Chakrabortty, 2013). It is perhaps not coincidental that spring 2013 saw unprecedented rioting in Swedish cities.

So my incredulity at the story of quality and high returns is generated by its naivety and absence of scepticism, its ability to ignore the bigger picture and the complexity it reveals, and its fatal tendency to over-generalise and de-contextualise research. The result is simplistic and reductionist conclusions supporting simplistic and reductionist thinking about early childhood education based on the assumption that a technical fix focused on one small area can solve problems that are structural and systemic, and can work anywhere, anytime irrespective of context. This exemplifies what philosopher and sociologist Edgar Morin calls 'mechanistic and fragmented thinking', which:

> perceives only mechanical causality while everything increasingly obeys a complex causality. It reduces reality to that which is quantifiable. Hyper-specialisation and reduction to the quantifiable produce a blindness not only to existence, the concrete, and the individual, but also to context, the global, and the fundamental.
>
> (1999, p. 70)

We need, Morin urges, to be thinking in context and thinking the complex, 'a kind of thinking that relinks that which is disjointed and compartmentalized, that respects diversity as it recognizes unity, and that tries to discern interdependencies' (p. 130). 'All knowledge of reality', he adds, 'is embedded in systems of interpretation' (p. 101). Yet this is exactly what the story of quality and high returns, and its supporting science, fail to acknowledge and act on. Amid the mass of numbers and statistical tests, the confident claims and expectations, the demand to know what works, precious little account is taken of complexity or context, little acknowledgement made of the need for interpretation and judgement.

Such simplified thinking is the hall-mark of much of the discussion about evidence-based policy and practice, a human technology with an important role in the story of quality and high returns, with its claims that evidence, scientifically derived, supplies objective, stable, replicable and universally generalisable knowledge that tells us what we should do. Indeed, this technology and its claims to reveal 'what works' lie at the story's heart, enabling the 'rigorous selection and application' of interventions; as such, it holds the key to minimising risk and maximising returns. Indeed, it is not unusual today to find story tellers adding weight to their narratives by including lists of programmes (most often from the United States) with a supposedly strong evidence base (e.g. Allen, 2011b; Wave Trust, 2013).

Evidence-based policy and practice, its disciples aver, removes uncertainty, permitting a regime of pure technical practice and calculability. But, typically, the tellers of the story of quality and high returns make no mention of the criticisms of evidence-based policy and practice and of the suppositions that underpin it. Perhaps they have never heard them, perhaps they choose not to do so, perhaps they simply dismiss them out of hand – we can't tell because they never refer to them. Whatever the reason, they ignore the nay sayers, those sceptical voices who raise reservations about evidence-based policy and practice, its powers of prediction and its dangers (see, for example, Pawson, 2006; Biesta, 2007; Hammersley, 2013). These reservations, which might be thought to at least merit acknowledgement and reflection, even refutation, include:

- The revisionist accounts of the nature of science in recent years that are 'significantly at odds with the assumptions built into advocacy of evidence-based practice' (Hammersley, 2013, p. 42), with their positivistic view of science as 'the only genuine form of knowledge . . . [able to] reliably reflect the nature of the world, or at least our experience of it, in ways that knowledge claims from other sources cannot' (ibid., p. 40).
- The dubious assumption that 'scientific evidence carries direct implications for practice that demand "implementation"' (ibid., p. 3), ignoring issues of complexity and context, the inescapable need for judgement, and science being 'necessarily an activity that is carried out by human beings within the social world' (ibid., p. 42). Scientists themselves, it is pointed out, do not

simply and logically derive conclusions from observations, but 'rely upon background knowledge, on past experience . . . and on personal, situated judgements (albeit ones that are open to future revision)' (ibid., p. 43).

- The substantive differences between medicine (where evidence-based practice has its origins) and education (to which it has spread), and the appropriateness, therefore, of transferring evaluative practice from one field to the other.

- The overblown claims for particular methods, such as the so-called 'gold standard' of the Randomised Controlled Trials and the 'systematic review', which take little or no account of the criticisms of the positivist model of science referred to above.

- The dismissal of political questions (as discussed below) in favour of exclusive attention to the technical question 'what works?' Such prioritising of decisions about means over deliberation about purposes and ends favours 'a technocratic model in which it is assumed that the only relevant research questions are questions about the effectiveness of educational means and techniques, forgetting, among other things, that what counts as "effective" crucially depends on judgments about what is educationally desirable' (Biesta, 2007, p. 5).

Cumulatively, these reservations should make us all wary of an uncritical and unqualified reliance on evidence-based policy and practice. As Ray Pawson, an expert on social research methodology, cautions, 'generating transferable lessons about interventions will always be difficult because they are never embedded in the same structures and contexts . . . [the] evidence base must attempt to get to grips with social processes of extraordinary complexity' (Pawson, 2006, pp. 30, 35). He goes on to warn against:

> the ludicrous idea that evaluators and reviewers are able to tell policy-makers and practitioners exactly what works in the world of policy interventions . . . and the [continuing] assumption about a one-to-one relationship between each past intervention, each evaluation and each future intervention. This is a foolhardy supposition. Social interventions are complex, active systems thrust into [other] complex, active systems and are never implemented the same way twice.
>
> (ibid., p. 170)

He adds that 'we should always be humble about predicting the path ahead on the basis of what we know about the one already trodden' (ibid., p. 167). So we should not discard evidence, but rather recognise that evidence never speaks directly. Evidence cannot tell us what to do, nor can it guarantee 'effective' interventions; we have to weigh it up, interpret it, evaluate it, all the time taking account of context and complexity, as well as political judgements about what is desirable.

For example, despite his cogent critique of evidence-based policy and practice as widely practised, Pawson identifies himself as a member of the 'empirical
tribe' of realists (as opposed to the 'critical tribe'), a 'branch of realism that says
it is worth trying to decide between alternative explanations even if you know
there is more to find' (ibid., p. 19). He does this through the process of 'realist
synthesis', in which evidence from studies of interventions in a common field
is worked with not to produce clear, consistent and universal answers, but
to help build theory: realist synthesis, he writes, operates through processes
of 'policy abstraction and theory-building rather than data extraction and
number crunching'. From his realist perspective, intervention programmes
represent theories about how to change behaviour, and the results, carefully
evaluated, enable theory to be continuously refined. Evidence in realist synthesis is always contextualised and perspectival; 'evidential truths are partial,
provisional and conditional' (ibid., p. 175). It cannot tell us what to do, or
guarantee 'effective' interventions. But it is still worthwhile, with the possibility of 'achieving some small betterment' (ibid., p. 167); and able to 'alert
the policy community to caveats and considerations that should inform decisions' (ibid., p. 100). This, then, is evidence not as a definitive answer, not
as a substitute for thought, but rather as a provocation to thought, a form of
documentation (a concept and practice to which I will return) that contributes to reflection, dialogue and deliberation. In short, thinking in context and
thinking the complex.

Incredulity at the story of quality and high returns, and its more grandiose
claims, does not mean doubting the value of early childhood education. I want
to make very clear that my critical stance towards the story of quality and high
returns does not mean I think early childhood education is unimportant and has
no worthwhile effects. On the contrary. I will argue its importance and discuss
potential effects in a less positivistic and a less economistic way in Chapter 4,
contending that early childhood education can play a significant part in creating
flourishing lives and democratic societies.

Nor does my incredulity at the more grandiose claims of the story of quality
and high returns mean that I dismiss the substantial body of positivistic research
that points to early childhood education having some specific effects. Rather I
question the meaning, the significance and the consequences of these effects.
Take, for example, the relationship between early childhood education, maternal employment and child poverty. One way in which early childhood services
are meant to contribute to child poverty reduction is the 'positive effect [they
have] on maternal employment levels in many countries, even given other
contextual influences' (Green and Mostafa, 2011, p. 4). There is clearly something in this argument. So, for example, child poverty fell by half under the
1997–2010 New Labour government in England, and about a quarter of this
fall can be linked to higher rates of employment among lone parents (Brewer,
2012, p. 33), some of which in turn was due to increased provision of early
childhood education.

I also have no reason to question the conclusion of most positivistic research that children attending 'good quality' early childhood education are better prepared for the subsequent regime of compulsory schooling and perform somewhat better, both before and after entry, when assessed against certain developmental or educational norms. See, for example, the results of the large-scale Effective Provision of Preschool Education (EPPE) study in England (Sylva *et al.*, 2008); the cross-national overview of long-term educational effects of large-scale or universal early years programmes by Christopher Ruhm and Jane Waldfogel (2011); or UNESCO's 2012 EFA Global Monitoring Report (UNESCO, 2012). Though note the contradictory findings from a recent follow-up to the US Head Start programme, which concludes that 'the evidence is clear that access to Head Start improved children's preschool outcomes across developmental domains, but had few impacts on children in kindergarten through 3rd grade' (Puma *et al.*, 2012, p. xvi).

Such results seem unsurprising. If combining employment and parenting is made easier by providing services that include safe and reliable care for children, it would be surprising if this had no effect on parental employment and child poverty. It would be surprising, too, if 'quality' early childhood education employed to ready young children for compulsory schooling had no effects: such powerful 'human technologies' geared to achieving this predetermined goal should make some difference.

But these predictable results also need more critical appraisal that puts them in perspective. The main reason for the fall in child poverty in England under a New Labour government was not increased maternal employment but financial redistribution through the tax and benefit system (Cribb *et al.*, 2012). Moreover, increasing 'in work' poverty due to increasing low-waged employment (Kenway, 2008; Hill, 2012) suggests that the equation of ↑childcare= ↑employment =↓poverty may be another instance of over-simplified thinking. Much will depend on the nature of the employment available as well as the costs of 'childcare'. In other words, parental employment by itself is not the solution to poverty and inequality; financial redistribution and a supply of decent jobs play an equally or more important part. It might be added that while access to 'affordable' early childhood education is an essential component of any strategy to reconcile work and family life, promote equal opportunities and combat social exclusion, once again by itself it is not enough; other components are needed for successful strategies, including a range of additional policies, changes in workplace culture and practice, and men assuming more responsibility for the care and upbringing of children. Moreover the good that early childhood education can do in reducing poverty and increasing employment can easily be reversed by changes in economic conditions – recessions, casualisation of labour, welfare cut-backs and so on.

If the employment and poverty effects need putting into perspective, so too do school effects. For example, Dumas and Lefranc (2010) conclude that a rapid increase in early childhood education in France in the 1960s and 1970s saw improvements in later school performance, even indeed in employment in later life. Even if such findings are unquestioningly accepted at face value, they represent a one-off improvement resulting from the move to universal early childhood education for children over 3 years of age; American policy-makers may not as yet have been persuaded to make this move, but many European countries have been and will have already gained any bonus associated with it. (Nor, one might add, is France today an outstanding example of economic success, at least viewed from a neoliberal perspective, while it retains its fair share of social exclusion and inequality, especially among its minority ethnic communities.)

The limits of the school effects of early childhood education should also be appreciated. The European Commission itself acknowledges, in advocating investment in early childhood education, that 'educational policies alone cannot address educational disadvantage' (2006, p. 10). Parental education, social class and parenting style remain powerful influences, with more effect on school performance than early childhood education (Waldfogel, 2004; Sylva et al., 2008; Penn, 2011); not to mention the privileging effect of private education at fee-paying schools.[7]

Last but not least, this critical appraisal of predictable results also raises questions about purpose and desirability, in particular whether it is the role of early childhood education, simply and unquestioningly, to prepare or ready children for a regime of compulsory school education – a regime that some would contend is increasingly conservative, standardising and narrow, conducted in schools that are increasingly testing sites and 'exam factories' (Coffield and Williamson, 2011). Such an unequal relationship between early childhood and compulsory education can have problematic consequences, in particular 'schoolification', an expressive term for primary schooling 'taking over early childhood institutions in a colonising manner' (OECD, 2006, p. 62), leading to a 'school-like approach to the organisation of early childhood provision', the adoption of 'the content and methods of the primary school' with a 'detrimental effect on young children's learning' (OECD, 2001, p. 129), and 'neglect of other important areas of early learning and development' (p. 42). While mathematics, language and science matter, the question is how best to work with them in early childhood education; while the problem is how to avoid them contributing to further schoolification by the spread of crude and over-simplified educational approaches that are at odds with the learning strategies of young children and that end up doing more harm than good. I shall return later to this important issue.

Early childhood education can make an important contribution to education overall and can provide important opportunities for learning and knowledge; that is not at issue. What is at issue is what relationship there should be between early childhood and compulsory education – indeed between all parts of the education system. Preparing or readying children is but one of several possible alternative relationships, and one which I would argue expresses the worst kind of unthinking instrumentalism, focused on means to achieving a taken-for-granted end, whilst avoiding political questions about education to which I will shortly come (for an extensive discussion of alternative relationships between early childhood and compulsory education, see Moss, 2013). Simply to say that children who have some 'quality' early childhood education perform somewhat better in compulsory schooling both states the obvious and begs too many questions to be useful.

It is time to draw this discussion to a conclusion. What feeds my incredulity at the story of quality and high returns is the great and simplistic redemptive expectations placed on early childhood education, and other early childhood interventions, which bear so little relationship to what they can reasonably be expected to achieve. A sense of proportion is needed, and is provided by Naomi Eisenstadt, who led the English government's ambitious Sure Start programme for its first seven years, when she reflects on 'what I have learnt and what I have achieved' (Eisenstadt, 2011, chapter 9). The rationale for this investment in services for young children was 'that if you could ameliorate the negative impact of poverty on children, you could break the cycle of deprivation', a view supported at the time by numerous research studies and programme evaluations of the sort I have discussed above. But in her retrospective reflections, Eisenstadt acknowledges the work of Wilkinson and Pickett, as well as of geographer Daniel Dorling (2010), with their emphasis on the centrality of inequality and their conclusion that more equal countries 'deliver better outcomes for all citizens across the income distribution' (ibid., p. 140).

While retaining her faith in the value of early intervention – 'I would argue that improving the lot of the poor is a social good in its own right, even if social mobility does not shift' – Eisenstadt now has serious qualifications about what it can achieve by itself:

> The most important lesson for me from the last 11 years is the need to address inequality as well as poverty and low attainment . . . We set out with Sure Start to improve the educational, social and emotional development of young children living in poverty so as to reduce the chances of growing up to be poor as adults. We have probably achieved the first part of that aim, but have been less successful in the second part . . . I believe that without significant redistribution of wealth across social classes, where you are born and who your parents are will remain a significant determinant of life chances . . . The expectation that early years services, however wonderful, could affect overall inequality was unrealistic. This shift will come from wider social reforms.
>
> (ibid., pp. 160–1)

Similar sentiments are expressed, more cogently and with the benefit of even more experience, by psychologist Edward Zigler, one of the founders of the Head Start Project in the United States, in a short commentary titled *Forty Years of Believing in Magic is Enough.* Early intervention programmes might, he conceded, reduce the academic achievement gap between children from poor and more advantaged homes, but they can never close the gap because:

> [t]here is no magical permanent cure for the problems associated with poverty . . . Expecting the achievement gap to be eliminated, however, is relying too much on the fairy godmother. Poor children simply have too much of an environmental handicap to be competitive with age-mates from homes characterized by good incomes and a multitude of advantages
> . . .
> Are we sure there is no magic potion that will push poor children into the ranks of the middle class? Only if the potion contains health care, childcare, good housing, sufficient income for every family, child rearing environments free of drugs and violence, support for parents in all their roles, and equal education for all students in school. Without these necessities, only magic will make that happen.
>
> (Zigler, 2003, p. 12)

A further and last reason that my credulity is strained by the story of quality and high returns is not only that its expectations are too great, but it is too narrowly focused on certain minority groups deemed to be problematic or failing. It forgets or overlooks the fact that more advantaged families are not waiting patiently for 'poor children' to take their 'magic potion' and catch up, simply marking time until the achievement gap has closed and the fabled 'level playing field' has been achieved. Not only is the relative situation of 'poor' children deteriorating under neoliberalism, as inequality increases. But more advantaged parents, driven by fear of their children failing in an increasingly competitive economy, haunted by the prospect they may end up losers rather than winners, are frantically deploying their formidable resources to ensure the educational, therefore economic, success of their offspring and will continue to do so:

> [T]he well-heeled have always bought social privilege. The best private nurseries and schools, the coaching, the acquisition of accomplishments, the elite university; anything that can secure a competitive edge for their offspring will be supplemented and supplanted [in the future] by gene therapy, a consumer choice for all who can afford it.
>
> (Rose and Rose, 2012, p. 153)

Put another way, middle-class parents are always more likely to thrive in an economic and education system built on neoliberal values of competition, markets and individual choice. They are able to deploy not only more money but also more knowledge, skills and contacts, or 'cultural capital',[8] than less advantaged groups (Ball *et al.*, 1994; Whitty *et al.*, 1998; Ball, 2003). Indeed, rather than there being one playing field for all, in need of levelling to give everyone an equal opportunity, it is more a case of there being numerous playing fields, each individually level and each hosting differently valued teams, with parents striving by hook or by crook to get their children moved up onto a more valued playing field to maintain distance from children in the poorer teams. So while the tellers of the story of quality and high returns may often talk about early childhood interventions breaking the 'cycle of disadvantage', they never mention the other side of the coin, the cycle of advantage, or how the two might be implicated in a systemic relationship of unequal income, wealth and power.

I repeat, early childhood education matters; I will give my reasons for saying so later. But it is not a game changer, removing or substantially reducing inequality and injustice at a stroke or, indeed, in the longer term. It is not magic and so much more is in play; the world is far too complex for simple solutions. If we truly want to tackle inequality and injustice, then we need redistributive policies and strong welfare states; we need to renew, extend and deepen democracy; and we need to nurture values of equality, solidarity and sustainability.

Two final thoughts on the mountain of positivistic research that plays such a prominent part in the story of quality and high returns. First, if only a fraction of this effort had been devoted to researching early childhood education from other disciplinary, theoretical and paradigmatic perspectives, in other words to working with other stories, we might by now have a better understanding of the full potentiality of early childhood education. Second, how sad that there has been so little dialogue between researchers and others working with different perspectives, between, if you will, different story tellers. Reviewing a book about the Minnesota Twin Study on the genetic and environmental influences on development, Michael Rossi takes issue with the author's conclusion that '[s]cience rests on data, not on dialogue', arguing that this 'gets it exactly wrong. The building blocks of science are data of one form or another, but dialogue is the basis on which science rests; discussion is what gives meaning to the numbers; the tales that I tell about data are what give it substance' (Rossi, 2013, p. 28).

Instead of exchanging and discussing each other's tales together, instead of dialogue, we have had decades of division. The positivists have sat round their camp fires and told each other the same old story, whilst attracting an attentive if somewhat uncritical audience of powerful people and organisations. While those telling other stories, such as the one I recount in Chapter 4, have sat round their camp fires, but talking mostly to themselves, the powerful unaware of and uninterested in their presence. A sad state of affairs indeed.

Governing the child – and others

There is, I have attempted to show, good cause for incredulity about the story of quality and high returns. But I don't like the story of quality and high returns for other reasons. It has a dangerously authoritarian streak, leading towards an ever-stronger governing of the child. Surprise and amazement, context and subjectivity, uncertainty and unexpected outcomes, experimentation and democracy find no place in the story of quality and high returns in its drive for evidence-based and 'tightly defined programmes', effective performance and predicted outcomes, investment and assured profit, with its attention focused on logging and measuring the expected, the already known, the norm. Faced by complexity and diversity, the unavoidable and rich messiness of life, the story calls for redoubling efforts to prescribe, standardise and control.

Swedish researcher Hillevi Lenz Taguchi describes this process of increased governing, of how a growing awareness of complexity and diversity has been accompanied not by finding ways to embrace and work with them, but instead by attempts to reduce them:

> [T]he more we seem to know about the complexity of learning, children's diverse strategies and multiple theories of knowledge, the more we seek to impose learning strategies and curriculum goals that reduce the complexities of this learning and knowing. Policy makers look for general structures and one-dimensional standards for practices. These are based on contemporary and updated developmentally appropriate practices . . . to provide consistent and equal quality for everyone by treating them with regard to the same universal, comparable and centralized standards . . . In fact, the more complex things become the more we seem to desire processes of reduction and thus increase control, but such reduction strategies simultaneously make us risk shutting out the inclusion and social justice we say we want to achieve.
>
> (2010a, p. 14)

The complexity and diversity reduction strategies that Lenz Taguchi describes involve the rigorous application of potent human technologies to ensure young children conform to 'the same universal, comparable and centralized standards', whether these be norms of child development or mandated learning goals. Pervading many of these technologies, providing both rationales and means for technical practices, and playing a powerful role in the story of quality and high returns, is the discipline of developmental psychology. Erica Burman has described the emergence of developmental psychology in the nineteenth century as 'prompted by concerns to classify, measure and regulate' (1994, p. 18), and this remains today one of its main functions in early childhood education, providing an abstract map of how children are supposed to be at any given age – 'developmental stages' – and producing an image of the scientific child to which I will return. By using these maps drawn from theories of child development, we 'lose sight of what is really taking place in the everyday lives of children and pedagogues, since reality is more complex, contextualised and perspectival than the maps we draw'; while, and here is the main contribution of child development to governing, 'the child becomes an object of normalization . . . with developmental assessments acting as a technology of normalization determining how children should be' (Dahlberg *et al.*, 2013, p. 39). We are back to checking if Johnny or Jemima have met our goals according to our measures, if they are normal, rather than seeing and documenting what Johnny or Jemima can actually do.

In these processes of complexity and diversity reduction, the otherness or singularity of the child is grasped, not respected, to make the Other into the Same, raising ethical issues to which I return in Chapter 4. The story of quality and high returns has no answer to diversity and complexity, except to treat them as threats to be tamed and controlled through ever-stronger governing. Certainly it has no way of realising their potentialities, wasting as Lenz Taguchi implies important new understandings and possibilities for education.

But this applies not just to children. The story of quality and high returns also means ever-stronger governing of adults, whether it be parents who need to understand, support and, where called on, participate in the human technologies applied to their children; or educators, who need as technicians to embody prescriptive and standardised methods and outcomes in order to apply proven human technologies with precision to achieve prescribed results. With its strong instrumentality, expressed in a will to achieve predetermined and standardised outcomes, and its belief in the power of prescriptive human technologies precisely applied – those 'tightly defined programmes' – the story of quality and high returns has but one ending: bringing children and adults alike within a pervasive and effective system of surveillance and control and, in the case of children, from an ever younger age.

Bad politics

The story of quality and high returns suffers from and inflicts the tedium of utter predictability, repeating its simple tale over and over again with little variation and no affect, couched in a monotonous and lifeless language. Focused on always already known and defined outcomes, intent to 'tame, predict, supervise, control or evaluate according to already determined standards' (Olsson, 2009, p. 185), there is no room for curiosity or imagination, for invention and the new. No one under the story's spell recognises or even looks for the unexpected or the previously unknown.

But if the story of quality and high returns fails to convince, if I dislike its will to govern and find it aesthetically stultifying, I dislike it as much for its politics. Part of the problem is the story's denial of the centrality of politics to education, indeed of any role for politics, exemplifying the erosion of politics before the neoliberal onslaught of economics and management. Driven by a will to govern, but also doubtless by a will to improve, deficiencies are identified by the story tellers and then 'rendered technical', a process that in the words of Tania Murray Li, 'confirms expertise and constitutes the boundary between those who are positioned as trustees, with the capacity to diagnose deficiencies in others, and those who are subject to expert direction' (2007, p. 7). Those who tell the story of quality and high returns thus treat early childhood education as, first and foremost, a technical practice, dominated by the technical question 'what works?' and with the technique of evidence-based policy and practice supposedly able to supply the one right, technical answer. The other side of the coin is that '[q]uestions that are rendered technical are simultaneously rendered non-political' (ibid.).

I would contend, however, that early childhood education, any education indeed, is first and foremost a political practice. What do I mean? Political theorist Chantal Mouffe defines 'politics' as 'an ensemble of practices, discourses and institutions which seek to establish order and organise human coexistence in conditions that are potentially conflictual . . . politics domesticates hostility'; while the 'political' can be understood as expressing and negotiating the conflictual in life, recognising a 'dimension of antagonism inherent in human relations' (Mouffe, 2000, p. 101). Li (2007) develops this agonistic theme by defining the practice of politics as 'the expression, in word or deed, of a critical challenge . . . It opens up a front for struggle' (p. 12).

Mouffe's definition might be extended with an added perspective: that the political involves taking responsibility for that which is of common concern (Biesta, 2004). The 'political', therefore, might be said to encompass issues that are both of public interest and subject to disagreement. While 'political practice' refers to the open and democratic deliberation and contestation that should follow from the recognition of alternatives about such issues of public interest and about which there are differences of opinion. But it is more than just a contest between differences of opinion; politics also involving contesting dominance, the 'refusal of the way things are' (Li, 2007, p. 12), and the story that claims it is the one and only truth.

Early childhood education is, in my view, primarily a political practice for two main reasons. First, because it is a matter of common concern, a public matter, an assertion I consider further in Chapter 4 when discussing the importance and meaning of 'public education'. Second, because there are conflicting views about it, which are expressed as divergent answers to certain political (or critical) questions. Mouffe defines such questions as 'not mere technical issues to be solved by experts . . . [but questions that] always involve decisions which require us to make choices between conflicting alternatives' (Mouffe, 2007). Some of the political questions for early childhood education are ontological. What is, in the words of Karl Mannheim (1893–1947), the 'diagnosis of our time'? What is our understanding or image, of the child, of the educator, of the early childhood centre? What does education mean? Some are epistemological. What paradigm do we adopt? What is knowledge? How do we learn? While others are axiological. What are the purposes of education? What are its fundamental values? What ethics?

If part of the bad politics of the story of quality and high returns is that it talks as if early childhood education is not a political practice, but merely technical, the other part is the political answers it does come up with – without acknowledging that this is what it has done, without acknowledging the presence of political questions, without acknowledging the possibility of alternatives. Ignoring the existence of politics and political questions does not mean they disappear or never existed in the first place: conflicting alternatives are there and choices made, even if neither is acknowledged. The story of quality and high returns comes up with answers to political questions, but they are mostly implicit and taken-for-granted, needing to be deduced by careful interpretation of what is said as well as what is not said.

As far as I can make these deductions, I dislike what I come up with. Here are some examples:

- A diagnosis of our time and a view of the future that presumes, without question, the desirability, inevitability and perpetuity of neoliberal capitalism and rampant novelty consumerism: 'there is no alternative', only more of the same. Faced by this necessity, the primary, indeed overriding, purpose of education is economic, acting as a 'means to develop human capital rather than promote democratic learning or citizenship objectives' (Hyslop-Margison and Sears, 2006, p. 3). The particular task facing early childhood education as the first stage of lifelong learning is to start the continuous process of producing and maintaining autonomous, enterprising and risk-managing subjects, a competitive, flexible and compliant workforce, and an informed, insatiable and individualistic body of consumers, so ensuring personal and national survival in a never-ending global rat race. As a Minister responsible for early childhood education in England put the matter in a speech: 'The 21st century will belong to those countries that win the global race for jobs and economic advantage. In order for every adult to fulfil their potential, they need to be properly equipped with essential skills from the very beginning of their lives' (Truss, 2013). The government policy paper that accompanied that speech, the vacuously titled *More Great Childcare*, insists that '[m]ore great childcare is vital to ensuring we can compete in the global race' (Department for Education (England), 2013, p. 6). Education, then, is perpetual preparation, continuous readying of the child, the youth and the adult for the next stage of lifelong learning, all driven by the ultimate goal: ensuring a pliant and passive labour force inscribed with neoliberal values and equipped to respond to the ceaseless, shifting demands of the market.
- A paradigm of positivism or regulatory modernity, with its basic tenets or foundations. What are these? The stable and coherent self, the transparency of language, the rationality of humans, the ability of reason to overcome conflicts between truth, power and knowledge, and that freedom involves obeying rational laws (Flax, 1990); and the value given to certainty and mastery, linearity and *predetermined* outcomes, objectivity and universality. Ontology and epistemology are central to paradigm. Regulatory modernity

believes in universals and essences that can be revealed and represented, to give us true knowledge of how the world really is:

[A prominent feature of the paradigm of modernity] is its claim to the transcendent status of irreducible universal knowledge. The basis for this claim lies in the idea that value-free, archetypal knowledge is possible and accessible by way of rational or dialectical scientific methods and standards of proof. One aspect of the superiority claimed by scientific knowledge is its purported insulation from the vagaries of human diversity and contingency by the exercise of reason. It is precisely because of this ostensible autonomy that modern knowledge lays claim to Universal Truth.

(Otto, 1999, p. 17)

Such ontological and epistemological positioning inscribes the dominant discourse in early childhood education, giving the story of quality and high returns a will to know and master the child, and a belief in the ability of scientific knowledge and technical practice to enact this will through early intervention.

- The image of the child as a stable subject and a fixed entity, with an essence that can be known, represented and predicted; as a reproducer of knowledge and values, whose task it is to acquire what we, in the adult world, have designated as normal and necessary (including those 'essential skills' for the global race); as the scientific child or child of nature, 'an essential being of universal properties and inherent capabilities whose development is viewed as an innate "natural" process – biologically determined, following general laws . . . [in] a standard sequence of biological stages that constitute a path to full realization' (Dahlberg *et al.*, 2013, p. 49); and as a unit of human capital, to be exploited in the interests of capitalism through 'being properly equipped with essential skills from the beginning of their lives' in a continuous process of lifelong learning. Pervasive, too, is the image of the 'poor' child, the child defined in terms of deficiency and need, vulnerability and disadvantage, a passive and incompetent child to be redeemed through high-quality, high-tech early intervention.

- The image of the educator as a transmitter and reproducer of predetermined knowledge and values; as a technician, trained in a range of discrete and measurable competencies that enable the effective application of pedagogical human technologies; and as a self-interested and essentially untrustworthy individual whose performance must be monitored, managed and moulded through the deployment of powerful managerial human technologies. This image is quite at odds with any concept of the educator as a professional, with an overriding responsibility towards her or his students, guided by a professional code of conduct, and 'who has traditionally [not] wanted to have the terms of their practice and conduct dictated by anyone else but their peers, or determined by groups or structural levers outside of their control' (Olssen and Peters, 2005, p. 325). In the story of quality and high returns, infused by neoliberalism, 'the patterning of power is established on contract, which in turn is premised upon a need for compliance, monitoring and accountability organized in a management line and established through a purchase contract based upon measurable outputs' (ibid.). So there is the emerging image, too, of the educator as autonomous contractor, whose job and remuneration will increasingly depend on delivering demonstrable 'value for money' – payment by results – contributing thus to ensuring a high return on investment.

• The image of the early childhood centre as a factory or processing plant – for the effective and efficient production of predetermined outcomes through the exact deployment of human technologies, outcomes that include equipping young children 'with essential skills' and readying them for compulsory schooling so they arrive 'ready to learn' in the mode required by that conservative institution. Or, in Foucault's terms, an enclosure for the production of docile and useful bodies through the exercise of disciplinary power.

• Education framed within the epistemological assumptions of regulatory modernity as a process of attaining certain defined developmental and learning goals, en route to reproducing knowledge of reality, a process in which the learner is 'independent and separate from other subjects as well as from the material environment, matters and artefacts in the world around them'. This is premised on a representational view of knowledge, which understands it to be an objective, stable and accurate representation of a pre-existing reality, a literal reproduction of the world. In this representational epistemology, learning is:

> a process that progresses in a linear fashion from a stage of a lower degree of cognitive complexity and abstraction in the individual child's language construction, to an increasingly more advanced conceptual stage . . . Knowledge is understood as cognitive constructs in language . . . believed to represent pre-existing things and phenomena in reality . . . [The learning subject] acts upon their world in order to discover the 'laws of nature' and uncover its hidden truths. These universal laws stand above and transcend humans . . . we see ourselves as 'beings-*in*-the world' (Barad, 2007: 160), who discover and learn about it, as we inhabit it as independent and free subjects and make use of it for our own benefit. Humans have, in line with this thinking, always sought a position of mastery over nature *in* the material world.
>
> (Lenz Taguchi, 2010a, pp. 17–18)

What we end up with is an education scathingly described by Olsson as 'driven by uncreative thought . . . embracing a trivialised idea of learning and knowledge expressed through the economic logic, and the right input-output relation . . . [and] where we shall be measured, weighed, quality assured, predicted, supervised, controlled, evaluated' (2013, p. 231). Instead of creative thought, we (children and adults) are locked into an idea of learning and knowledge that is 'about "thinking right" and about reproducing knowledge that already exists' (ibid.), where questions and answers are givens, and which leaves no space for invention, for the new, for the interesting, for the remarkable and for the surprising.

I disagree profoundly with these and other (implicit) political answers embedded in the story of quality and high returns, and will offer some of my own answers to the key political questions in Chapter 4.

But there is one further reason for levelling this accusation of bad politics. Putting too much faith in early childhood education as a 'magic potion' is not only misleading; it is dangerous too. Social, economic and political problems are transformed into technical problems with technical solutions – 'rendered technical'. By pretending there is a relatively easy fix for many of the profound problems that confront our societies, and by implying that the cause of these problems lies with individual failings that can be rectified by 'early interventions' and 'tightly defined programmes', the story of quality and high returns distracts attention from structural inequalities and lets injustice off the hook. After all, the poor have their Head Start or their Sure Start and if they don't do well with that behind them, then they only have themselves to blame. It is a story of and for the status quo.

Helen Penn, in her critique of the Human Capital approach that plays so large a part today in early childhood education, in particular in the story of quality and high returns, argues that as it has developed under neoliberalism it takes:

> inequity for granted or at worst ignores it . . . [It] does not raise questions regarding social justice in analysing the situation of poor children, nor does it consider redistribution as part of the possible solutions/redress . . . [Instead the] basic assumption is that it is possible to provide interventions for young children that directly, or indirectly, teach them how to compete or succeed, and this in turn will lead to poverty reduction.
>
> (Penn, 2010, pp. 53, 61)

Picking up on the same theme, Donald Gillies contends that '[f]undamental inequity is entirely elided in the Human Capital Theory model: any inequities of outcome can be attributed to the shortcomings of individuals in respect of their choices or capital returns. The overarching economic, social, and political system is essentially absent from any analysis, let alone criticism' (2011, p. 235). Jerome Kagan, eminent Harvard psychologist, suggests that the investment rationale so pervasive in today's early childhood education has traction in the United States because not only is it a seductive idea but the alternative, to recognise deep inequality, is too painful (Kagan, 2000).

We have a strange situation. Whilst the understanding and practice of education has narrowed, the expectation placed on it has broadened to a remarkable extent, to serve as magic cure and elixir of success. Writing about the education system in the United States, in particular in urban areas, Jane Anyon maintains that 'We have been counting on education to solve the problems of unemployment, joblessness, and poverty for years', but as education did not cause these problems, 'education cannot solve them' (Anyon, 2005, p. 3). Education, she continues, can augment macroeconomic policy, but that policy itself should be the priority; education can all too easily become a substitute for interventions that would actually lower poverty and inequality, such as a large rise in minimum wage, investment in urban job creation and enforcing laws against racial segregation in housing and hiring.

While looking beyond one country and based on 30 years of cross-national comparative research, Wilkinson and Pickett conclude that:

> [t]he evidence shows that reducing inequality is the best way of improving the quality of the social environment, and so the real quality of life, for all of us (including the better-off) . . . It is clear that greater equality, as well as improving the wellbeing of the whole population, is also the key to national standards of achievement and how countries perform in lots of different fields . . . If you want to know why one country does better or worse than another, the first thing to look at is the extent of inequality . . . And if, for instance, a country wants higher average levels of educational achievement among its school children, it must address the underlying inequality which creates a steeper social gradient in educational achievement.
>
> (Wilkinson and Pickett, 2009, pp. 29–30)

We live at a time when wealth has become increasingly and incredibly concentrated at levels last seen in the 1920s, not just in the United States but globally,[9] and when the wealthy, the top 1 per cent, behave with ever-increasing detachment and irresponsibility[10]; when the existing economic model has shown itself to be unsustainable and inimical to flourishing; when politics and policy-making come increasingly under the influence of the rich and powerful; when democracy, equality and sustainability have been undermined. It is, under such conditions, not surprising if we turn to technical experts to solve essentially political problems, experts who mostly 'exclude the structure of political-economic relations from their diagnoses and prescriptions' and who focus more 'on the capacities of the poor than on the practices through which one social group impoverishes another' (Li, 2007, p. 7). It is, I believe, no accident that in these circumstances, early childhood education has been put forward, along with other 'early interventions', as a simple, cheap and technical solution to complex and difficult political problems.

From this perspective, early childhood education, as it emerges in the story of quality and high returns, is part of the problem, not the solution. At a time of growing crisis, the story of quality and high returns distracts attention from critical analysis of the causes and effects of inequalities and other injustices, and of the radical solutions needed to rectify them, solutions involving redistribution of power, income and wealth, the development of new economic models, and (re)committing to democracy, equality and sustainability. No need, the story implies, to struggle politically to produce more equal, more democratic and more sustainable societies; no need to confront and challenge the deep-seated and powerful opposition to such a struggle. For all can be solved by quality early intervention, with high returns to investors as a bonus. This is, it seems to me, not only unconvincing but downright dangerous.

The story of markets

A diverse market [in early childhood services is] the only show in town.
(Archer, 2008)

Imagine arriving at your supermarket and finding members of a rival brand advising on how best they should display their goods . . . What has this to do with childcare? Well, this is exactly what the [English] Government is expecting the best nurseries to do in an effort to raise standards across the board. In the spirit of partnership working, both the private and main-tained [public] sectors will be expected to spend time sharing best practice with other nurseries, even if they are competitors . . . [To] ignore the com-merciality [*sic*] of such a request to the private sector is simply not realistic . . . Why should funds not be available to private companies that choose to offer 'consultancy advice'? I would be willing to set up such a training support group within my company – but please, let such a scheme be both realistic and commercial.
(Bentley, 2008, p. 12)

Market-based [early childhood] services have the potential to limit public expenditure and allow greater choice and control for parents.
(EC Communication, 2011, p. 6)

I now turn to the second story about early childhood education that flourishes today, very much on the up if not yet quite as prominent or widespread as the story of quality and high returns. It is the story of markets. This story says that early childhood education is best provided through developing a market in competing providers and services, in which the consumer can choose the service best suited to her or his needs, preferences and pocket. This way of doing things has, its proponents contend, a number of benefits: better meet-ing needs and preferences (choice); driving up standards (quality); providing best value for money (efficiency); protecting consumers against the self-interest and overweening power of providers (empowerment); improving or closing failing services (discipline); and stimulating new solutions to meet unmet and new consumer demands (innovation). Competition, the shibboleth of neo-liberals, is the driving force delivering these benefits (Cleveland and Krashinsky, 2004), together with individual choice, the other side of the same coin, between them supposedly ensuring the most efficient allocation of resources. Furthermore, although markets can and do include public providers, the true neoliberal claims that the private for-profit sector can always do the job better, seeking a nirvana of marketisation and privatisation: a market of competing entrepreneurial businesses.

Where the private sector does have a substantial presence, we begin to see the emergence of a second level of marketisation, a new chapter in the story of markets in early childhood education. Not just a first level where places in early childhood centres are traded in a market, with rival providers competing for the custom of parent-consumers. But also a market where early childhood centres themselves are traded, these centres being understood first and foremost as assets that can be bought and sold for profit, their value measured in terms of occupancy and financial return. The financialised flavour of this market – with its focus on asset values and its wheeling and dealing in 'nursery businesses' – is captured in the language of a business economist, working for a company that describes itself as the 'UK's foremost and most highly regarded provider of information and market intelligence on the independent health, community care and childcare sectors':

> In the near term, investment activity in the nursery market [i.e. the buying and selling of nurseries] is likely to be subdued as business asset values are below trend, and credit markets are only gradually opening up. More cautious future market expectations mean investors are looking to secure only high quality businesses at realistic prices. This selective activity is reflected in the nursery business property market, where a large number of properties are listed but the number of transactions is currently low as customers have been more restrained.
>
> (Blackburn, 2012, p. 57)

Another sample of how the market and trade in centres have become taken-for-granted parts of the early years landscape, at least in the UK, a country which has the highest proportionate level of for-profit provision in the world,[11] comes from *Nursery World*, a weekly early years magazine, whose news section regularly records nursery deals and which produces a supplement called 'Nursery Chains', focused on businesses owning a clutch of nurseries:

> Bright Horizons has bought nursery group kidsunlimited for £45m [million] in a move that sees the second largest UK chain add 64 settings and a childcare voucher business. The £45m deal – the largest acquisition of this year – brings the total number of nurseries owned by Bright Horizons

[*sic*] Family Solutions in the UK to 203, offering 15,500 childcare places. The international company, which has headquarters in the US, operates more than 750 childcare centres worldwide . . . Courteney Donaldson, director of childcare at Christie + Co, which advised Bright Horizons on the acquisition, said, 'Over the past year or so, the nursery, childcare and education marketplace has been the stand-out sector in terms of the vibrancy of its transactional marketplace, particularly across the corporate and regional marketplace'.

(Morton, 2013, pp. 6–7)

The names of the key players (or brands) – 'Bright Horizons' and 'kidsunlimited' – attempt to project an aura of warmth and aspiration, albeit tackily. But the whole exercise is inscribed with the stilted language and managerial practice of business and finance: 'chain', 'voucher business', 'solutions', 'headquarters', 'transactional marketplace', 'corporate and regional marketplace'. And despite the attempt at warm words bandied round by the companies – 'We [at Bright Horizons] have long admired the kidsunlimited brand focus on [yes!] quality outcomes' – there is no getting away from the fact that we are witnessing an exercise in corporate ambition and financial muscle, as Bright Horizons ingests kidsunlimited to close the gap on the biggest UK chain, the 'Busy Bees Group', with its 214 nurseries and 19,509 places.[12]

Returning to what might be termed first-level marketisation, a trade in early childhood education places with providers competing for the business of parents, this has been spreading for some time and well beyond just one country. The second report of the OECD *Starting Strong* review of early childhood policies in 20 member states noted that the:

> marketisation of early childhood services has been promoted in recent years in OECD countries . . . To limit public expenditure, and allow greater choice and control by parents are among the reasons advanced. Vouchers and parent subsidies are favoured over direct funding of services in the expectation that parental purchase of services will bring private entrepreneurs, new funding and greater dynamism into the provision of services – all this with lesser cost to government.

(OECD, 2006, p. 115)

The spread, though, is not even. Marketisation has gone furthest in Anglophone countries, Africa and the Asia Pacific region. In Europe, it has become the dominant mode of delivery in England and the Netherlands (Lloyd, 2012, p. 4). But everywhere, like the wider neoliberal story, the story of markets is extending its reach. (For a fuller discussion about the marketisation of early childhood education, see Lloyd and Penn, 2012).

Why I don't like the story of markets

Again, I dislike the politics, an objection to which I'll return. The language used in the story again reveals an impoverished, instrumental view of education dominated by economic thinking and relationships. But the story is not just deeply unappealing. It is not convincing, lacking credibility even in its own terms; once again, it invites incredulity.

How do markets in early childhood education work in practice? Or, put another way, are the claims made for markets convincing? Australian early childhood researcher Jennifer Sumsion has studied the story of markets in her country, where it has gained primacy in early childhood education since the early 1990s, driven by government commitment to 'consumer choice, competitiveness, profit maximisation and a downsizing of government's role in favour of private sector expansion . . . and the assumption that privatisation will enhance the efficiency of childcare provision' (2006 p. 101). However, she concludes, there is a 'lack of empirical evidence to support assertions about the "automatic superiority" (Crouch, 2003, p. 9) of market-dominated provision of social services generally (Meagher, 2004) and childcare specifically'.

Having reviewed the wider literature, I would agree (Moss, 2009, 2012). Admittedly the evidence is patchy. It is striking that those countries that have gone furthest down the marketisation road have signally failed to research and evaluate the *system* of early childhood education for which they have opted. Having willed markets in early childhood education into existence, they have neglected to enquire into how they work in practice and to what effect. Instead, we are left with bits and pieces of research, fragments that provide only limited insights.

Piecing together these fragments, it soon becomes clear that any discussion of or evidence about markets needs to be strongly contextualised and qualified. There is, in practice, no such thing as *the* market in early childhood education, a universal, unmediated and pure nexus of market relationships. Instead there are many, diverse and local markets, varying in: the extent and nature of regulation; the respective roles and modes of private and public funding; the density of supply and demand; the public/private mix of providers; not to mention the social, cultural and economic contexts within which they are located.

At best it can be said that the case for markets in early childhood education, judged in their own terms, is not proven.[13] It is not, for example, established that they are more efficient or more innovative. (Innovation, of course, is not necessarily always a good thing, for example, financial innovations brought about the 2008 financial crisis. This example also highlights the question: who gains from innovation? Innovation, in short is a political issue, not just a technical matter.)

What is apparent is that markets in early childhood services do not behave as markets are supposed to do. Sumsion finds that 'in Australia and internationally, evidence abounds of an "imperfect" market for childcare services that fails to conform to the principles of so-called market rationality' (2006, p. 101). From the Netherlands, economist Janneke Plantenga concludes that '[t]he childcare market [in her country] is an unusual and atypical market . . . [M]arket competition does not seem to matter much' (2012, p. 70). Whilst Stephen Ball and Carol Vincent echo the point, arguing from their research that the 'childcare market [in the UK] just does not work like markets are supposed to . . . and indeed it is a very inefficient market' (2006, p. 38).

One reason is the level of regulation and public funding. Governments are often reluctant to allow market forces full play in early childhood education, for example imposing systems of regulation (standards, curricula, etc.) and inspection and providing subsidies to parents to enable those on lower incomes to participate on a more equal (though not fully equal) footing in the market. I shall return to this market management later, in the next chapter.

But the reasons run far deeper, to the nature of the 'product' that 'businesses' in early childhood 'markets' purport to 'produce' and 'sell' to 'consumers', indeed to the very notion of commodification and contractual relationships that such terms express. Both Plantenga in the Netherlands and Ball and Vincent in the UK put their fingers on the problem:

> [Where] the quality of the product may depend directly on the personal relationship . . . raising efficiency by the introduction of market forces is almost impossible, because *the client does not fit into the idealised image of a mobile, detached consumer.* This conclusion may be even more relevant if the service is provided to a third party, as is often the case with care and welfare services.
>
> (Plantenga 2012, p. 75; emphasis added)

> The services which are required by consumers are complex and unusual. As our respondents unanimously see it, they want 'safety, happiness and love' . . . This is in a sense an impossible market. The *financial exchange is inadequate as a way of representing the relationship involved.*
>
> (Ball and Vincent 2007, p. 38; emphasis added)

In the story of markets, parents must adopt the role of *homo economicus*, the economically rational utility maximiser, 'the strictly egocentric, self-absorbed person who is "rational" in the peculiar sense of mainstream economics' (Häring and Douglas, 2012, p. 164). This means acting as informed, calculating consumers, 'mobile and detached', weighing up costs and benefits to arrive at a best buy and prepared to chop and change nursery supplier if the supplier fails to deliver or if a better deal turns up; in the same way, market savvy consumers are urged to switch between banks or fuel companies or broadband suppliers. But in early childhood education such market rationality in practice seems seriously impaired, rendering the market imperfect. People, in short, don't behave as marketeers think they should; financial exchange, as a consequence, 'is inadequate as a way of representing the relationship involved'.

Take the key task of being an informed consumer. This is hard enough at the best of times, because:

> [c]onsumers do not usually have easy access to all of the information they would need to judge effectively the value of what is on offer. Reliable and comparable information about the relative quality of different products, even those from the same supplier, often is not available or is manipulated by sellers. Moreover, most consumers would probably not have the background information or time necessary to make use of that information were it available.
>
> (Hammersley, 2013, p. 25)

But the problem is even more acute when it comes to services, such as early childhood education, not directly experienced by purchasers. Writing of the Netherlands, Plantenga observes that 'quality in particular can only be judged to a certain extent by parents' (2012, p. 70), since it is children not parents who actually attend services. Or, as Laura Sosinsky puts it, 'parents are the purchasers, and not the recipients of childcare and are not in the best position to judge its quality' (2012, p. 142). But making informed judgements is made even harder because:

> many parents have never purchased childcare before, and by the time they learn what they need to know, their children are old enough so that the parents may never purchase childcare again . . . [Furthermore, working parents have] little time to seek out and evaluate childcare, even if they knew entirely what they were looking for.
>
> (Cleveland and Krashinsky, 2002, p. 39)

Experience in the Netherlands confirms that:

> information is a real problem. The consumers [assumed to be parents] do not know every supplier and quite often receive information through informal networks. Furthermore the consumer is only partly able to check the quality of services . . . As a form of self-regulation, the sector has adopted a quality agreement with rules about a pedagogical plan, child–staff ratios, group size and accommodation. Parents, though, seem to value different aspects of quality, for example active play, the provision of different activities and short journeys. As a result, parents may overestimate a service's quality.
>
> (Marangos and Plantenga, 2006, p. 19)

So the market condition of well-informed consumers may be hard to achieve. But there is a further problem. What to do if the early childhood service does not live up to expectation? Faced by such failure, dissatisfied *homo economicus* might well switch suppliers – just as they might a bank or a gas supplier. Most actual parents don't: '[a] typical feature of the childcare market is that parents rarely switch once they have opted for a certain childcare provider' (Plantenga 2012, p. 70). The author explains this in terms of 'high switching costs', including a concern for the adverse effects of 'switching' on children – in other words, young children may be very upset by being moved from one supplier to another.

But this reluctance to assume the role of *homo economicus* is not confined to parents. The (male) nursery owner[14] quoted at the start of this section may be dismissive of 'the spirit of partnership working', likening nurseries to competing supermarket brands. This is a man who has truly entered into the market spirit. But the (female) workforce, working daily with children and parents, may be less inclined to adopt this entrepreneurial stance. Two studies by Jayne Osgood involving (female) English practitioners found that they emphasised caring, collaboration and community, values that were perceived to be at odds with, and at risk from, government reforms that emphasised competitive entrepreneurialism and favoured rationality, commercialism and measurability:

> [T]he ethic of care and approaches to management that female managers tend to adopt can be regarded as oppositional discourses to the masculine managerialism . . . embedded in government policy designed to promote entrepreneurialism . . . They were resistant to viewing children as financial commodities, but this became inevitable when seeking to make a profit.
>
> (Osgood, 2004, pp. 13, 16)

This offers an example of how markets and market thinking are not able to 'express and promote many values important to [education], such as mutually shared caring concern' (Held, 2002, p. 32).

The work of a new generation of behavioural economists, who apply the psychology of human behaviour to micro-economic decisions, has also cast doubt on the existence of the species *homo economicus*. Many studies and experiments that have 'tested the notion of *homo economicus* have unfailingly found it wanting', undermined by 'strong feelings of solidarity, fairness, cooperation and revenge [that] seem to be hardwired into human nature' (Häring and Douglas, 2012, p. 165). While Will Hutton and Philippe Schneider conclude that:

> [i]t is no longer axiomatic that the majority of people, the majority of the time, can be assumed to make choices that are unambiguously in their best interests . . . The mystery isn't why we make so many poor economic choices, but why we persist in accepting economic theory that predicts we are biased toward making good ones.
>
> (2008, p. 16)

Similar doubts have led Plantenga to conclude that, in early childhood education, 'market control by parents will always be limited' (2012, p. 75). Ball and Vincent go further, arguing that the current problems are irresolvable 'in so far as there are important paradigmatic differences between the nature of market relations and the nature of the social relations embedded in childcare . . . [T]he market is an exchange relationship rather than a shared relationship based on shared values' (Ball and Vincent, 2006, p. 48).

Of course, it may be possible over time to reshape the subjectivity and behaviour of people, to turn parents into informed and calculating consumers of early childhood education, to construct from the present unpromising material an authentic *homo economicus* perfectly suited to acting out the story of markets. But even if this were to be possible, is it something we want? Do we want a species consisting of billions of *homo economicus*? Can our species, faced by grave crises that endanger us all, survive such an evolution? Would not ideal markets, premised on exchange between egocentric individuals driven solely by self-interest, dissolve social ties (Held, 2002)? Would not realisation of *homo economicus*, the self-interested individual, 'curtail any collective transformation of the conditions of existence' (Read, 2009, p. 36)? More specifically, do we want to commodify early childhood education and render all relationships economic? Do we really want these relationships – between children, parents, educators and services – reduced to economic calculation and contractual exchange? Will that make for a better world? These are important political questions, ignored by those who tell the story of markets.

Which brings me to the political reasons for my dislike of the story of markets. I will not run through all the political questions I have argued are central to a choice of story, to show why I react so unfavourably to the answers embodied in the story of markets. Just four will suffice. I don't like the image of parents and of educators as *homo economicus*, and its underpinning assumption that every relationship in life should be reducible to a calculation of utility maximisation. I don't like the image of the early childhood centre as a business and as a tradable asset, whose primary purpose is to sell a product and generate a profit. And I don't like the image of the child in the story of markets.

Indeed, the child is a problem. Markets are premised on a contractual relationship between service suppliers and service consumers. But who, in the case of early childhood education, is the consumer? It could be argued that children are the direct consumers and it is certainly they who have most first-hand experience of the product. But most studies of and advocates for the market assume parents[15] are the consumers: they have the money, they make the choice and they buy the service, so they are allotted the lead role of consumer in the story of markets. Children are unlikely to have a strong voice in the choice or the continuing use of a service; they 'cannot easily communicate with the parent about what kind of care is being delivered' (Cleveland and Krashinsky, 2002, p. 39). So despite being the direct recipients of early childhood education, children are not protagonists in the exchange transaction: they are not consumers, whilst reference to children's rights or citizenship is noticeably absent in the story of markets. In this story the image of the child is, in effect, reduced to that of a passive object, which parents pay providers to care for and, perhaps, educate.

Finally, I view the story of markets as inimical to my answer to the question 'what are the fundamental values of early childhood education?', an answer that, as I shall develop in Chapters 4 and 5, has democracy at its core. This profound incompatibility is well expressed in a book by philosophers of education Wilfred Carr and Anthony Hartnett, whose title – *Education and the Struggle for Democracy* – suggests a political dimension unknown or alien to those who see nurseries purely as businesses trading commodities in the marketplace:

> Any vision of education that takes democracy seriously cannot but be at odds with educational reforms which espouse the language and values of market forces and treat education as a commodity to be purchased and consumed . . . 'Freedom of choice' will be a major principle in determining educational policy, [but] the notion of 'choice' will not simply refer to the rights of individuals to pursue their narrow self-interests in a competitive marketplace. Instead it will be recognised that, in a democracy, individuals do not only express personal preferences; they also make public and collective choices related to the common good of their society.
>
> (Carr and Hartnett, 1996, p. 192)

So as with the story of quality and high returns, so too with the story of markets. I respond to the story with incredulity, doubting the claims it makes. And I respond to it with distaste, for the bad politics it represents. Markets and their attendant values and relationships may have their place in some areas of economic life – but not I contend in areas that are predominantly political, social, cultural and ethical, areas that require 'public and collective choices' and have a major bearing on the 'common good', areas such as early childhood education. When organisations such as the European Commission blithely say, as quoted above, that marketisation of early childhood education gives 'greater choice and control for parents', I am left wondering not only what evidence they work with to produce this conclusion, but also what they mean by 'choice' and 'control', indeed if they can imagine 'choice' and 'control' as being exercised in ways other than market participation – by, for example, democratic means and the exercise of public and collective choice and control.

But how and why did early childhood education come to this pass? How, as a senior English civil servant put the matter, did a 'diverse market [in early childhood services become] the only show in town' in a country like England? How did the story of markets come to be told and gain so many listeners who find it plausible and persuasive? And what has amplified the story of quality and high returns, enabling it to achieve an even wider reach? To understand this, I have to turn to the rise and rise of a bigger, more epic story, a meta-narrative of recent decades: the story of neoliberalism.

Notes

1 This indiscriminate use of 'quality' is not confined to early childhood education. Try the simple exercise of counting how often you see or hear the word in use about you in the course of a day!

2 OECD's 'quality toolbox' contains a number of 'policy levers', including curriculum and standards; workforce conditions, qualifications and training; engaging families and communities; and advancing data collection, research and monitoring. Pull the levers, to provide 'quality' early childhood education, and high returns are promised including 'better child well-being and learning outcomes as a foundation for lifelong learning; more equitable child outcomes and reduction of poverty; increased intergenerational social mobility; more female labour market participation; increased fertility rates; and better social and economic development for the society at large' (www.oecd.org/edu/school/startingstrongiii-aqualitytoolbox-forearlychildhoodeducationandcare.htm).

3 The per capita GDP of the United States in 2010 was $46,588 compared with an average for all OECD countries of $33,971. Only Luxembourg, Norway and Switzerland had higher levels of per capita GDP (OECD, 2013).

4 In his 2013 State of the Union address, President Obama noted that 'fewer than 3 in 10 four-year-olds [in the United States] are enrolled in a high quality preschool program'. He proposed additional federal funding to assist states 'to expand high-quality preschool to reach all low- and moderate-income four-year-olds from families at or below 200% of poverty' (Obama, 2013). By contrast with this belated and partial extension, many European countries already have near universal provision not only for 4-year-olds, but also for 3-year-olds.

5 One consequence of the United States being the only member state of OECD that provides no universal entitlement to maternity or parental leave is that many children are placed in 'childcare' from a very early age, i.e. during their first year. In Sweden, with 13 months of parental leave paid at 80 per cent of earnings, there are virtually no children under 12 months of age in preschools; the number rises rapidly after 12 months, the age at which all children are entitled to a preschool place.

6 Despite the extreme hostility to taxes amongst sectors of American society, taxation in the United States as a percentage of GDP is amongst the lowest within OECD member states: 24.8 per cent in 2010 against an OECD average of 33.8 per cent and over 40 per cent in Denmark, Finland, Norway and Sweden (www.oecd.org/ctp/tax-policy/revenuestatisticstaxratioschangesto20102012edition.htm).

7 As the English Education Minister, a member of the right-wing Conservative Party, commented in a speech in May 2012, 'it is remarkable how many positions of wealth, influence, celebrity and power in our society are held by individuals who were privately educated'. This includes more than half of the cabinet members in the current UK government (*Daily Telegraph*, 2012).

8 Cultural capital consists of 'cultural habits and . . . dispositions inherited from' the family that are fundamentally important to school success (Bourdieu and Passeron, 1990 [1964], p. 14).

9 The Global Wealth Report 2012 concludes that 'the bottom half of the global population possess barely 1% of total wealth. In sharp contrast, the richest 10% own 86% of the world's wealth, with the top 1% alone accounting for 46% of global assets' (Credit Suisse, 2013, p. 13).

10 Henry (2012) arrives at a conservative estimate of $21 to $32 trillion for the amount of global private financial wealth 'invested virtually tax-free through the world's still-expanding black hole of more than 80 "offshore" secrecy jurisdictions' (p. 5). The owners of this staggering amount of wealth have essentially absolved themselves of any responsibility for society or the wider public good.

11 A report on the nursery market in the UK in 2009–10 (Laing and Buisson, 2010), estimated there to be 662,835 places in nurseries providing full day care, more than three-quarters in the for-profit sector; put another way, for-profit providers accounted for 81 per cent of the estimated £3.9 billion value of the UK 'childcare market'. Most of these providers are small, 'one nursery' businesses, though the share of nursery chains is increasing.

12 In November 2013, the Busy Bees Group was itself bought out by the private equity arm of the Ontario Teachers Pension Plan, whose other UK investments include airports, gas distribution and the operator of the national lottery.

13 The same can be said for the field of compulsory education, a recent OECD review on 'Markets in Education' concluding:

> Over the last decade a substantial body of research has emerged related to market mechanisms in education worldwide. Several reviews have been conducted and have come to quite similar conclusions regarding effects of policies aimed at increasing parental choice and school competition. In general, if any effects are found, they are small.
>
> (Waslander et al., 2010, p. 64)

14 While I know of no research on the subject, it is my impression that men are far more likely to be owners or senior managers of nursery businesses (i.e. the entrepreneurs) than they are to be workers in these services (i.e. the educators and carers). If this is the case, then it is another dimension of the strong gendering that characterises early childhood education.

15 In practice, the assumption is that the consumer and purchaser of services is the mother, as reflected in the widespread usage of terms like 'childcare for working mothers' and the common assumption that 'childcare' costs are a charge on the mother's earnings.

Chapter 3

The story of neoliberalism
A grand narrative of our time

Something is profoundly wrong with the way we live today. For thirty years we have made a virtue out of the pursuit of material self interest . . . Much of what appears 'natural' today dates from the 1980s: the obsession with wealth creation, the cult of privatization and the private sector, the growing disparities of rich and poor. And above all, the rhetoric which accompanies these: uncritical admiration for unfettered markets, disdain for the public sector . . . the delusion of endless growth.

(Judt, 2010, pp. 1–2)

The effect [of neoliberalism penetrating 'common sense' understandings] in many parts of the world has increasingly been to see it as a necessary, even wholly 'neutral', way for the social order to be regulated.

(Harvey, 2005, p. 41)

Economics are the method; the object is to change the heart and soul.

(Thatcher, 1981)

Whenever particular stories come to crowd out others, when they come to dominate the field, we need not only to interrogate these stories critically but also to ask why they get to be so influential. What is it about the times we live in that gives these stories such exposure and influence, and leads us to adopt their language and rhetoric? How is it we come to treat these stories as 'natural' and 'neutral', as true representations of the world, as statements of fact not fictions? Why do we embed as 'common sense a whole bundle of beliefs – ideas beyond question, assumptions so deep that the very fact they are assumptions is only rarely brought to light'? (Hall *et al.*, 2013, p. 13). We need, in short, a historical perspective that both relativises dominant stories, reminding us that there are many stories that have been and could be told; and that relates the current prominence of such stories to a particular temporal context.

That context, I believe, is the rise of neoliberalism as the dominant political economy. It is this phenomenon that is referred to above by historian Tony

Judt (1948–2010) when he wrote that for 'thirty years we have made a virtue out of the pursuit of material self interest . . . [and shown] uncritical admiration for unfettered markets'. It is this transformative change – the emergence of the story of neoliberalism as a meta-narrative of our age – that has provided a nurturing environment for the story of quality and high returns and now for the story of markets, giving them traction and momentum.

The rise of neoliberalism to prominence can be traced back to the 1970s, when it took advantage of the opportunities afforded by economic shocks, the onset of profound technological changes and the faltering of the social democracy and Keynesianism that it was to replace as a dominant regime.[1] It then gathered pace in the Reagan/Thatcher decade of the 1980s, to achieve hegemony as an economic regime during the 1990s. The USA and the UK may have taken the lead in this spread of the story of neoliberalism, but there has been a turn to neoliberalism in the political economy practically everywhere since the 1970s, so that it can be said today that 'almost all states have embraced some form of neoliberalism' (Harvey, 2005, p. 3).

This is not the first time that a liberalism of 'unfettered markets' has figured as a dominant regime of political economy, at least in Europe. There was a previous manifestation that thrived in the early stages of industrialisation in the nineteenth century, sometimes referred to as an age of laissez-faire capitalism, before being subdued by the rise of the 'social state', from the early years of the twentieth century, with its greater regulation of free-wheeling capitalism and greater recognition of the social:

> In the face of rising political unrest and evidence of the malign effects of irregular employment, poor living conditions and squalor, socialists and social liberals were now demanding more extensive social intervention to mitigate what were now seen as the inevitable social consequences of capitalist economic arrangements. Whatever their differences, in each case the term 'social' implied a kind of anti-individualism: the need to conceive of human beings as citizens of a wider collectivity who did not merely confront one another as buyers and sellers on a competitive market. Hence at least some aspects of the economy required to be politically governed in the name of the social, in order to dispel a whole range of conflicts . . . and to ensure social order, social tranquillity, perhaps even social justice.
>
> (Rose, 1999, p. 118)

But the liberalism of unfettered markets never went away. It went underground, where it was kept alive over the years by committed story tellers. Its recent resurgence is an instance of 'hegemonic globalisation' (Chapter 1), of what Harvey terms '[a] minority tradition becoming majoritarian' and an 'economic doctrine plucked from relative obscurity and transformed into a central guiding principle of economic thought and management' (2005, p. 2). The story went from the sidelines to centre stage because those committed story tellers bided their time and kept telling and refining their story, waiting for the opportunity to spread the word to a wider and more receptive audience, more on which in the final chapter.

In this chapter, I explore the story of neoliberalism and examine its bearing on both the stories of quality and high returns and of markets, making clearer the relationship between neoliberalism and the two dominant stories in early childhood education. But before doing so, I need to make two points clear. First, while it is necessary to sketch out some general features of the story of neoliberalism, it is important to avoid the idea that it is some monolithic entity, with a definition and practice that is homogeneous, universal and static, on which all agree, handed down *ex cathedra* from some economic papacy in a set of principles to which all true believers must strictly adhere. It is not 'an overarching system or mechanic totality that simply shapes subjects' (Nxumalo *et al.*, 2011, p. 195), but rather 'a complex, often incoherent, unstable and even contradictory set of practices that are organised around a certain imagination of the "market"' (Ball, 2012a, p. 3). Like the Catholic Church, neoliberalism's followers live in many places, come in many shapes and sizes, have other perspectives that matter in their lives; like the Catholic Church, neoliberalism may provide its followers with a frame of reference, a way of approaching life, but it does not control every thought and action and does not exclude other influences and beliefs. So rather than a monolithic thing, it is perhaps more useful to think of assemblages of ideas and practices that form 'multiple, heterogeneous, and at times incongruent connections' (Nxumalo *et al.*, 2011, p. 195), and that exert a powerful but not overwhelming influence.

Second, while I think neoliberalism – indeed any dominant regime of political economy – is important for understanding dominant stories in fields like education, I want to avoid being over-deterministic. I have no wish to reduce early childhood education simply to being a function of the prevailing political economy. For example, as I shall discuss later on, the story of quality and high returns in particular has a more complex relationship with neoliberalism, the former's will to govern being at seeming odds with the rhetoric of individual freedom and choice that forms a central part of the neoliberal story. It transpires that there are other influences at play, which in part gain their influence because neoliberalism contains its own contradictions, once we get behind its rhetoric.

So, and this is a point to which I will return in the last chapter, while neoliberalism has a powerful effect on education today, and we should seek to understand this effect, it is not omnipotent. There are contradictions, there are other stories to be heard, there are possibilities for resistance, there are changes in hand and in prospect since nothing stays the same. All of which gives cause for hope.

So what is the story of neoliberalism?

> [Neoliberalism's] bundle of ideas revolves around the supposed naturalness of 'the market', the primacy of the competitive individual, the superiority of the private over the public . . . [T]he free possessive individual engaging with others through market transactions, remains the touchstone.
>
> (Hall *et al.*, 2013, pp. 13–14)

The story of neoliberalism is a story about everything and everyone, offering a comprehensive worldview about how all human life can and should be reduced to a set of economic relationships and values. It is a story on an epic scale, a 'meta-narrative' that claims to explain everything, claims to offer the one right answer to every question, claims to be a universal panacea for every problem, need or desire the human species may have; it is a story to end all stories, a story of the end of history. As such, its influence has become pervasive: 'neoliberalism as worldview has sunk its roots deep into everyday life' (Mirowski, 2013a, p. 28).

It is a story about a particular form of capitalism in which certain ideas are particularly prominent. Many, such as Foucault, would see competition as neoliberalism's main idea or first principle. As Susan George observes 'competition is central [to neoliberalism] because it separates the sheep from the goats, the men from the boys, the fit from the unfit   [supposedly allocating] all resources, whether physical, natural, human or financial with the greatest possible efficiency' (1999, p. 3).

Competition works through the medium of markets and the transactions that take place therein between buyers and sellers. Markets are unparalleled information processors: 'central to neoliberalism is a core conviction that the market really does know better than any one of us what is good for ourselves and for society' (Mirowski, 2013a, p. 79). And if markets know best, then they should be pervasive, everything being fair game for marketisation, including of course early childhood education, since all things are viewed as commodifiable, deemed tradable commodities whose value is defined as their market value – their exchange value in a free market (Radin, 1996). Everything, in short, can be reduced to monetary value and that value is determined by the interplay of supply and demand in market relationships; Oscar Wilde's observation that '[n]owadays people know the price of everything and the value of nothing' would be dismissed, for 'price' and 'value' are, to the true neoliberal, one and the same.

Inequality is the basis, the driver of competition (Ball, 2013), inherent and necessary, since 'inequality has the capacity to sharpen appetites, instincts and minds, driving individuals to rivalries' (Lazzarato, 2009, p. 117). It is at the heart of neoliberalism, not just some unfortunate by product, for it drives the ideal market system and progress (Mirowski, 2013a). Some may express concern at the worldwide trend towards concentration of income and wealth in recent years, but such inequality is, in the neoliberal story, simply 'the playing out of a neoliberal script to produce a more efficient and vibrant capitalism' (Mirowski, 2013b, p. 8).

Also important to neoliberalism's identity, in most accounts, are individualisation and the primacy of individual choice, with freedom consisting of the unfettered exercise of such choice; insecurity and flexibility, ensuring responsivity to market signals; relationships based on exchange and contract; the superiority of all things private, including private enterprise and entrepreneurship; and the discipline of profit. Combine these values with the operation of markets and, so the story goes, standards will be driven up, prices driven down, preferences matched to purchasing power, innovation constantly stimulated, and utilities maximised.

Neoliberalism is not confined just to things, those goods and services that are bought and sold every day. It is a meta-narrative that extends into every facet and niche of life, offering a comprehensive approach, economic in nature and applicable to all human behaviour (Becker, 1976). The market, neoliberalism believes, 'should be the organizing principle for all political, social and economic conditions' (Giroux, 2004, p. 1); while Harvey adds that market exchange is valued in neoliberalism as an ethic, 'acting as a guide to all human action' (2005, p. 3). In this totalising story, private relationships do not escape the neoliberal gaze, which reaches right down into marriage, family life and child-bearing and rearing. These 'private' relationships, too, are conceptualised in predominantly economic terms, foregrounding rational calculation and optimal returns.

Everything, therefore, right down to the most intimate of relationships, is reducible to the logic and practice of the market place, and in that market place, each and every one of us is deemed a rational utility maximiser in constant pursuit of self-interest: the *homo economicus* we have already met in the previous chapter, 'malleable rather than committed, flexible rather than principled – essentially depthless' (Ball, 2012a, p. 31). The world supposedly consists of such autonomous, risk-managing and self-interested individuals, for whom dependence and interdependence, solidarity and risk-sharing, stability and long-term commitment are dangerous words, capable of infecting and corrupting the perfect subject of neoliberalism. We are, as Stephen Ball puts it, re-formed by neoliberalism, which is itself:

> made possible by a 'new type of individual', an individual formed within the logic of competition – a calculating, solipsistic, instrumentally driven, 'enterprise man' . . . The individual, the institution, our social relations become modelled on, microcosms of, the business.
>
> (2013, p. 132)

Neoliberalism, therefore, 'thoroughly revises what it means to be a human person' (Mirowski, 2013a, p. 58), calling forth a perpetual market trader, not only trading in goods and services – but in him or herself. For *homo economicus* is an entrepreneur of the self, maximising his or her own market value, ensuring (and here I return to familiar territory) the full exploitation of his or her 'human capital', one of 'an intricately linked set of overlapping propositions' developed by neoliberals (Mirowski, 2013b, p. 2). 'Human capital', a concept originating with economist Gary Becker and that figures so prominently in the story of quality and high returns, has been identified by Foucault as the 'signal neoliberal departure . . . that undermines centuries of political thought that parleyed humanism into stories of human rights . . . [instead reducing] the human being to an arbitrary bundle of 'investments', skills sets, temporary alliances (family, sex, race), and fungible body parts' (Mirowski, 2013a, p. 59). And in this world of autonomous, self-governing individuals, weaving their way through life's myriad markets and transactions, of every man and woman for him or herself, of endlessly calculating the choices that give the best return, in this world there is no place for class or any other communal identities or solidarities nor for collective risk-sharing, problem-solving and choice making.

Markets, capital, investments, returns. Not surprisingly, in such a context, the idea of contract – with its insistence on exchange, pre-specification, compliance, monitoring and accountability (Olssen and Peters, 2005, p. 325) – is also pervasive, defining all relationships and spelling out agreed inputs and expected outputs:

> The gist of the contract is that the duties of the partners have been negotiated, defined and agreed before any action is undertaken. What the partners are expected to do, what they may be called to do, what they may be reprimanded for not doing – is all spelled out and circumscribed in advance . . . Attention of both partners is to be focused on the task at hand – the delivery of a certain commodity, the performing of a certain service for a certain sum of money – not on each other. Their interest in each other neither needs, nor is encouraged to reach beyond the performance of the contractually agreed task.
>
> (Bauman, 1993, p. 58)

Such contractual relationships assume that everything can be known, quantified, costed and calculated, creating a constant calculus of profit and loss, costs and benefits, investment and returns in an endless flow of accountability. Contractual relationships of whatever sort are based on such calculations, what you expect to give and take from each relationship, paying close attention to specified and mutually advantageous exchange in a process of rational utility maximising. Predictability about inputs and outputs is to be valued as providing firm ground for making calculations, for risk management, for being in control: uncertainty, surprises, unpredicted outcomes, and unassessed or unassessable risks are to be avoided.

Not surprisingly, given this attention to exchange, contract and calculation, the emergence of neoliberalism has supported a process of repositivisation to meet a 'rage for accountability', based on measurability; as the Dark Mountain Project observes, in this way of thinking 'anything which cannot be measured cannot matter', indeed fatally undermines the calculation of profit and loss so central to this economic regime. With its reductive need for and belief in simplicity, certainty and objectivity, neoliberalism pins its hopes on a 'social science of variables' that claims an accurate, stable and ultimate representation of reality (Lather, 2006); a social science that behaves as if it was a natural science, able to control for variation and so to discover universal, stable and objective theories and laws, and a social science firmly located in the paradigm of regulatory modernity. To this end, complexity and messiness, diversity and context, the social and the cultural must and can be controlled, reduced and tamed, spurred on by a belief that there must be one right answer for every question, one calculable rate of return on any investment.

Neoliberalism is, first and foremost, a story of the victory of economics and the defeat of the social, reversing the process that produced the social state of the twentieth century with its belief that 'some aspects of the economy required to be governed in the name of the social'. Under the logic of neoliberalism's ideas, the social, and also the political, collapse into the economic, so that 'all aspects of social behaviour are reconceptualised along economic lines' (Rose, 1999, p. 141) and policies are depoliticised, reduced to economic calculation. Ball has described this process in the education field:

> education is increasingly, indeed perhaps almost exclusively, spoken of within policy in terms of economic value and its contribution to international market competitiveness . . . Within policy this economism is articulated and enacted very generally in the joining up of schooling to the project of competitiveness and to the 'demands' of globalisation and very specifically through the 'curriculum' of enterprise and entrepreneurship.
>
> (Ball, 2007, pp. 185–6)

Judt, too, recognised the triumph of the economic over all other dimensions of human life and saw profound consequences in this victory born of neoliberalism:

> For the last thirty years, in much of the English-speaking world (though less so in continental Europe and elsewhere), when asking ourselves whether we support a proposal or initiative, *we have not asked, is it good or bad? Instead we enquire: Is it efficient? Is it productive?* Would it benefit gross domestic product? Will it contribute to growth? This propensity to avoid moral considerations, to restrict ourselves to issues of profit and loss – economic questions in the narrowest sense – is not an instinctive human condition. It is an acquired taste.
>
> (Judt, 2010, p. 86; emphasis added)

So loud, so confident, so influential has the story of neoliberalism become over the last 30 years, that it is easy to forget there is nothing innate or essential, natural or neutral about it. Neoliberalism is just another story, and one that is, in Tony Judt's words, 'an acquired taste'. But though the taste may not be universally acquired, although it may not totally govern all souls, neoliberalism now forms a central part of the contemporary context, a context I contend that has greatly enhanced the appeal of certain stories in early childhood education in recent decades.

Neoliberalism and early childhood education

The story of neoliberalism has provided a nurturant environment for the spread of both stories that dominate early childhood education today – quality and high returns and markets. All three stories have much in common. Their way of thinking, the logic that inscribes them, is profoundly economistic, recasting everyone as economic actors, competitive entrepreneurs of the self and reserves of exploitable human capital; reducing everything to a calculation of economic costs and benefits; foregrounding relationships of exchange and contract; and making the maximisation of returns the central criterion for deciding how to relate and behave. They are all imbued with the paradigm of regulatory modernity, with its ontological and epistemological assumptions. They all treat education as a commodity, whether as the object of social investment, to be purchased as a means to high returns (individual, corporate, societal); or as the object of market transactions between parent-consumers and provider-businesses.

This shared economistic perspective is inscribed with a shared instrumental and performative rationality and a shared belief in leadership, managerial methods and other technical practice. Conversely, neither the meta-narrative of neoliberalism nor the more specific early childhood education stories of quality and high returns and of markets have much interest in or time for democracy, whether in politics, governance or everyday life. Indeed neoliberalism is 'profoundly suspicious of democracy' (Harvey, 2005, p. 66), which is viewed, at best, as an irrelevance, at worst as a potential hindrance to markets and their efficient functioning, and hence to performance and high returns. The citizen fades away to be replaced by the consumer; democratic politics gives way to the rule of experts, technicians and managers.

True, some neoliberals would argue that markets provide the purest form of democracy, through the unrestricted exercise of individual preferences. But I would disagree with this understanding of democracy, siding with Gert Biesta when he says that 'the behaviour of consumers in a market where their aim is to satisfy their needs . . . should not be conflated with democracy, which is about public deliberation and contestation about the public good and the just and equitable (re)distribution of public resources' (2010, p. 54). I will put democracy at the heart of my story about early childhood education, developing my understanding of democracy further in subsequent chapters.

One other connection with neoliberalism should be noted, one I have already touched on in the last chapter when I spoke of the story of quality and high returns letting 'injustice off the hook'. This is a story about early childhood education that gives neoliberalism a good conscience. It claims, through the magic of early intervention, to ensure equality of opportunity to every child, offering a 'Head Start' or 'Sure Start' to the poor and needy, implying any subsequent inequalities are down to individual, familial or cultural failings or to personal preferences, not class or other forms of privilege and not systemic injustice. A grossly unequal distribution of income and wealth does not matter, just as long as everyone has an equal start in life and an equal opportunity to become part of the gilded elite, through the beneficent effects of 'evidence-based' early intervention programmes. More equality of outcome, costly to the elite but vital for personal and societal well-being (Wilkinson and Pickett, 2009), is ditched for the modest price of installing a bogus equality of opportunity – bogus because offering early childhood education or other early interventions does not and cannot possibly ensure a genuinely equal start in life, since so many other factors are at play, not least the capacity and will of advantaged families to keep well ahead of the game.

At the same time, the story of quality and high returns also claims to offer amelioration of the multitude of social ills that neoliberalism seems to exacerbate. Early intervention offers balm to the inflamed conscience; it will fix these ills or, at least, reduce them substantially. Left and right alike can subscribe to the story of quality and high returns, either for its egalitarian promise or its safeguarding of the status quo.

But is the relationship between the three stories as simple as that? Are there not some apparent and rather glaring contradictions? Doesn't the story of markets imply primacy for individual choice and freedom, even if this means parents making the 'wrong' choice for their children's development and well-being by opting for poor quality? Doesn't the story of quality and high returns, by contrast, involve strong governing and constraints on freedom, for example by governments specifying technologies and outcomes such that the free market is regulated and no longer really free, minimising the possibility of 'wrong' choices? Isn't the story of markets, with its rhetoric of freedom and individual choice, much closer to the spirit of neoliberalism than the story of quality and high returns, with its emphasis on prescribed inputs and outputs?

Take, for example, the case of England. Here, as we have seen, there is a well-established market in the provision of early childhood services, apparently now so natural and neutral that a civil servant can casually assert in public that a 'diverse market [in early childhood services is] the only show in town' (Archer, 2008). Parents are deemed consumers, exercising individual choice among a welter of businesses operating in a 'childcare' or 'early education' market, and few today would bat an eyelid at this characterisation of early childhood education. This appears the very personification of the story of markets and indeed the story of neoliberalism.

But this is no free market; it is intensely governed externally, by the state. There are national regulations covering standards, curriculum and learning goals (the Early Years Foundation Stage – EYFS); a national system of surveillance and inspection extending to every individual centre and childminder in the country (the Office for Standards in Education, Children's Services and Skills – OFSTED); a national system of assessment of young children's performance (the EYFS Profile assessment that requires educators to assess children against 17 early learning goals), to determine if a 5-year-old has attained a national norm (the 'Good Level of Development'); and public subsidies for lower-income parents to spend on 'childcare' services. While at the same time, more and more attention is given to managing the performance of publicly funded interventions, through an increasing emphasis on 'evidence-based' programmes and payment by results.[2] The epitome of the story of quality and high returns.

A potent economism runs through both stories. But whereas the story of markets urges the practice of freedom by the individual consumer, the story of quality and high returns insists on governing the child and regulating the market. To quote the sub-title of a recent English government policy paper, the search is underway for both 'raising quality and giving parents more choice' (Department for Education (England), 2013). What is going on?

Several observers have noted a strain of governing running through the neoliberal project, expressing a will to standardise, manage and control. Harvey attributes this to the social incoherence and inherent instability brought on by neoliberalism leading to an increasing authoritarianism, which he considers to be a distinctly 'neoconservative' answer:

> to one of the central contradictions of neoliberalism. If 'there is no such thing as society but only individuals' as Thatcher initially put it, then the chaos of individual interests can easily end up prevailing over order. The anarchy of the market, of competition, and of unbridled individualism . . . generates a situation that becomes increasingly ungovernable. It may even lead to a breakdown of all bonds of solidarity and a condition verging on social anarchy and nihilism.
>
> (2005, p. 82)

Educational theorist Michael Apple (2004, 2005) has also described an alliance between neoliberalism and neoconservativism apparent in education policies in the US and the UK, producing a characteristic mix: markets, competition and individual choice in provision of services and the allocation of children to them; and an increasingly authoritarian system of governing these same services and children, through prescriptive standards, high stakes testing and other modes of management. Apple also points to a third party in the alliance, a particular fraction of the middle class who have thriven with education being treated as a predominantly technical and managerial subject, to be governed by experts and managers: '[t]hese are people with backgrounds in management and efficiency techniques who provide the technical and "professional" support for account-ability, measurement,"product control", and assessment that is required by the proponents of neoliberal policies of marketisation and neoconservative policies of tighter central control in education' (Apple, 2005, p. 20). What might be termed a new governing class.

But it is not just the incipient chaos of neoliberalism with its attendant risk of negative results, nor the influence of neoconservatives who worry that total laissez-faire will have bad consequences for the fabric of society and the order of things that drives the governing implicit in the story of quality and high returns. It is also the demands of achieving a neoliberal regime and, with it, the promised benefits. Unlike nineteenth-century 'unfettered market' liberalism, which had no time for the state, twenty-first-century neoliberalism is not at all in favour of the minimalist state: 'its major distinguishing characteristic is instead to infuse, take over, and transform the strong state, in order to impose the ideal form of society . . . to redefine the shape and functions of the state, *not to destroy it*' (Mirowski, 2013a, pp. 40, 56; original emphasis). For neoliberalism is not an innate condition; it is 'an acquired taste' and the acquisition of this taste requires active intervention by a strong state acting as 'both producer and guarantor of a stable market society' (Mirowski, 2013b, p. 2). A complex web of rules, regu-lations and procedures needs to be put in place to build and maintain a world of markets. Armies of lawyers, accountants and managers need to be educated, recruited and deployed to enact these rules, regulations and procedures. Last but not least, the remainder of the population have to play their part in this story, grasping the plot and learning their roles in it.

Neoliberalism makes much of individual choice and personal freedom. Yet it insists there can be no choice or freedom about neoliberalism or about the subject of neoliberalism, who we must be – for the paradox is that without insisting on the neoliberal subject, neoliberalism itself must ultimately fail. *Homo economicus* is a necessity, not an option. What Margaret Thatcher meant when she said that economics was the method but the object was to change the heart and soul was that behind the changed economic relationships that neoliberalism strove to introduce was a deeper, more totalising purpose: to re-form the subject as *homo economicus*, reaching down into the deepest recesses of humanity to shape and govern our desires and fears, our expectations and hopes, our assumptions and understandings, our beliefs and values – our very sense of who we are.

So it is no good saying, as a parent, that you don't want to assume the role of consumer exercising individual choice between individual nursery businesses in a market of nurseries; it is no good saying, as a parent, that you would rather assume the role of citizen, using the local, public nursery and participating democratically in its everyday life along with fellow citizens. That will never do. It is the wrong answer that shows you unsuited to a neoliberal world, unable to enact the neoliberal subject, a failure of neoliberal conditioning. The souls of current and future generations must be governed and formed to avoid such failings and to generate subjects with, in Judt's words, 'uncritical admiration for unfettered markets, disdain for the public sector . . . [and belief in] the delusion of endless growth'.

Lynn Fendler, in an evocatively titled chapter *Educating Flexible Souls*, provides another example of the heavily qualified freedom of neoliberalism, drawing specifically on early childhood education. She starts from the prominence that flexibility has gained 'as the cutting-edge solution to the challenges of productivity in a fast-moving [neoliberal] global economy' (2001, p. 119). Neoliberalism calls for 'flexible' and 'fluid' ways of being, for the flexible subject where flexibility is inscribed into his or her innermost being and, she argues, it is 'the goals and objectives of education [that] reinscribe the values of flexibility through curricular and pedagogical practices'. She goes on to analyse the way that three educational discourses, widespread in contemporary early childhood education, constitute this 'subjective flexibility': whole child education, developmentally appropriate curricula, and interactive pedagogy.

Fendler makes a further important point about the value of flexibility in neoliberalism. Just as the value of freedom does not extend to our being free to choose what kind of subject we wish to be, so the value of flexibility does not extend to any discretion about the other ends to be pursued. Flexibility is strictly limited to means not ends. This, Fendler contends, is apparent in much early childhood education, where flexibility can be extended to how the young child arrives at an outcome – just as long as no flexibility is permitted in determining the outcome:

> Flexible interactive pedagogies are not necessarily instances of freedom or emancipation but rather effective and efficient technologies for attaining predetermined, socially stipulated objectives. It is significant, then, that the developmental goals are specified and integrated into the pedagogical discourse, more or less explicitly. And because the developmental goals are specified, there is no theoretical possibility for the subject to have any features or characteristics other than those specified as normal – as defined by their developmental appropriateness. *The notion of flexibility, then, may pertain to the course of interaction. However, there can be no flexibility or variation in the outcome per se*; the outcome of current pedagogies is paradoxically limited to a response-able and response-ready subject.
>
> (ibid., pp. 133–4; emphasis added)

What might be termed free play but no free outcomes!

The problem confronting neoliberalism becomes apparent. It wants to reduce life and the world to the magic of untrammelled market relationships, in the belief that this will inevitably bring the best of all possible worlds. Remove regulation, reduce the social state, let the market have full rein is the mantra. But at the same time it needs the state, with all its regulatory strength, to play an active role in the formation of this market, clearing away all obstacles to its free operation, ensuring (the much quoted) level playing field between competing entrepreneurs, guaranteeing the sanctity of contracts. It also wants an ideal subject for this market place, entrepreneurial, flexible and self-serving; but, as I have already argued, *homo economicus* is not an expression of an innate human nature. So once again external intervention is needed, state assistance in 'educating flexible souls'. The required subject must be constructed, through the inculcation of a neoliberal subjectivity and a consequent self-regulation that strives to live up to this subjectivity, what Foucault terms 'governmentality' or governing the self through the conduct of conduct.

It is, therefore, neoliberalism itself that calls forth an authoritarian regime – apparent in the story of quality and high returns – that operates alongside and tempers all the talk of free markets and free choice. This is a response both to the social instability that untrammelled neoliberalism breeds; and to neoliberalism's need to bulldoze market conditions into place and to govern the soul to produce the kind of subject required for the working of free markets and free choice. But there is a third reason why neoliberalism produces enhanced governing: survival.

Faced by an increasingly competitive global economy, a juggernaut seemingly intent on following a predetermined path at ever-increasing speed and capable of devouring all in its way, nation states feel impelled to intervene. Take the example of lifelong learning, which nation states increasingly advocate and provide. To survive in a harsh environment of continuous and intensifying competition and creative destruction, the state must ensure its citizens are continually equipped to meet the ever-changing demands of neoliberal capitalism, their human capital fully exploited and at the market's disposal; this is part and parcel of being a flexible neoliberal subject and lifelong learning is the answer. This is what Keri Facer terms 'future proofing', education's presumed role of equipping the country, the enterprise and the individual to compete in the global economic (rat) race, making them fit for purpose in an inevitable, unchangeable and neoliberal world of more of the same – only more so: never-ending competition, a never-ending search for how to keep one step ahead, a never-ending struggle to climb over the opposition. Informed by neuroscience, such lifelong learning is now understood by economists and politicians to mean from birth, not from some arbitrary compulsory school starting age, part of a continuous process of preparing the flexible and compliant subject to continually adapt to the changing needs of the labour market and rootless capital. The state, therefore, if it has not done so before, must build up early childhood education, and not any old education, but an education of quality and high returns.

Where important national interests are at issue, then even a state otherwise given over to neoliberalism will regulate the market to try to ensure it protects and furthers these interests. So while marketisation of early childhood education is on the rise, no countries allow free rein to the market, indeed interventionism is growing: through inspection regimes, setting standards, introducing curricula with prescribed goals, overseeing the education of workers, providing subsidies for parents, establishing entitlements to a period of free early childhood education, and even in some cases compelling children to attend.[3] Neoliberalism calls for state intervention to further its aims and ensure its survival, while the state regulates markets and governs children and adults alike to further its aims and ensure its survival under the neoliberal regime – and does so with all the human technologies at its disposal, technologies that have become ever more effective over time and with the deployment of increasing resources.

Markets may increasingly be seen as the best way to deliver services, in particular through private and often business providers, and as the best means to allocate children to these services via the medium of individual parental choice. But countries, or rather governments, don't trust markets to deliver quality and high returns. That calls for substantial regulation and sufficient technical capability to achieve those expert-derived and market-required outcomes that nation states hope will ensure success in an increasingly competitive global race. In other words, markets tempered by quality for high returns.

Confronted by neoliberalism, with its global markets and an elite capitalist class, both deterritorialised and both able to move resources wherever they choose at the press of a button, nation states have lost sovereignty. But they have not been hollowed out. Instead, they turn their power inwards on their territorialised citizens; 'to make the contemporary wave of neoliberalism work, the state has to penetrate even more deeply into certain segments of political-economic life and become more interventionist than before . . . [deepening] its grasp over certain facets of social processes, driven away from performing other functions' (Harvey, 2005, pp. 65, 180). The state may not be willing or able to govern global capitalism: but it can and increasingly does govern the souls of its people, not least through education.

Neoliberalism is, from my perspective, just another story, albeit a very ambitious one that claims to know the meaning of life and how it should be lived. It is a way some people have found to weave reality, then gone a step further to impose their reality on the rest of us as if it was true: DONA again. I began this section with Tony Judt, a trenchant critic of neoliberalism and an advocate of alternatives, whose premature death in 2010 removed a forceful and passionate critic of neoliberalism. I end with his words, about the need for and difficulty of telling another story about the political economy that provides the context for early childhood education:

> Why is it that here in the United States [and I would contend, elsewhere too] we have such difficulty even *imagining* a different sort of society from the one whose dysfunctions and inequalities trouble us so? We appear to have lost the capacity to question the present, much less offer alternatives to it. Why is it so beyond us to conceive of a different set of arrangements to our common advantage? Our shortcomings – excuse the academic jargon – is *discursive*. We simply do not know how to talk about these things.
>
> (Judt, 2009, p. 86; original emphasis)

Notes

1 However, the neoliberal project was being discussed and taking shape from the late 1940s. The first meeting of the Mont Pèlerin Society was held in 1947, and this group – a closed, members-only debating society – subsequently expanded in numbers and geographical coverage to become 'the premier site of the construction of neoliberalism' (Mirowski, 2013a, p. 29), and a key part of what Mirowski (ibid.) terms the Neoliberal Thought Collective.

2 At the time of writing, the English government is trialling payment by results in Children's Centres in 27 local authority areas, as part of a wider trend across government and as a prelude to a possible general extension of this practice. Writing to local authorities in June 2011, a senior civil servant refers to the government wanting 'to use payment by results to incentivise a focus on the proposed core purpose of children's centres: to improve child development and school readiness among young children and to reduce inequalities' (Jeffreys, 2011, p. 1).

3 Nine out of 28 European Union member states (Bulgaria, Croatia, Cyprus, Greece, Hungary, Latvia, Luxembourg, Poland and Romania) now require children to attend early childhood education, mostly for a year, but for 2 years in Luxembourg and, soon, for 3 years in Hungary.

Chapter 4

Transformative change

The story of democracy, experimentation and potentiality

Early childhood education, I would argue, is in need of transformative change, moving away from the much-heard story of quality and high returns and from the up-and-coming story of markets, stories I find both implausible and unpalatable. We need, to quote the words of Tony Judt that concluded the last chapter, to 'conceive of a different set of arrangements to our common advantage', and we need to 'know how to talk about these things'. We need, in short, to tell and hear more stories, old and new.

There are so many other stories that could be told about early childhood education, and I welcome the prospect of a world where a multitude of stories are heard and none claims a monopoly of the truth. Indeed, as the books in this series demonstrate, other stories are already being told about early childhood education for those who care to hear. The problem is that the two stories I have so far discussed are so beguiling in their promise, so certain in their delivery, so assertive in their claims and so in tune with the dominant regime of our time, that other stories are marginalised, going either unheard or listened to by small audiences.

I add my voice to those of other dissident story tellers, offering an other story in this chapter, which I title the story of democracy, experimentation and potentiality. I begin the chapter by giving an outline of this story, before going into its origins in more detail to explain why I choose to tell it. This leads again into the territory of political questions, putting forward the answers that I give to these questions, answers that supply the threads from which I weave my story. I pay particular attention to the answer to one question: democracy and experimentation as two fundamental values in early childhood education, both also playing a prominent part in realising potentiality. As these give such a distinctive identity to my story, I dwell at some length in the next chapter on the meaning of these values and their implementation in practice in education.

The story I tell in the next two chapters differs in many ways from both the story of quality and high returns and the story of markets. All of these stories agree on the importance of early childhood education. But they do so for very different reasons and employ very different reasoning. They see the world in very different ways and have very different hopes and expectations. These differences are expressed in the vocabulary each story deploys. So it is here that I begin.

Different story, different vocabulary

'[Q]uality' is a choice not a necessity. You don't have to work with the concept, though you may choose to do so.

(Dahlberg *et al.*, 2013, p. xxii)

Language matters. We should pick our words carefully, being self-conscious about meaning. So before starting on the story of democracy, experimentation and potentiality, I want to highlight the importance of language in story-telling in general and in early childhood education stories in particular.

I have tried to be very careful and self-conscious in my choice and use of words. No reference is made in my story to words or terms such as 'evidence-based', 'child development', 'programmes', 'quality', 'investment', 'outcomes', 'returns', 'assessment scales', 'human capital', 'business', 'consumer' or 'market'; words or terms that proliferate in the story of quality and high returns and in the story of markets and that proclaim and affirm the instrumental, the technical, the managerial, the reductive, the economic. Instead I speak of 'projects', 'potentialities' and 'possibilities'; 'uncertainty', 'wonder' and 'surprise'; 'in-between', 'lines of flight' and 'rhizomes'; 'images', 'interpretations' and 'meaning-making'; 'democracy' and 'experimentation'. These are words that foreground relationships and responsibility, immanence and emergence, diversity and complexity, the ethical and political. I use another vocabulary not only to reflect and express another way of thinking about the subject of early childhood education, but because an alternative vocabulary can help to free us from the hold that other stories have upon us.

Take 'quality' for example. The word and its use in early childhood education have been thoroughly critiqued and problematised (Dahlberg *et al.*, 2013). 'Quality' is not neutral and not natural, but a constructed concept saturated with values – for example, a belief in objective, stable and universal means and ends – and complicit as a management tool in governing early childhood education. Worse, the word masks the political nature of education, the notion that education is first and foremost a political question. Instead of talking about political questions and allowing for different, possibly conflicting, answers to them, instead of arguing about what we think is a good or desirable education and why we think this, we take the easy way out and slip into using the shorthand of 'quality' – and by so doing delegate to experts to tell us what we should think and do. For it is experts who are supposed to know and tell us what 'quality' means, offering norms for technicians to work to and to which managers can require compliance. So through the use of 'quality', the political is rendered technical and managerial and we absolve ourselves from responsibility for education; we leave it instead to 'them' to say what should happen and to manage and evaluate performance. Neoliberalism's disdain for democracy is perfectly expressed in the word 'quality' and its pervasive use.

Admittedly some argue that 'quality' is compatible with democracy, that (in the words of OECD's Quality Toolbox) 'defining and assuring quality should be a participatory and democratic process, involving different groups, including children, parents, families and professionals who work with children' (OECD, 2012, p. 38). But if a world of value plurality and multiple perspectives is assumed, with a democracy of conflicting alternatives not rational consensus (a distinction discussed further in the next chapter), then the end result is multiple definitions of quality – which would render the concept useless by turning a technical statement of fact ('Quality is . . .') into a political judgement of value ('From our perspective quality means . . .'). That was always the 'problem with quality', how to square context, complexity and multiple perspectives with the need for a standardised measure of effectiveness in producing standardised outcomes.

That is why, despite occasional talk of participation and democracy, 'quality' invariably ends up as a search for some universal technical statement of fact. That is why international measures of quality, such as ITERS (the Infant/Toddler Environmental Rating Scale) and ECERS (the Early Childhood Environmental Rating Scale), have such widespread and growing appeal. That is why, writing with Gunilla Dahlberg and Alan Pence, I concluded that:

> [t]he 'problem with quality' cannot be addressed by struggling to reconstruct the concept in ways it was never intended to go. If we try to make an accommodation with, for example, subjectivity or multiple perspectives, then an increasingly desperate search for quality will prove to be a wild goose chase. For the concept of quality in relation to early childhood institutions is irretrievably modernist . . . It is about a search for definitive and universal criteria, certainty and order – or it is about nothing . . . The problem with quality is not really a problem once we recognize that it is not a neutral concept, but that it is a concept which we can choose to take or leave.
>
> (Dahlberg et al., 2013, p. 111)

I choose to leave it. I find no place for 'quality', either in its vapid form as a meaningless feel-good label or in its more troubling use as shorthand for tightly defined human technologies that act as effective means to produce predetermined outcomes. Choosing not to use 'quality' frees me up to think differently. I choose instead to title my story in a way that proclaims what I value and desire, clearly stating what for me would make for a good early childhood education: democracy, experimentation, potentiality. I do so in the knowledge that others may not agree. My title is, in short, an unashamedly political label for an unashamedly political story.

Because 'quality' has become such a revered term that its rejection may seem sacrilegious, I should make my position absolutely clear at the risk of some repetition. I question, problematise, reject and wish to get beyond 'quality'. But that does not mean I am some callous advocate of cut-price nurseries as a cheap and profitable solution to the 'childcare challenge' – parking places for young children. Quite the reverse. I want all young children to be entitled to good early childhood education, as a public service provided as a matter of right. Furthermore, I want to tell a story that makes clear what I mean by 'good', without insisting the meaning I give is self-evident, neutral and uncontestable.

Or take another example of contested vocabulary, 'investment'. I find this a harder call than 'quality'. My immediate response to the word, as indeed to the concept of 'social investment', is rejection because of its economistic connotations, its calculative tenor, its instrumental rationality and its impoverished image of the child as a reservoir of future capital. But this response may be too hasty, too coloured by a certain 'thin' idea of investment, when there are 'thicker', more appealing readings to be had. Nathelie Morel, Bruno Palier and Joakim Palme point to an approach to social investment in the Nordic countries that 'successfully combine[s] social and economic goals . . . [and] strong protection with heavy social investment, with the aim to promote social equality and gender equality' (Morel et al., 2012, pp. 358–9). They continue this line of argument by stating that 'egalitarian societies are more successful in implementing social investment policies' and that 'it is not just equality of opportunity ("social justice") but also equality of outcomes that matter' (p. 363). This 'thicker' version of social investment they term a Social Democratic approach, compared to 'a "Third Way" approach based on a more "anglo-liberal" perspective on social policy' (p. 360), one that feels closer to the thinking of neoliberalism.

'Investment', too, can have broader, non-pecuniary connotations. The dictionary refers to investment in terms of 'to lay out for profit', a definition very much in line with the story of quality and high returns. But it also offers another sense of the word, as 'to give rights, privileges or duties', which might sit more easily with the story I am about to tell, with its undertones of early childhood education as an entitlement of citizenship. Perhaps, also, investment might be understood as being about putting or placing one's faith or belief in others, for example as when philosopher and educational reformer John Dewey (1859–1952) refers to 'a working faith in the possibilities of human nature', or headteacher Alex Bloom (1895–1955) calls for teachers to have 'a larger faith in the natural fineness of the child and in his inner potential'. In this case I might understand putting resources into education as investing faith and belief, and doing so without being able to know, predict or calculate exactly what will come from it. This is investment as part of a relationship of hope, obligation and incalculable hospitality, not a relationship of calculable exchange. This is investment in potentiality, in that which cannot be known in advance.

'Investment', then, may not be a completely lost cause; perhaps in the future the word might be reclaimed and used again. For the moment, though, I choose to forego it. It seems to me to have become too tainted by its close association with the story of neoliberalism and the story of quality and high returns, with their economistic rationality and their narrow calculus of costed inputs and pre-defined outcomes, their use of tightly prescribed technologies ('high quality'), and their reduction of the child and adult to a repository of 'human capital'. Today's talk of 'investing in children' too readily takes us down a slippery slope of increasingly governing the child in the interests of an unexamined life in an unexamined future. To avoid confusion and to make alternatives clear, better to avoid the word for the moment, and work with a different vocabulary.

A story of democracy, experimentation and potentiality

The metaphor that might best represent my image of the school is that of a construction site, or a permanent laboratory, in which children's and teachers' research processes are strongly intertwined and constantly evolving . . . Learning does not proceed in a linear way, determined and deterministic, by progressive and predictable stages, but rather is constructed through contemporaneous advances, standstills, and 'retreats' that take many directions . . . The construction of knowledge is a group process. Each individual is nurtured by the hypotheses and theories of others, and by conflicts with others, and advances by co-constructing pieces of knowledge with others through a process of confirmation and disagreement. Above all, conflict and disturbance force us to constantly revise our interpretive models and theories on reality, and this is true for both children and adults.

(Rinaldi, 2006, pp. 126, 131–2)

From time to time though [in early childhood education], there are moments where something new and different may happen, something that increases all participants' capacity to act and create interesting connections and features in between teachers and children as well as between the form and content of the practice. These are the moments of the lines of flight . . . When something new and different is coming about, when the lines of flight are created and activated in the practices, it is never taking place as a rationally planned and implemented change by specific individuals. Rather, there are from time to time magic moments where there seems to be something entirely new and different coming about. This is recognized only by the tremendous intensity and, very often, the physical expression of goose bumps that take possession of participants.

(Olsson, 2009, pp. 62, 63)

Early childhood institutions can be understood as public forums situated in civil society in which children and adults participate together in projects of social, cultural, political and economic significance . . . Forums provide a locus for active citizenship through participation in collective action and the practice of democracy. A strong and vibrant civil society requires this type of engagement by active citizens in forums – and out of such activity may come new social movements.

(Dahlberg *et al.*, 2013, p. 78)

Education is the right of all, of all children, and as such is a responsibility of the community. Education is an opportunity for the growth and emancipation of the individual and the collective; it is a resource for gaining knowledge and for learning to live together; it is a meeting place where freedom, democracy and solidarity are practiced and where the value of peace is promoted. Within the plurality of cultural, ideological, political, and religious conceptions, education lives by listening, dialogue, and participation; it is based on mutual respect, valuing the diversity of identities, competencies, and knowledge held by each individual.

(Comune di Reggio Emilia, 2009, p. 5)

[The school] as a physical space and a local organization . . . may be one of the most important institutions we have to help us build a democratic conversation about the future. A physical, local school where community members are encouraged to encounter each other and learn from each other is one of the last public spaces in which we can begin to build the intergenerational solidarity, respect for diversity and democratic capability needed to ensure fairness in the context of sociotechnical change. Moreover, the public educational institution may be the only resource we have to counter the inequalities and injustice of the informal learning landscape outside school . . . It is therefore the time both to defend the idea of a school as a public resource and to radically re-imagine how it might evolve if it is to equip communities to respond to and shape the socio-technical changes of the next few years.

(Facer, 2011, p. 28)

The authors writing above are telling a story about early childhood education that is very different to the story of quality and high returns or, indeed, the story of markets: what might be called the story of democracy, experimentation and potentiality. Compare them, for instance, with the authors quoted on pages 17 and 18 in Chapter 2. This is a story, first and foremost, about early childhood education as *public* education, by which I mean an education that is both for all citizens and the responsibility of all citizens; in which all citizens (children, young people and adults) have an interest and which is a public good; that provides a shared experience in a public domain (as distinct from the private or market domains), defined by David Marquand as 'a space where strangers encounter each other as equal partners in the common life of the society, a space for forms of human flourishing that cannot be bought in a market' and, as such, 'fundamental to a civilised society' (Marquand, 2004, p. 26); and that contributes to the production of public values, such as democracy, equality and sustainability.

In this story, early childhood centres are public spaces and public resources, open to all citizens as of right. They are places for realising potentiality, the potentiality both of citizens and of early childhood education. This potentiality is great but its full extent is unknown and unknowable; it is, quite simply, incalculable. As the philosopher Baruch Spinoza (1632–1677) puts it '[w]e never know in advance what a body can do'; or in Dewey's words, human experience 'can have no end until experience itself comes to an end'. Potentiality is, put simply, a matter of and . . . and . . . and . . .

Part of the potentiality of early childhood education in early childhood centres lies in the opportunities they provide for learning, by children and adults. But we cannot know, we cannot predict, we cannot control what directions that learning will take, since it does not 'proceed in a linear way, determined and deterministic'. We cannot know what will emerge from the encounters that take place between children, between children and adults and between adults, every one an active subject, a protagonist with a wealth of potentials and seeking 'every day to understand something, to draw out a meaning, to grasp a piece of life' (Rinaldi, 2006, p. 112).

Learning is important, and I return to it later in this chapter, but it is by no means the full extent of the potentiality of early childhood education. Part of the potentiality resides in the limitless possibilities early childhood centres can offer for a wealth of other relationships and activities, serving as a resource for all those living in their catchment areas. They can be meeting places where, as Facer puts it in her book *Learning Futures*, 'we build a democratic conversation about the future . . . intergenerational solidarity, respect for diversity and democratic capability'. They can be agoras where, as the regulations for the Reggio Emilia municipal schools (for children from birth to 6 years) state, 'freedom, democracy and solidarity are practiced and where the value of peace is promoted'. They can be collective workshops for the initiation of projects and for the 'production of ideas, images, knowledge, communication, cooperation, and affective relations . . . [which] tends to create not the means of social life but social life itself'. This is what political philosophers Michael Hardt and Antonio Negri call 'immaterial production', including knowledge but much else besides, and 'produced not by individuals but collectively in collaboration . . . [creating] a common, social nature of production' (Hardt and Negri, 2005, pp. 146, 187); while the benefits of this production – the centre's output as a public space, a workshop of projects and a creator of new knowledges – are secured for the whole community and for the common good.

The idea of encounter plays an important part in this story, encounters with difference, with the unknown and with the unfamiliar. Such encounters are not only between children and teachers, but with and between staff, parents and the other members of the centre's local community. They are not only between people but also with material objects; and not only with material objects but also with the immaterial – different ideas, perspectives, understandings. Drawing on the quotations that begin this section, such encounters may provoke 'conflict and disturbance'; they may force us, children and adults alike, 'to constantly revise our interpretive models and theories on reality'; they may generate 'lines of flight . . . when something new and different is coming about, magic moments'. And such encounters are made possible by early childhood education being recognised as a right and the early childhood centre operating as a public space, a forum and a collective workshop.

The creativity that lies at the heart of the story of democracy, experimentation and potentiality happens not by swaddling early childhood education in a closely woven mesh of predetermined means and ends – knowing the end point and the route to it even before starting. On the contrary, it happens by enabling the unexpected and the new to emerge and escape all attempts to tame, predict, supervise, control and evaluate them against preset goals. It happens by nurturing an openness to the unpredictable and new, a willingness to experiment and make new connections. It happens, too, because early childhood education, in this story, is inscribed with the values of democracy, the ethics of an encounter, and with an image of the rich child, born with a hundred languages, an avid meaning-maker from the very start of life – about all of which, more below.

The challenge here is to turn away from trying to know what a child or an adult or a centre is, to resist transmitted representations, to let go of expert assurances of guaranteed outcomes and returns; and to turn instead towards the child and the centre as an unknowable potentiality, a not-yet, a becoming, a multiplicity, a case of and . . . and . . . and. So my story is about an open-ended early childhood education in a centre that occupies and contributes to an unfinished world, a place of infinite possibilities, giving constant rise to wonder and surprise, magic moments and goose bumps, and a source of hope and renewed belief in the world; a place, too, where 'freedom, democracy and solidarity are practiced and where the value of peace is promoted'.

In this story, democratically elected and accountable bodies – such as the local authority in England or the *kommun, commune* or *comune* in Sweden, France or Italy respectively – fund, support and (to an extent) provide early childhood education and centres as 'education is the right of all, of all children, and as such is a responsibility of the community'. But they do so also because, to return to Dewey and his account of democracy, they have 'faith in human nature in general [and] faith in the capacity of human beings for intelligent judgment and action if proper conditions are furnished'. My story speaks of such public involvement as an act of political belief, not of economic investment, founded on a positive image of the citizen and her or his potential, less *homo economicus* and more *homo sapiens*.

Given this belief in human beings and their potential, these bodies – we might call them 'educative communes' to reflect their political status and their educational responsibility – recognise the great importance of providing public institutions that can help to realise this potential as part of an emancipatory project. They recognise, too, the vital role these institutions can play in sustaining a healthy democratic society, maintaining solidarity and social cohesion, creating local knowledge and other immaterial products, and enabling citizens to engage in conversations about the future. But they also recognise that there is nothing inevitable about this role, no way of guaranteeing it by buying into particular technologies or expertise; there is only the possibility that this role might be realised through endless hard work, sustained commitment, democratic participation and continual openness to experimentation and new thinking. For this is a story of transformative change that turns from an early childhood education of immobility and reproduction to an early childhood education of constant movement and creativity.

Apart from funding and supporting early childhood education and providing some centres, educative communes also actively encourage all centres to work together in networks to help realise more fully their potential for learning and other projects. Collaboration not competition is the order of the day. They also work with these centres and networks to construct a local educational project, with its own pedagogical identity and building its own body of local knowledge.

While great weight is given to the singularity and the unknown potentiality of citizens and centres, and great value is attached to unexpected and surprising outcomes, this early childhood education is not without a shared sense of direction. The democratic decision to provide public support for early childhood education and centres comes with some conditionality. There is a national policy that defines a common structure for early childhood education, including entitlement, funding and the workforce. All publicly supported centres work with certain democratically agreed values and goals, set out in a national curriculum. But there is scope for interpretation, opportunities for review and space for additional local values and goals, with national values including democracy and experimentation leaving many openings to innovate and to create new local projects and practices. Moreover, early childhood centres are democratically accountable for the work that they do and the way in which they do that work, providing a variety of documentation that forms the basis for evaluations through open and participatory processes of dialogue, deliberation and meaning-making; in centres themselves, in neighbourhood forums and at the level of the educative commune, a democratic accountability made to the whole citizenry. I return in later chapters to consider these issues in more detail.

Answering political questions

Where does my story come from? Why do I tell it? How have I come to create it? First I must admit it lacks originality, drawing inspiration and ideas from many older stories. Democracy, experimentation, potentiality all have a long and honourable place in some educational traditions and an august roll-call of advocates; I stand, in this respect, on the shoulders of giants. I acknowledge these influences, and recognise that this is the way stories develop; they are told and retold and evolve in the retelling.

But what draws me to these traditions and to previous narrators is the politics of early childhood education, in other words a view that stories are built around answers to the sort of political questions raised in Chapter 2, those 'not mere technical issues to be solved by experts . . . [but questions that] always involve decisions which require us to make choices between conflicting alternatives'. I have contended that the stories of quality and high returns and of markets are also based on answers to such questions, but do so implicitly, concealing the political process and choices behind a veneer of supposedly objective and true statements; faced by such obfuscation, I had to do my best to deconstruct the stories to find what those answers might be. I will, instead, take the political questions raised in Chapter 2 in order, tackling them head on and setting out my answers, to elaborate my story and explain its origins and rationale.

What is the diagnosis of our time?

> It was the best of times, it was the worst of times, it was the age of wisdom, it was the age of foolishness, it was the epoch of belief, it was the epoch of incredulity, it was the season of Light, it was the season of Darkness, it was the spring of hope, it was the winter of despair.
>
> (Dickens, 2012, p. 1)

> Of all humanity's delusions of difference, of its separation from and superiority to the living world which surrounds it, one distinction holds up better than most: we may well be the first species capable of effectively eliminating life on Earth.
>
> (Dark Mountain Project, 2009a)

> There is no single vital problem, but many vital problems, and it is this complex intersolidarity of problems, antagonisms, crises, uncontrolled processes, and the general crisis of the planet that constitutes the number one vital problem.
>
> (Morin, 1999, p. 74)

We live in a time of technical and scientific marvels, of unparalleled access to information and communications, of unequalled global trade and travel. Those with the requisite resources have better health, greater longevity and more material comforts than at any previous time in history. For some this is undoubtedly the best of times, the 'spring of hope'.

But that will not do as a diagnosis of our time. For it might also be said that for mankind as a whole and as a species this is also the worst of times, 'the winter of despair'. We live in an economic regime of neoliberalism, a turbo-charged market capitalism under which inequality is rising and which, to draw on a quote from Tim Jackson in Chapter 1, incarcerates us in an 'iron cage of consumerism', constructed by a relentless drive for novelty – new production and new consumption in a lethal embrace – which in turn feeds an obsession with growth and the equating of growth with prosperity. This is a regime that is harmful to people, driven as it is by anxiety:

> The extended self is motivated by the angst of the empty self. Social comparison is driven by the anxiety to be situated favourably in society. Creative destruction is haunted by the fear of being left behind in the competition for consumer markets.
>   Thrive or die is the maxim of the jungle. It's equally true in the consumer society. Nature and structure combine together here to lock us firmly into the iron cage of consumerism. It's an anxious, and ultimately a pathological system.
>
> (Jackson, 2009, p. 65)

But the system is not just ultimately pathological. It is also unsustainable, inflicting massive harm to the environment. A report to the European Commission on *The World in 2025* (Gaudin, 2008) argues we cannot carry on as we have been without putting the future of our species at risk. For if we do, if the globalisation of a market economy and excessive consumption continues and spreads even further, 'it appears to lead to a global collapse' (ibid., p. 6).

The future then, at least if we want a future, cannot be simply more of the same; and education cannot be reduced to an economic imperative of improving competitive advantage by 'educating flexible souls' (to use Fendler's poignant term) needed to people a world of presumed endless growth. The global race we are urged to excel in, the race to compete successfully in a global market, is a race to the abyss. A new economic model is called for, a model that increases equality, reduces anxiety and exists within limits. This means a profound change of relationship with our environment: instead of trying to control the planet, after the 'industrial age gave the illusion that mankind could master the world without mastering itself' (Morin, 1999, p. 88), humanity must exert self-control. This calls, too, for a new subject, renouncing *homo economicus*, self-interested and exploitative, in favour of *homo sapiens* who adopts the attitude of the carer or gardener:

> more than a Producer, she/he is the guardian of life perpetuation, and also a poet modelling life as an artist . . . a guard of nature. She/he is not running away, leaving the weed [*sic*] invading the garden. She/he accepts the responsibility of modelling nature. She/he is on duty to care for nature, but also, this is the important point, she/he takes pleasure and accomplishment as an artist, because, ultimately, gardening is an art.
>
> (Gaudin, 2008, p. 75)

Hand in hand goes a different relationship to prosperity, making the turn from equating prosperity with continual growth and its attendant environmental depredations, to equating prosperity with flourishing while leaving a vastly less material impact on the environment. As Jackson comments in his report, *Prosperity without Growth*, 'the possibility that humans can flourish and at the same time consume less is an intriguing one. It would be foolish to think that it is easy to achieve. But it should not be given up lightly' (Jackson, 2009, p. 7). It will mean weaning ourselves off novelty-based and status-driven consumption, the driver of materialistic individualism and a major contributor to our unsustainable growth-based economy:

> Structural change must lie at the heart of any strategy to address the social logic of consumerism . . . [First] to dismantle the perverse incentives for unproductive status competition. [Second] to establish new structures that provide capabilities for people to flourish – and in particular to participate meaningfully and creatively in the life of society – in less materialistic ways.
>
> (ibid., p. 11)

In a world of enormous inequality, within and especially between countries, where so many are so far removed from the profligate material conditions of the minority, planetary sustainability calls for a 'new macro-economics for sustainability' that 'must abandon the presumption of growth in material consumption as the basis for economic stability' and 'ensure distributional equity' (ibid., p. 10).

But an economy surviving only by a diet of massive over-consumption, in which perpetual growth is seen as the solution to all problems, is not the only reason for a profoundly troubling diagnosis of our time. For it is part of a much larger and even more serious scenario: we are 'the first species capable of effectively eliminating life on Earth'. Mankind has had this fearful capacity since the advent of nuclear weapons: as Edgar Morin observes, Hiroshima brought the planet into a 'Damoclean phase [in which] humanity must live with the possibility of self-destruction' (1999, p. 16); and with the development and proliferation of these weapons, this capacity has been greatly enhanced.

But there are other reasons for fearing mankind's capacity to eliminate life on earth – or at least severely damage it: global warming and associated climate change, with a two-degree Celsius increase in global surface temperature, which world leaders agreed in 2009 'was the line over which global society should not step' (Berners-Lee and Clark, 2013, p. 22),[1] likely to be exceeded by the end of the century (International Panel on Climate Change, 2013, section E.1); spreading toxicity and other forms of environmental degradation; resource depletion; loss of bio-diversity, with some, indeed, already warning that we are on the brink of a sixth mass extinction of other species, distinguished from the previous five by its man-made causes (see, for example, Gibbons, 2011); not to mention the proliferation of nuclear weapons of unimaginable destructive power.

Each of these threats is deadly serious in its own right; each is already causing great damage to human life, other species and the wider environment; and each is related to the others to form a 'deadly intersolidarity of problems'. We may try and keep them in separate compartments, looking occasionally at one in isolation before turning aside to concentrate again on the 'global race', getting back to business as usual, the short-sighted business of producing, consuming and polluting more and more. But as Stephen Emmott, head of Computational Science at Microsoft Research in Cambridge, puts it, adding his warning to Edgar Morin's, 'our activities are not only completely interconnected with, but are now also interacting with, the complex system we live on: Earth' (2013, p. 38).

We cannot continue as we are and we have little time in which to change direction. All of the science 'points to the inescapable fact that we are in trouble. Serious trouble . . . [and] one thing that is predictable is that things are going to get worse' (ibid., p. 117). We are, Emmott concludes, facing problems the scale and nature of which are 'immense, unprecedented and possibly unsolvable', in short 'an unprecedented emergency' (ibid., pp. 182, 195). Driving this point home with striking imagery, in January 2012, '[f]aced with inadequate progress on nuclear weapons reduction and proliferation, and continuing inaction on climate change, the Bulletin of the Atomic Scientists . . . moved the hands of its famous "Doomsday Clock" to five minutes to midnight' (www.thebulletin.org/content/media-center/announcements/2012/01/10/doomsday-clock-moves-1-minute-closer-to-midnight).

So, my diagnosis of our time is not good, far more winter of despair than spring of hope. The condition of the patient, our species, may or may not be terminal but is, at best, very ill from a combination of an unhealthy economic system, self-destructive weaponry and a fouled and disturbed environment. Science and technology may have forged ahead, but politics and ethics have remained trailing in their wake – consequently, 'our cleverness, our inventiveness and our activities are now the drivers of every global problem we face' (Emmott, 2013, p. 6). Furthermore, a hegemonic economic regime that spurns democracy, collaboration and the public domain in favour of intense competition, extreme individualism and excess consumption is at total odds with what is needed to address the threats to human life on earth and to rebalance our world to prosperity without growth.

I cannot say with any degree of confidence that I know what this diagnosis means for education – in early childhood or beyond: I have no pat answers. It is clearly far, far more than just adding a few more items to the curriculum. What I am certain of, however, is that the diagnosis of our time must play a central part in all discussions about the future of all education. We cannot implicate education in the continuation of a ruinous economic system and self-inflicted environmental disaster, that deadly global race. We need to find a more responsible, less compliant and more optimistic role, not least contributing to democratic deliberation and new thinking about a safe and sustainable future.

What is our understanding or image of the child? Of the educator? Of the early childhood centre?

'What is your image of the child?' That political question has been the starting point for the 50 year project of early childhood education in Reggio Emilia. To ask the question is to recognise that there are 'hundreds of different images of the child' and that each one of us has an image that 'directs you as you begin to relate to a child' (Malaguzzi, cited in Hoyuelos, 2013, p. 60). I have already mentioned some in my discussion of the story of quality and high returns in Chapter 2. To answer the question is to make a political choice from amongst so many possibilities, a choice that is of the utmost significance for policy, provision and practice.

My *image of the child*, already touched on, is what Loris Malaguzzi termed the 'rich' child: a child born with great potential that can be expressed in a hundred languages[2]; an active learner, seeking the meaning of the world from birth, a co-creator of knowledge, identity, culture and values; a child that can live, learn, listen and communicate, but always in relation with others; the whole child, the child with body, mind, emotions, creativity, history and social identity; an individual, whose individuality and autonomy depend upon interdependence, and who needs and wants connections with other children and adults; and last but not least, a citizen and a subject of rights. To have the image of a 'rich' child is not to deny that many children are poor in the sense that they live in material poverty, have lives and prospects blighted by inequality, and have to contend with other conditions that deny any hope of a flourishing life. But to have this image of the 'rich' child, whatever her or his material circumstances, is to have a constant reminder of potentiality, dwelling on what each and every child brings to early childhood education and what early childhood education can contribute to the realisation of that potentiality – not on what education should be doing to compensate for or rectify deficiencies.

In Reggio Emilia, they also speak of the 'competent child', an image that complements the 'rich' child. Competence here is not understood in the narrow technical sense of acquiring certain specified skills or information through training, but in a broad sense to describe a way of being:

> Competent in relating and interacting, with a deep respect for others and accepting of conflict and error. A child who is competent in constructing, in constructing himself while he constructs his world and is, in turn, constructed by the world. Competent in constructing theories to interpret reality and in formulating hypotheses and metaphors as possibilities for understanding reality. A child who has his own values and is adept at building relationships of solidarity. A child who is always open to that which is new and different. A possessor and builder of futures, not only because children are the future, but because they constantly re-interpret reality and continuously give it new meanings.
>
> (Rinaldi, 2006, p. 123)

My *image of the educator* is similar, 'rich' and competent with enormous potential, an active learner co-constructing knowledge in relationship with others, not least children, with the school as a 'a place where adults and children learn together' (Hoyuelos, 2013, p. 126). Like the child, she has the potential of a hundred languages:

> The hundred languages of the children have to become the hundred languages of the teacher. The teacher can have a hundred languages if she or he can discover her competence by listening and not only talking. The teacher can be competent in expressing and communicating with the hundred languages and using a hundred media when [*sic*] she or he can connect – theory and practice, time and space, hands and mind, school and society, dreams and passion, strength and joy.
>
> (Rinaldi, 2006, p. 195)

This educator is a reflective practitioner, a theorist and a critical thinker, aware that 'when you do practice, it's because you have a theory . . . [and that when you] think, it's because there is a practice behind it' (ibid., p. 191). Aware, too, and curious about the many paradigmatic positions and theoretical perspectives that are available, respecting this diversity whilst also able to make choices between conflicting alternatives; indeed able to listen to others' stories and ask questions of them, but also to create and tell her own stories. She is also a researcher and experimenter, seeking new understandings, new knowledge, new ideas, these identities manifested in various ways: 'as a way of thinking, of approaching life, of negotiating, of documenting'.

Such an educator is able to work with the 'rich' and competent child I have envisaged, through adopting certain roles described by Aldo Fortunati:

> An active and constructive child stimulates the teachers to place more attention on the organisation of opportunities than on predefining objectives . . . [The role of the teacher is] removed from the fallacy of certainties and [reassumes] the responsibility to choose, experiment, discuss, reflect, and change, focusing on the organisation of opportunities rather than the anxiousness to pursue outcomes, and maintaining in their work the pleasure of amazement and wonder.
>
> (2006, pp. 34, 38)

This view about the educator's role was echoed by Loris Malaguzzi, who saw it as 'not to pass on "learning", but to create different learning conditions' (Hoyuelos, 2013, p. 126):

> the objective of education is to provide the child with situations in which he can be active and initiate his own learning . . . [and] to increase the child's possibilities to invent and discover . . . We need more creators of

contexts that promote learning, rather than acts or situations that transmit content . . . We need to produce situations in which children learn by themselves, in which children can take advantage of their own knowledge and resources autonomously, and in which the minimal intervention of the adult is guaranteed . . . What I want to do is activate within children the desire and will and great pleasure that comes from being the authors of their own learning.

(ibid., pp. 126, 268, 269)

Although this does not mean the educator never intervenes, but should only do so when the 'children's "fuel"' is almost exhausted, using judgement built from practice, relationships and reflection.

My image of the educator also includes elements of what has been termed a democratic professionalism. This concept is based on 'participatory relationships and alliances. It foregrounds collaborative, cooperative action between professional colleagues and other stakeholders. It emphasises engaging and networking with the local community' (Oberhuemer, 2005). This, again, means recognising, welcoming and respecting diversity, of values, of ideas, of understandings. As the educator Paulo Freire (1921–97) writes, 'I must respect positions opposed to my own, positions that I combat earnestly and with passion' (2004, p. 66). The educator-as-democratic professional may offer her "reading of the world", but at the same time her role is to 'bring out the fact that there are other 'readings of the world', different from the one being offered as the educator's own, and at times antagonistic to it' (Freire, 2004, p. 96).

To recap *my image of the early childhood centre*, it is as a public space or forum, a place of encounter between citizens, both children and adults, and as a collaborative workshop or laboratory for the use of these citizens. As such it is a place of infinite potentiality – a site of many, many projects and other possibilities. Education (the meaning of which I discuss below) will be important. But there can be much else going on besides, including those projects that are specified by the democratic bodies that initiate and support these centres and others that arise from encounters between citizens and in response to the opportunities and needs of the children, families and communities that centres serve. To take but a few general examples (and more specific examples can be found later on page 136), these projects may involve co-constructing knowledge (learning) for children and adults; providing various forms of family support, especially for parents of young children; building social solidarity and community cohesion; helping to resist dominant discourses, for example through pedagogical documentation discussed later, and other forms of oppression experienced by local families and communities; sustaining minority cultures and languages through recognising, valuing and nurturing diversity; contributing to the local economy, both by supporting employed parents and by centres themselves providing good employment opportunities; experimenting with new pedagogical and community projects; and promoting gender and other equalities.

Two further points should be made about my image of the early childhood centre. First, these centres can provide a safe and secure place for children whilst their parents are at work (or doing other socially or personally valued activities) – what some would term 'childcare'. By providing this, centres contribute to various projects, such as developing the local economy and promoting equalities. But this should be seen as just one of the purposes that centres can perform. Early childhood centres, in my understanding, are multi-purpose services that include 'childcare' among their many purposes; they are *not* 'childcare services', i.e. services defined first and foremost by the provision of care for working parents, a narrowly defined concept that too readily perpetuates an idea of centres as businesses selling a commodity (care) and being only for some families (those wanting to purchase care). Furthermore, centres provide care – or as I propose below, an ethic of care – to *all* children who come to them, irrespective of their parents' employment status.

Second, and returning to my earlier problem with the term 'investment', I cannot and should not seek to justify early childhood centres on the basis of calculated returns – payment by results. Rather they are justified, first and foremost, as one of a small number of social institutions (schools are another) that are fundamental to the cohesion and creation of a democratic society. Fundamental because they provide spaces for encounter between citizens – ever more important in our increasingly privatised and individualised world – and opportunities for deliberation, collective choices and local projects, the scope and significance of which cannot be predicted in advance or from a central point.

Spinoza's comment that '[w]e never know in advance what a body can do' expresses a belief in the immanent, unknowable and unlimited potentiality of the individual, a belief well suited to the image of the rich and competent child and educator. The same can be said of early childhood centres – 'we never know in advance what a centre can do'. But this means that we need to have sufficient faith in such collective endeavours not to seek to control them through 'tightly defined programmes' and pre-specified goals and methods, imposing an iron will to know that leaves no scope for the unknown and unexpected, for wonder and surprise.

What does education mean?

The debate about the meaning of 'education' has a long history. One difference of opinion, particularly apparent today, and expressive of the political nature of education, is between a narrower and a broader understanding. The former emphasises cognition (above all other facets of human being), the acquisition of a limited and prescribed range of mainly work-related competences and skills, and the attainment of predefined standards or norms. The latter emphasises fostering all facets of personhood (not just the cognitive), general health and wellbeing, relationships with and inclusion in a wider community and the ability to work together with other members of that community: what some might in shorthand refer to as 'holistic' education. The former sees education as a process of achieving autonomy and fitness for prescribed purpose, and treats care and nurturance as quite separate and lesser activities. The latter sees education as a process of upbringing and increasing participation in the wider society, with the goal that both individual and society flourish (Moss and Haydon, 2008). It treats care and nurturance as intrinsic, therefore inseparable, parts of education, not least because education is understood as a relational and ethical practice, with relational and ethical purposes. The former might be termed 'education-in-its-narrower sense', the latter 'education-in-its-broadest-sense'.

'Education-in-its-broadest-sense' has much in common with the German concept of *bildung*, which has influenced Continental European debates about the meaning of education. Or rather, I should say a broad understanding of the concept of education has much in common with a particular understanding of the concept of *bildung*. Rooted in the tradition of humanism and enlightenment, and often linked to the educational theorist Wilhelm von Humboldt (1767–1835), *bildung* in this understanding refers to the *process* of an individual striving to reach her or his full potential, as well as to an *ideal* – having, for instance, reached a state of reflexivity towards one's self, others, and the world (Luth, 1998). Gunilla Dahlberg develops this understanding of *bildung* in a discussion of the concept's importance for a Swedish government commission in 1994 on the future of the school:

> Now '*bildung*' has many different interpretations, for example it is sometimes treated as transmission of pre-determined facts; it then gets lost in a narrow goal-governed idea of education. But the Commission reclaimed another idea of *bildung*, which views knowledge as consisting not only of facts but also meaning-making and understanding, as well as skills and a dimension that relates to the uniqueness of a situation and one's ability to value that situation. It also recognised knowledge as always contextualised and constructed, but without losing its instrumental aspects . . . [Donald Broady, a researcher, wrote] for the Commission about the classical German conception of *bildung*: the human being is, or should be, a being that constructs her/himself into something not decided beforehand. *Bildung* is, hence, an active undertaking, which implies an increase in the individual's possibilities for freedom. Donald related his thinking to Kant's well-known paper *What is Enlightenment?*, in which Kant encourages us to have courage to use our own reason without direction from someone else.
>
> (Dahlberg, 2013, pp. 83–4)

The notion of 'education-in-its-broadest-sense' is also similar in many respects to another concept with its roots in Germany but with an extensive reach across continental Europe: social pedagogy. Its distinctive identity has frequently been lost in translation, pedagogy often being translated into English as 'education' or 'the science of education' (with 'pedagogues' similarly mis-translated as 'teachers'). One group of English researchers, who have worked over several years to understand the Continental tradition of social pedagogy and its application today in services for children and adults, describe it as implying:

> an approach to work with people in which learning, care, health, general wellbeing and development are viewed as totally inseparable, a holistic idea summed up in the pedagogical term 'upbringing'. The pedagogue as practitioner sees herself as a person in relationship with the child as a whole person, supporting the child's overall development.
>
> (Boddy *et al.*, 2005, p. 3)

To summarise. My understanding of education is holistic; it involves the creation or realisation of the self as a subject, not following a predetermined route but creating something new and unique; it strives to bring about a subject able to think and speak for herself; but it is also about the self in relation to others and the wider society, so that self-realisation is not confused with autonomy but presumes interdependence, obligation and responsibility. It is, in short, education as an emancipatory project of realising potentiality, without 'emancipation from bonds to other people' (Readings, 1996, p. 189).

What paradigm do we adopt?

The effect of paradigm, the mindset we adopt through which we make sense of the world and our place in it, is so pervasive and profound that it is difficult to understand how any education – early childhood or otherwise, and including the education of educators – can proceed without addressing this most basic of questions. For the answer, and therefore the position adopted, changes everything. My answer and position might be broadly called post-foundational, a paradigm that encompasses a variety of theoretical perspectives including post-modernisms, post-structualisms and post-colonialisms.

This paradigm challenges the basic tenets, or foundations, of the paradigm of regulatory modernity, which plays so large a part in the story of quality and high returns. Post-foundationalism values complexity and context, uncertainty and provisionality, subjectivity and interpretation. Ontologically, it adopts a social constructionist approach, in which the world and our knowledge of it are socially constructed, a process in which all of us, as human beings, are active participants in relationship with others: 'the world is always *our* world, understood or constructed by ourselves, not in isolation but as part of a community of human agents, and through our active interaction and participation with other people in that community' (Dahlberg *et al.*, 2013, p. 24; original emphasis).

Epistemologically, too, the paradigmatic position is very different:

> Post-structuralists, building on critical philosophies of science, reject the possibility of absolute truths and universally ordered systems of knowledge. Instead, knowledge is understood as produced by an 'economy of discourses

of truth' and meaning emerges from the interaction of competing knowledges. Some knowledges justify and support dominating meanings and practices while other knowledges, usually marginal, challenge hegemonic discourses . . . This perspective doesn't make scientific knowledge 'untrue'. Rather, *it demands that we understand Truth in a different way, as the contingent product of particular, situated ways of comprehending the world and not as something that is absolute and immutable which pre-exists social relations and awaits discovery* . . . [T]he central issues become those of understanding the conditions in which certain discourses or world-views are privileged and how the distinctions they produce between true and false can be contested.

(Otto, 1999, p. 17; emphasis added)

From this perspective, there is not and cannot be some position outside the world from which objective, stable and universal knowledge can be revealed and dispassionate and irrefutable judgements made. It recognises, too, the inextricable relationship between knowledge and power, in which power functions through knowledge and what is deemed knowledge is a function of power, and the inevitability of position and context. There can, for example, be no neutral, stable and generic measure of 'quality', nor can evidence 'tell' us anything. Instead, post-foundationalism views knowledge as unavoidably partial, perspectival and provisional. It offers a world of multiple local practices, perspectives and knowledges, so that different people will interpret – make meaning – of evidence in different ways and will arrive at different views about what constitutes, for example, good education in a process that is inescapably political. For the paradigm lends itself readily to the primacy of political practice, with its view of a world in which we constantly face conflicting alternatives.

Post-foundationalism, in short, relativises, because there can be no one objectively right answer in a world of multiple perspectives: there is no position 'out there' from which I can objectively view, know and evaluate the world. But this should not be confused with anything goes, a world of aesthetic and moral equivalence. Being situated in a post-foundational paradigm does not mean being unable to evaluate and judge, that we cannot make aesthetic or moral choices. We can and must, though it is demanding on us to have to do so. For we must take responsibility for this process and for our choices, not abdicate responsibility to someone or something else: some purportedly universal code or some supposedly neutral measurement yardstick or some allegedly objective expert, claiming universal knowledge and truth. We have, for example, to decide through making choices in response to political questions what we think is a good early childhood education, not fall back on some expert definition and measure of 'quality' that pretends to be a technical and apolitical specification.

Sociologist Zygmunt Bauman, in his writing about postmodern ethics, has emphasised the greater, not lesser, responsibility that the post-foundational paradigm calls for, insisting that to adopt a post-foundational position offers no easy way out from making choices:

Choices between good and evil are still to be made, this time, however, in full daylight and with full knowledge that a choice has been made. With the smokescreen of centralized legislation dispersed and the power-of-attorney returned to the signatory, the choice is blatantly left to the moral person's own devices. With choice comes responsibility. And if choice is inevitable, responsibility is unavoidable . . . What this new condition does spell out, however, is a prospect of a greater awareness of the moral character of our choices; of our facing our choices more consciously and seeing their moral contents more clearly.

(Bauman, 1995, p. 7)

If I were to sum up why I have chosen this post-foundational paradigmatic position, I would offer three main reasons. First, it helps us to think critically, for example about power relations – 'the rationalities and techniques by which one governs the conduct of others' (Ball, 2013, p. 143). Not that power and its effects are intrinsically bad; power is productive and can be beneficial. But we need to be aware of the omnipresence of power relations. They are everywhere, and we are all participant in them: 'In human relations, whatever they are – whether it be a question of communicating verbally . . . or a question of a love relationship, an institutional or economic relationship – power is always present: I mean the relationship in which one wishes to direct the behaviour of another (Foucault, 1987, p. 11).

For this reason, we need to remember that 'everything is dangerous', the issue being not one of intent but of effect: benign motives may have unintended or even malign effects, and early childhood education is no exception.

Second, it offers a possibility to escape from the will to know and master that features so prominently in the paradigm of regulatory modernity, with its consequent need for 'taming subjectivities as well as learning processes; predicting, controlling, supervising and evaluating according to predetermined standards' (Olsson, 2009, p. 6). Instead, in the post-foundational paradigm, there is no certainty to be had, no correct position to be found and taken, no absolute truth to be discovered and enforced – and that turns out to be a benefit not a bane. Post-foundationalism offers the possibility to open up for movement and experimentation in subjectivity and learning, no longer constrained by prescribed outcomes and norms that are justified by absolute truth claims. Instead of the predictability and repetitiousness of the dominant discourse in early childhood education, with its desire to fix or position the child in her or his already known, developmentally appropriate place, the post-foundational paradigm holds out the prospect of an early childhood education of events and lines of flight, of surprise and wonder. If regulatory modernity has a will to know and a drive to master, post-foundationalism does not know what a body can do – and is at ease with not knowing, whilst excited at the potentiality of this condition.

Third, it provides hope for responding to the diversity and complexity of the world in ways that are welcoming and respectful, and do not seek to reduce it to a unified whole by trying to make the Other into the Same. This response to diversity and complexity, to tame and comprehend them by reductive modes of simplification, standardisation and technical practice, is inherent in the paradigm of regulatory modernity and pervasive in the dominant discourse of early childhood education. The challenge to early childhood education, to education overall, is 'to think another whom I cannot grasp', for it poses educators with profound questions: 'such as how the encounter with Otherness, with difference can take place as responsibly as possible – as something which the so-called 'free thought' cannot grasp through categories, classifications and thematizations' (Dahlberg, 2003, p. 270). I shall return to this issue when I discuss below my answer to 'what ethics?'

What is knowledge? How do we learn?

These two questions are posed together, since they are so closely connected, the one entirely dependent on the other. Both, in turn, lead to a further question: what pedagogy?

Deborah Osberg and Gert Biesta outline different approaches to these questions in two articles, which take as their starting point the:

> current need to update the epistemology of schooling [that] originates from *a general trend in epistemology which moves from a static, passive or representational view of knowledge towards a more active and adaptive one.* With the former knowledge is held to be an accurate representation of a pre-existing reality. With the latter it is held that knowledge is caught up with the activity and situations in which it is produced.
>
> (Biesta and Osberg, 2007, pp. 15–16; emphasis added)

The former idea of knowledge, what Charles Taylor calls 'modern representational epistemology' (1995, p. 5), underpins contemporary schooling – and indeed the story of quality and high returns. The belief in a true knowledge that accurately represents an independent and pre-existing reality has defined the task of modern schools as transmitting this knowledge. But this idea of knowledge, bred of the paradigm of regulatory modernity, needs replacing by the latter idea of knowledge, what Osberg and Biesta term an 'emergentist' epistemology and define as the creation of new properties:

> [C]ontemporary understandings of emergence have retained the idea that emergence introduces properties that are novel and sometimes even inconceivable or unimaginable . . . Strong emergence therefore presents a direct challenge to determinism (the idea that given one set of circumstances there is only one logical outcome) . . . [If] we think of knowledge (or knowing) not as *determined* by our engagement with the present, but as *emerging* from our engagement with the present . . . each knowledge event

– which is to say each taking place of knowledge (knowing) – is necessarily *also radically new*.

(Osberg and Biesta, 2007, pp. 33, 34, 40; original emphasis)

Put another way, 'in an emergent universe we cannot rely on the rules of the past to dictate what we should do in the future'.

From the perspective of an emergentist epistemology, knowledge is not a 'correct representation of an independent reality . . . real life as it really is' (Biesta and Osberg, 2007, pp. 17–18). Nor is learning the transmission of a description or representation of reality from a person who knows to another who does not, without mediation or interpretation, an 'unproblematic transference with full conservation of intent' (Roy, 2004, p. 297). It is not about the child, in this way, reproducing a true representation of a known and pre-existing world.

From the perspective of an emergentist epistemology, knowledge is the creation of something new, of new properties 'that have never existed before and, more importantly, are inconceivable from what has come before' (Osberg and Biesta, 2007, p. 33). Knowledge is a social construction, and learning is the process of constructing knowledge 'collectively in often unpredictable interactions among teachers, children and young people, texts, family members, media and objects, and through events and experiences' (Thomson *et al.*, 2012, p. 2). Or, as Lenz Taguchi (2010a) puts it, learning is 'a collaborative process of meaning making that emerges *in-between* learners, and learners and matter in the learning context' (p. 20). Moreover, learning that is 'inclusive of complexity, diversity and multiplicity cannot have a fixed origin, end point or linear trajectory' (p. 22).

Carlina Rinaldi describes how the municipal schools in Reggio Emilia adopt this epistemological perspective:

> Learning does not take place by means of transmission or reproduction. It is a process of construction, in which each individual constructs for himself the reasons, the 'whys', the meanings of things, others, nature, events, reality and life. The learning process is certainly individual, but because the reasons, explanations, interpretations, and meanings of others are indispensable for our knowledge building, it is also a process of relations – a process of social construction. We *thus consider knowledge to be a process of construction by the individual in relation with others, a true act of co-construction*. The timing and styles of learning are individual, and cannot be standardized with those of others, but we need others in order to realize ourselves.
>
> (Rinaldi, 2006, p. 125; emphasis added)

What is created in such processes, what new properties emerge, is not readily controlled, indeed is quite unpredictable; we do not know what a body can do. So instead of the image of knowledge as a ladder or tree, following orderly and predetermined step-by-step sequences to a preset goal, moving onwards and upwards towards the known end, other images come to mind. One immediately familiar image is Loris Malaguzzi's metaphor of knowledge as like a 'tangle of spaghetti'. Another, less familiar image is the *rhizome*, developed by Deleuze and Guattari (1999; see also Deleuze and Parnet, 1987). Knowledge-as-rhizome is something that shoots in all directions with no beginning and no end, but is always *in between*, with openings towards other directions and places. It is a *multiplicity* functioning by means of connections and heterogeneity, a multiplicity which is not given but constructed.

Knowledge then is created in networks of relationships, not only with other people but also with matter, both having agency, 'the possibility of intervening and acting upon others and the world' (Lenz Taguchi, 2010a). It results from what Deleuze and Guattari envisage as the provocation of an encounter with difference – hence one reason for the importance and potential of diversity. From that provocation comes a line of flight, 'an event of unthought possibilities that leaps away from immobile, fixed and structured (stratified) spaces regulated by taken-for-granted habits of mind and body' (ibid., p. 22), and signifying the creation of something new. Through this can emerge new meanings, new theories, new understandings, the possibility of escaping the clutches of the already known, the circular orbit of the given problem and the given answer. The philosophy of these two Frenchmen 'insists on creative thought, on inventing and on that which is not yet', reflecting the longing of children for 'the actual act of invention, for the new, the remarkable, the interesting, and to be taken seriously in one's littleness' (Olsson, 2013, p. 231).

Learning, then, 'resembles a complex web of interconnections' (Lenz Taguchi, 2010a, p. 15) and knowledge is a product of such connectivities. Education should do everything possible to foster connections, resisting the boundaries raised by subjects and disciplines and the separation of rationality, imagination, emotion and aesthetic; and ever conscious of the damage caused by 'education and culture which prefer to separate [rather] than to work on connections' (Vecchi, 2004, p. 18). By the same token, learning is unpredictable and follows no predetermined direction: 'it can begin anywhere and go any place' (Lenz Taguchi, 2010a, p. 27). Rinaldi takes a similar view when she says that 'learning does not proceed in a linear way, determined and deterministic, by progressive and predictable stages, but rather is constructed through contemporaneous advances, standstills, and "retreats" that take many directions' (2006, pp. 131–2).

Lenz Taguchi sums up the consequences for understandings of knowledge and learning when moving from an approach inscribed with a representational epistemology to one inscribed with an emergentist epistemology. It means a shift from:

- end-point goals and values *to* learning 'in the middle of things in collaborative processes of negotiation and renegotiation';
- vertical and hierarchical relationships between human organisms and material reality *to* a horizontal and non-hierarchical 'flattened-out' relationship in which we cannot separate the learner from what is learned;

- linear *to* rhizomatic learning processes;
- a notion of an independent responsible learning subject *to* interdependence, collaboration, and a mutual responsibility for learning;
- the individual learner and her or his cognitive development *to* collaborative processes of meaning-making in material-discursive intra-actions[3];
- the notion that there is only human agency *to* understanding both human and non-human organisms and matter as performative agents;
- representations of the world in language *to* invention and creation of new concepts, ideas, problems of investigation and strategies of doing;
- identifying lack and deviation *to* affirmation of difference, diversity and new inventions (Lenz Taguchi, 2010a, p. 29).

It is worth dwelling on these answers to the questions, of what knowledge is and how we learn, since they point very clearly to profound differences with the story of quality and high returns. For at the heart of that story is an understanding of knowledge and learning that holds firmly to ideas of linearity and predetermination, certainty and closure, to be realised through the logic of the programme, the prescribed technology applied to the learner and proven to work in delivering prescribed outcomes: or, as Malaguzzi put it, '[a] map, specified in its details, of actions or events that have to occur for a certain outcome to be achieved and that result in a final, predetermined reality' (Hoyuelos, 2013, p. 179). Indeed, Malaguzzi extends this critique to Vygotsky's theory, finding it depicts a learning process that is extremely linear, moving:

> from one ability to a greater one, which turns out to be dangerous because not always, at least not from all points of view, is the zone of potential development further advanced than the zone of real development . . . Besides the idea of an individual possessing greater or lesser ability is dangerous in the sense that it looks at development in a progressive form like an ascending arrow decided by the adult.
>
> (ibid., pp. 124–5)

By contrast, the story of democracy, experimentation and potentiality, with its image of the rhizome and its associated concepts of emergence and being in between, with its love of complexity and uncertainty, believes 'in a child who is full of potentialities and capabilities that cannot be determined . . . [living a childhood that is] an adventure full of unexpected possibilities' (ibid., p. 332). Rather than programming, with its sole pursuit of known answers to pre-specified questions, this calls for project work, providing freedom for children to experiment, research and move, and creating an environment for theory-building, listening and meaning-making, an environment where connections can readily be made and where the unexpected is expected and welcomed. Which brings me to the follow-up question: 'what pedagogy?'

Biesta and Osberg propose (following Ulmer, 1985) a 'pedagogy of invention', which they describe as emerging from 'a complexity inspired epistemology' in which 'knowledge does not bring us closer to what is *already* present but, rather, moves us into a *new* reality which is incalculable from what came before . . . knowledge is not conservative but *radically inventionalistic*' (Biesta and Osberg, 2007, p. 46; original emphasis). They also propose an innovatory image of the school, which discards the common image of schools as 'places where the rules of the past are taught in order to take care of the future . . . replicating the past and holding the world still' (ibid., p. 47). Instead of teaching children about a pre-given world, Osberg and Biesta argue schools must be places:

> where meanings can be *responsibly* negotiated and hence where the new is *allowed* to appear . . . We believe that if we rethink the purposes of schooling using insights from complexity and deconstruction, which suggest an emergentist relationship between the world and our knowledge of it, then we must think of schools as not as [*sic*] places where the meanings of a *present* world (which is also a world that has always already passed) are replicated and hence preserved. Instead schools can be thought of as places where new worlds are *allowed* to emerge, or to say this differently where the world is renewed.
>
> (ibid., p. 49; original emphasis)

The early childhood educators in Reggio Emilia have gone further, from theorising the pedagogical implications of an epistemological shift to putting them to work on an everyday basis in their municipal schools, in what they term a 'pedagogy of relationships and listening'. In this pedagogy, learning is a process of co-constructing meaning, always in relationship with others through continuous theory-building, theory testing and theory rebuilding, with others acting as careful listeners to theories as they are put forward:

> For adults and children alike, understanding means being able to develop an interpretive 'theory', a narration that gives meaning to events and objects of the world. Our theories are provisional, offering a satisfactory explanation that can be continuously reworked; but they represent something more than simply an idea or a group of ideas. They must please us and convince us, be useful, and satisfy our intellectual, affective, and aesthetic needs (the aesthetics of knowledge). In representing the world, our theories represent us.
>
> Moreover, if possible, our theories must please and be attractive to others. Our theories need to be listened to by others. Expressing our theories to others makes it possible to transform a world not intrinsically ours into something shared. Sharing theories is a response to uncertainty.
>
> (Rinaldi, 2006, p. 64)

Through such pedagogy, which is not tied to pre-existing understandings, new meanings are created, in schools where 'new worlds are allowed to emerge . . . [and] the world is renewed'.

This discussion of learning and knowledge does not mean there is no place in early childhood education for beginning the acquisition of important skills or techniques, for example literacy and mathematics. These matter, and of course there must be a place for them. But the issue becomes what that place is, so as to ensure the acquisition of skills and techniques is not at the expense of creating knowledge and living a flourishing life, a danger that Dewey recognised and cautioned against in words that should adorn the walls of every education ministry in the world:

> What avail is it to win prescribed amounts of information about geography and history, to win ability to read and write, if in the process the individual loses his own soul; loses his appreciation of things worth while, of the values to which these things are relative; if he loses desire to apply what he has learned and, above all, loses the ability to extract meaning from his future experiences as they occur.
>
> (Dewey, 1938/1988, p. 49)

Further, how should the acquisition of skills and techniques relate to children's own learning strategies and the wider pedagogy? Can they work in partnership or will they oppose each other to the detriment of both?

So to say literacy and numeracy matter is not to say much. Everyone would agree. What matters far more is how they are learnt and how they fit into the far bigger picture of an education-in-its-broadest-sense and an emergentist epistemology; how to avoid crude and over-simplified approaches that may do more harm than good. Swedish researcher Liselott Mariett Olsson, writing about a project 'The Magic of Language' (discussed further in Chapter 7), shows how it is possible to 'find ontological and epistemological perspectives on language that align themselves with, and are close to children's own strategies for learning language, reading and writing'. Put another way, this is about going with the flow by starting from 'children's own learning strategies and production of knowledge', rather than 'trying to fit children's learning into preformed theories and practices' and in so doing, to 'tame, standardise and trivialise learning' (Olsson, 2012, p. 90). Another Swedish researcher, Gunilla Dahlberg, makes a similar point but applied more broadly:

> This preparation for school discourse, which starts in Sweden today, has led in recent years to more talk about mathematics, language, natural sciences – but again in a very simplified way. I mean the idea of learning as transmission of facts, of reproducing knowledge that is already known; rather than learning as a process of meaning making. With this simplified approach, we don't listen to and work with children's strategies for learning, how they make meaning, so we lose a great amount.

Of course, maths, language and science are important. But if we only looked and listened, we'd see, for example, that children in preschool were using maths all the time. We prefer to test and diagnose at a distance rather than participate to better understand what children are actually doing, for example through pedagogical documentation. We then easily miss the possibility to challenge, deepen and extend children's learning processes.

(2013, p. 88)

The final word on this subject goes to the political theorist Hannah Arendt (1906–1975) and her reminder of the hope that children bring to the world through their potential for creating the new – and the danger of older generations crushing this potential. My hope, she writes:

always hangs on the new which every generation brings; but precisely because we can base our hope only on this, we destroy everything if we so try to control the new that we, the old, can dictate how it will look. Exactly for the sake of what is new and revolutionary in every child, education must be conservative; it must preserve this newness and introduce it as a new thing into an old world.

(Arendt, 1993, pp. 192–3)

What are the purposes of education?

'What is education for?' is another well-worn question, but none the less remains topical and important and as far as ever from consensus. I would like to suggest four purposes that chime with, indeed emerge from, my answers to other political questions: education for survival, flourishing, values and emancipation. I return first to the diagnosis of our time.

Arguing that the current life-threatening juncture we find ourselves at as a species makes earlier ideas of 'education for progress' no longer viable, historian of education Richard Aldrich argues instead for 'an education for survival', with two main aims: to make preparations for survival following any catastrophes; and to foster '"living well" to prevent or reduce the incidence of major catastrophes that threaten human and other species and the Earth itself' (2010, p. 11). Picking up on this theme, Osberg and Biesta suggest that 'one function of schooling is to teach the young how to take care of the world . . . because we care about and wish to take responsibility for the future, the world that will emerge' (2007, p. 47). To which I would add that the multi-purpose early childhood centres envisaged above might also teach the same care to adults as to children. This emphasis on caring suggests the importance of the kind of relational ethics in early childhood education that I discuss below: an ethics of care and an ethics of an encounter, both of which emphasise responsibility for the other and the planet and contest a way of relating to others and the environment that foregrounds calculation, grasping and mastery.

If 'living well' contributes to one purpose of education, survival, it is also important for another, promoting personal well-being or flourishing. The concept of flourishing, or as some might term it personal well-being, 'is pivotal to sound thinking about education' (White, 2005, p. 3). Human flourishing, Erik Olin Wright proposes, 'is a broad, multidimensional umbrella concept, covering a variety of aspects of human well-being . . . [including] the absence of deficits that undermine human functioning . . . [and] the various ways in which people are able to develop and exercise their talents and capacities, or, to use another expression, to realise their individual potentials' (Wright, 2010, p. 13). These potentials can and do take many forms – intellectual, emotional, spiritual, artistic, physical, and more – none of which is inherently more worthy than others; living well requires attention to all of our potentialities, a holistic idea that recognises their interconnectedness. Such broad generalities do not lead, of course, to a precise and generally agreed definition of flourishing. Nor is such a definition likely, since 'what is human flourishing?' is yet another political question to which there are varied and, in some cases, conflicting answers. What education can do, though, is provide copious opportunities for democratic deliberation on this question and experimentation with provisional answers.

So taking the two sides of living well – the environmental and personal – into account I might perhaps develop Aldrich's concept and propose an 'education for survival and flourishing', understood as living well *and* within limits, a reminder that personal flourishing cannot be divorced from collective, even species flourishing. Those limits include at least two important and interrelated dimensions. The limits imposed by what the planet itself can bear – the limits of sustainability; and the limits imposed by social justice – the limits of distributional equity.

A third purpose of early childhood education resides in the reproduction, renewal and emergence of societal values. I choose these terms carefully to represent the unfinished and contentious nature of values. Some will retain their public importance and backing over time, justifying reproduction; others lose their relevance and appeal as conditions and understandings change. But even those values that maintain their importance and backing need constantly holding up to question to ask whether the meanings we attach to such values need rethinking and re-envisioning in response to new conditions, new understandings, new perspectives, recognising the contestability and fluidity of such meanings. Furthermore, over time new values (just like new images or understandings of the child) can emerge and need to be taken into early childhood education.

A final purpose for education that complements the other three – survival, flourishing and values – is what might be termed emancipation. What do I mean? A good starting point is the definition of Enlightenment by the philosopher Immanuel Kant (1724–1804) as 'man's release from his self-incurred tutelage . . . [tutelage being] the inability to use one's understanding without the guidance of another person' (Kant, 1784) – or, to put it more simply, the possibility for children and adults to think and act for themselves. Developing this theme, and following Foucault, emancipation is not an impossible escape from power, but the possibility of transgression, not being governed for example by dominant discourses or taken-for-granted assumptions and practices. It is developing the capacity to see that there are alternatives, that it is possible to think and act differently, that life could be different, that there are many truths and knowledges, that there are other stories to tell – though, at the same time, to appreciate that these alternatives are not all of equal value, and that choices may need to be made.

Viewed in this way, emancipation is:

> practical critique that takes the form of a possible transgression (Foucault, 1984, p. 45). Transgression means doing things differently in order to show – or to prove, as Foucault would say – that things can be different and that the way things are is not necessarily the way things should be . . . Thus, the emancipatory potential of transgression lies in the possibility of no longer being, doing, or thinking what we are, do, or think . . . it is seeking to give a new impetus . . . to the undefined work of freedom.
>
> (Biesta, 2013, p. 7)

One important task in this emancipatory project for education and educational centres is transgressing the story of an inevitable future, to which the only response is preparation for the global race. This calls for contesting the prevalent idea of education as 'future proofing', the concept I introduced in Chapter 2 that envisages the purpose of education as fitting children to perform flexibly and compliantly in a pre-given and inevitable future of more of the same, engendering an uncritical and passive acceptance of what fate seems to hold in store for us. Taking seriously my answer to the question 'What is our diagnosis of the time?', 'future proofing' is positively harmful given the dysfunctional economic regime that currently ensnares us and the scale of the dangers confronting us. We cannot continue as if the future will be or must be or should be simply a projection of the present. Transgression is essential. We need to create something new, a future which provides us all with hope, a future in which we can all believe in the world again, a world that is renewed.

Facer refers to this transgressive emancipatory and creative work as 'future building'. It questions a pre-given and inevitable future of more of the same; it understands, in Paulo Freire's words, 'history as opportunity, not determinism' (Freire, 1996, p. 77). It views the purpose of education, and the school where it takes place, as providing:

a powerful democratic resource and public space that allows its young people and communities to contest the visions of the future that they are being presented with, and to work together through the spaces of traditional and emergent democratic practice, to fight for viable futures for all.

(Facer, 2011, p. 15)

This chimes with Osberg and Biesta's analysis and their proposal for an emergentic epistemology, with its attention to the emergence of new properties that are not based on the past:

In an emergent universe we cannot rely on the rules of the past to dictate what we should do in the future. For this reason it is misguided to think of schools as places where the rules of the past are taught in order to take care of the future. Such an attitude succeeds only in replicating the past and holding the world still. Schools, rather, should be thought of as places where the world is renewed.

(Osberg and Biesta, 2007, p. 47)

An emancipatory education expressed, inter alia, through future building implies education playing an important part in shaping the future – environmentally, societally and individually, helping to navigate a course towards survival and contributing to flourishing. And the enactment of future building through democratic practice, with the school serving as a 'powerful democratic resource', contributes also to another purpose, the reproduction and renewal of values, in particular what I will later contend is a fundamental value: democracy.

I am not saying that survival, flourishing, values and emancipation, however qualified and elaborated, are the only purposes of education. There is, for example, an economic purpose too, though as already indicated, what that is and how it would be consistent with the other purposes I have proposed needs far more thought and deliberation – as indeed does the shape of a future economy that contributes to survival, flourishing, values and emancipation. In any case, it is high time that we once again separated the economic from the social, and put the former in its place, as a means to an end, as an adjunct to flourishing, and not as the be all and end all of life on earth.

What ethics?

Two ethical ideas lie at the heart of my answer to this question: an ethics of care and an ethics of an encounter. They have some important features in common. Both are relational ethics: they concern how we should relate to each other, and hence are of central importance to a relational activity like education. Both question the possibility and desirability of autonomy, or at least autonomy as an unqualified goal involving the abandonment of obligations, since both assume there is no way we can or should want to escape some degree of dependency and interdependency. Both are situational and contextual, requiring an ethical sensibility and ethical judgements, not the strict application of tightly defined and universal codes. Both foreground responsibility – for other people, other species and for the environment – so speaking to the demands of an education for survival and flourishing. Both are radically at odds with neoliberalism, with its relational ethics of calculative exchange and contractual proceduralism, an ethics interpreted and overseen by the lawyer, the manager and the accountant.

Political scientist and feminist scholar Joan Tronto, a leading exponent of an *ethics of care*, describes it as involving both particular acts of caring and a general habit of mind that should inform all aspects of life and which includes attentiveness, responsibility, competence and responsiveness (Tronto, 1993). With Berenice Fisher, Tronto further defines caring as 'a species activity that includes everything we do to maintain, continue and repair our "world" so we can live in it as well as possible . . . That world includes our bodies, our selves and our environment, all of which we seek to interweave in a complex, life-sustaining web' (Fisher and Tronto, 1990, p. 40). Note here the similarity to the previous discussion of 'living well', both individually and in relation to others and our planet. Note, too, that care as an ethic is both about what we do and about a certain sensibility; it should pervade everything we do and every relationship – to ourselves, to others and to our planet. Care as an ethic, as a relational ideal, moves us well away from a narrow view of care as simply a bundle of tasks that can be commodified and traded, a view embodied in the impoverished term 'childcare for working parents' and the economistic notion of a market in 'childcare services'.

An ethics of care started life as a reaction to an ethics of justice, an ethic based on the application of universal principles such as rights. An ethics of care, instead, positively values the particular, the need to take account of context, situation and the other, though it is argued that there is 'no need to abolish the justice paradigm for care ethics to receive attention . . . [only] the creation of a more caring form of justice' (Diedrich *et al.*, 2003, p. 37). In its respect for particularity, 'the care ethic, or care perspective, can be viewed as a reaction to the whole history of Greek metaphysical reduction in western philosophy' (ibid., p. 34). The *ethics of an encounter*, originating in the work of the philosopher Emmanuel Levinas (1906–1995), similarly questions such long-established habits of thought, contesting a Western philosophical tradition that has given primacy to knowing, the will to know that all too often has been at the expense of the Other:

> [K]nowledge – and therefore theory, or history – is constituted [in this tradition] through the comprehension and incorporation of the other . . . In western philosophy, when knowledge or theory comprehends the Other, the alterity of the latter vanishes as it becomes part of the same . . .

In all cases the other is neutralized as a means of encompassing it: ontology amounts to a philosophy of power, an egotism in which the relation with the other is accomplished by assimilation into the self.

(Young, 1990, pp. 44, 45)

Levinas contests the implicit violence, the 'ontological imperialism', in this process of knowing by assimilation, which he describes as 'grasping' the Other to make the Other into the Same, primarily by identifying the knower with the known:

[T]he problem can be stated in the following way: as soon as I finish a conversation with another person, as soon as I pause to reflect, I have the opportunity to think. Once I think, I will try to understand what my discussion partner is saying in categories already familiar to me . . . *Essentially I will translate the vocabulary of the other into my vocabulary, imposing my ideas of what the other has said. In this way, I have reduced the otherness of the other (his alterity) to the sameness of my thought.* I do not allow the other to appear in her light, but the light I lend to her.

(Diedrich *et al.*, 2003, p. 42; emphasis added)

By grasping through such logocentrism, by seeking to know through the application of 'categories already familiar to me', we reduce otherness rather than adopting an ethical stance that respects the alterity of the Other, the Other's absolute otherness or singularity: an ethical stance that acknowledges this is an Other whom I cannot represent, whom I cannot classify into a category, whom I cannot assess against a norm or goal, whom I cannot seek to understand by imposing my framework of thought. This means I have to abandon the security and certainty that comes from making the Other into the Same through incorporating the Other into an existing schema, my existing schema. This means trying to forego the will to know, to give up (or at least relativise) the habits of millennia.

Bill Readings, in his book *The University in Ruins*, considers some of the pedagogical implications of an ethical position that has much in common with Levinas. He develops a critique of the 'enlightenment narrative' of education as a search for truth that produces an autonomous subject – an individual learner – made free of obligations by what they learn and the development of reason; and of the neoliberal narrative of education as a project of self-accreditation and entrepreneurship, a process of consuming knowledge in preparation for the market. He seeks instead to rebuild a notion of pedagogy as first and foremost an ethical practice that recognises and values both our absolute otherness – our singularity – and relationships, in particular our 'obligation to the existence of otherness' and an understanding of community based on 'the model of dependency' (Readings, 1996, p. 190).

Developing themes that have been introduced earlier in this chapter, Readings argues that from his ethical position education is 'not primarily a matter of communication between autonomous subjects functioning as senders and receivers', and teaching 'should cease to be about merely the transmission of information and the emancipation of the autonomous subject' (p. 154). Instead education is about 'drawing out the otherness of thought' and is, in Blanchot's words, 'an infinite attention to the other' (ibid., pp. 156, 160). An education inscribed with this relational ethics requires listening to thought, which:

> is not the spending of time in the production of an autonomous subject or an autonomous body of knowledge. Rather, to listen to Thought, to think beside each other and beside ourselves is to explore an open network of obligation that keeps the question of meaning open as a locus of debate. Doing justice to Thought, listening to our interlocutors, means trying to hear what cannot be said but that which tries to make itself heard. And this is a process incompatible with the production of (even relatively) stable and exchangeable knowledge.
>
> (ibid., p. 165)

This, it might be said, is describing a pedagogy of relationships and listening inscribed with the ethics of an encounter.

Dahlberg has also pointed to the enormous implications of such relational ethics for education:

> Putting everything one encounters into pre-made categories implies we make the Other into the Same, as everything which does not fit into these categories, which is unfamiliar and not taken-for-granted has to be over-come . . . To think another whom I cannot grasp is an important shift and it challenges the whole scene of pedagogy. It poses other questions to us pedagogues. Questions such as how the encounter with Otherness, with difference, can take place as responsibly as possible.
>
> (Dahlberg, 2003, p. 270)

To which I would add that the ethics of an encounter poses a great challenge to the story of quality and high returns, with its calculative ethos and its will not only to know but to govern and control through the application of tech-nologies – including 'pre-made categories' that seek to apply totalising schemas to make the Other into the Same. No thought is given here as to how 'the encounter with Otherness, with difference, can take place as responsibly as pos-sible'; indeed ethics (like politics) is noticeable by its absence from this story as it is told, rendered inaudible and implicit (since ethics, like politics, can never be absent). Instead of that story's desire for consensus and closure – compliance with universally agreed norms – and its reduction of relationships to cash and contract, an ethics of an encounter recognises and welcomes irreducible other-ness and dissensus and relationships of incalculable responsibility and obliga-tion. The university says Readings, but it could as well apply to any educational institution including the nursery or preschool, is 'where thought takes place besides thought, where thinking is a shared process without unity. Thinking together is a dissensual practice' (1996, p. 193).

What are the fundamental values?

Erik Olin Wright, who I have already introduced in Chapter 1 along with his concept of 'real utopias', proposes three principles – or values – as the foundations for what he terms an 'emancipatory social science' and a just society:

> Equality: in a socially just society all persons would have broadly equal access to the material and social means needed to live a flourishing life.
>
> Sustainability: future generations should have access to the social and material means to live flourishing lives at least at the same level as the present generation.
>
> Democracy: in a fully democratic society, all people would have broadly equal access to the necessary means to participate meaningfully in decisions about things which affect their lives.
>
> (Wright, 2012)

I have already argued the importance of equality for a well-functioning society and of sustainability for a society with any worthwhile future. So I readily accept these values as being necessary for a just society. I also agree on the centrality of democracy to a just society, and will discuss its meanings and applications in the next chapter. In short, I acknowledge these to be foundational values for all aspects of society, including early childhood education, and for flourishing lives.

I would, however, add a number of other values to this trio, values that are also fundamental to my concept of education. *Solidarity* expresses a commitment to collaboration, collegiality and mutual support on matters of shared interest; it recognises individuality, but acknowledges that this is always constructed in relation with others and is enabled by and enacted through common purpose, collective effort and sharing risk (e.g. public education, public health, public space). It is a value that also expresses interdependency, obligation and responsibility, and contests a self-interested autonomy. *Diversity* acknowledges the alterity of the Other, the singularity of human beings, as well as the irreducible multiplicity of values, perspectives, identities and ways of life. If solidarity and diversity might seem to be at odds, Michael Hardt and Antonio Negri in their book *Multitude* discuss the possibility, indeed necessity, of a relationship between singularity (absolute otherness) and commonality. While insisting on singularity – 'a social subject whose difference cannot be reduced to sameness' – they also insist that there is nothing to 'prevent the singularities from acting in common' and forging solidarities (Hardt and Negri, 2005, pp. 99, 100, 105):

> Once we recognise singularity, the common begins to emerge. Singularities do communicate, and they are able to do so because of the common they share. We share bodies with two eyes, ten fingers, ten toes; we share life on this earth; we share capitalist regimes of production and exploitation; we share common dreams of a better future. Our communication, collaboration, and cooperation, furthermore, not only are based on the common that exists but also in turn produce the common. We make and remake the common we share every day.
>
> (ibid., p. 128)

What Hardt and Negri contest is a binary of two conflicting opposites: either atomised individualism or an aggregate that subsumes all difference into a faceless and standardised mass or a chaotic and incoherent mob. What they suggest in its place is a productive and constructed relationship between the diversity of singularity and the productivity of solidarity – or, to be more precise, solidarities.

Uncertainty and *subjectivity* are two values whose importance lies in their recognition of, indeed welcome for, irreducible diversity and, therefore, for there being other perspectives and knowledges, other ways of thinking and acting. These values support an open-endedness, 'an obligation that keeps the question of meaning open as a locus of debate', which is the opposite of the closure that comes from a will to know and the certainty that there is one true answer to any question discernible by objective observation and reason. Both also mean taking on responsibility, for making choices when there is not and cannot be certainty, universal truth, or an objective yardstick.

Surprise, as a value, is about the importance attached to the not predicted, the not expected, the truly new and original. The philosopher Martin Buber (1878–1965) regarded surprise as being central to education, writing that 'a real lesson is neither a routine repetition nor a lesson whose findings the teacher knows before he starts, but one which develops in mutual surprises' (Buber, 1947/2002, p. 241). The value of surprise sustains both dialogue and creativity. Surprise is a sign that true dialogue is happening (Stern, 2013), a dialogue in which neither party knows where the relationship is headed, what the outcomes may be, a point made forcefully by Rinaldi when she speaks of dialogue 'not as an exchange but as a process of transformation where you lose absolutely the possibility of controlling the final result' (2006, p. 184). While creativity involves the making of connections that generate material and immaterial production that is new and surprising.

Both uncertainty, subjectivity and surprise are also highly supportive of the final value I want to foreground: *experimentation*. By which I don't mean the conducting of randomised controlled trials or the study of objects in carefully regulated laboratory conditions. What I do mean by experimentation and how this value relates to the value of democracy forms the subject of the next chapter.

Notes

1 Though even this 2°C target appears 'to be much more dangerous than previously thought, both from the perspective of specific "predictable" risks and, even more pertinently, in terms of the chance of crossing a climatic tipping point. [This target] is much more than we should risk but much less than we are heading for' (Berners-Lee and Clark, 2013, pp. 23, 24).

2 Claudia Giudici, a *pedagogista* Reggio Emilia, explains the theory of the hundred languages like this: 'When we speak of languages we refer to the different ways children (human beings) represent, communicate and express their thinking in different media and symbolic systems; languages therefore are the many fonts or geneses of knowledge' (Vecchi, 2010, p. 9).

3 'Material–discursive intra-actions' refer to the work of the feminist theorist Karen Barad who argues that the discursive (notions and beliefs) and the material (objects and artefacts) are mutually implicated in intertwined relations.

> The relationship between the material and the discursive is one of mutual entailment. Neither discursive practices nor material phenomena are ontologically or epistemologically prior. Neither can be explained in terms of the other. Neither is reducible to the other. Neither has privileged status in determining the other. Neither is articulated or articulable in the absence of the other; matter and meaning are mutually articulated.
>
> (Barad, 2007, p. 152)

Chapter 5

Democracy, experimentation and democratic experimentalism

It is perhaps invidious and seemingly arbitrary to extract just two parts of my story, just two out of the many answers generated by political questions, and give them the privileged treatment of their own chapter and indeed of naming after them my story of early childhood education. To the extent I have an answer to the charge, it would be this. Democracy is a requirement for an inclusive, diverse and participatory politics of early childhood education, in which political questions and answers can be freely discussed and contested, deliberated and collectively decided upon; it is in this sense the *sine qua non* of all that follows, the guarantor of a rich and varied story-telling culture. Democracy, too, is a requirement for an early childhood education of potentiality: as Sarah Amsler puts it, democracy 'promises the possibility of open and alternative futures . . . [it] is the only political arrangement that is commensurate with the ontological character of possibility itself' (2012, p. 19). But democracy is also, as will be discussed, a value, practice and way of relating that underpins so much else that I consider desirable in early childhood education; it matters on the stage of large-scale collective decision-making, but also in the smaller-scale but vital matters of how we live our everyday lives.

Experimentation – or, as I shall emphasise, democratic experimentation – is of particular importance because as a value, but also as a practice and way of relating, it enables an opening up of potentiality, whether it be the potentiality of people or of institutions, such as early childhood education. It is driven by a desire to create something new: to find ways whereby the immanent can emerge or lines of flight can be generated from encounters with difference. It may well be that in early childhood education there are some predetermined goals that we seek to achieve, some values, skills and information we decide, democratically, that we want public education to reproduce; but in the story of democracy and experimentation such normative goals are not pursued at the expense of the love of and desire for creativity and innovation, for wonder and surprise that are at the heart of experimentation as a value.

The idea of democracy as a fundamental value in education is not an original thought. If it appears to some as unusual or inapposite in early childhood education, or indeed in any form of education, it is because historical amnesia is one of the afflictions of contemporary education policy. Instead of having a respectful regard for the past, we obsess over how best to fit children for their neoliberal future; we dash forward clutching precariously to the juggernaut of 'creative destruction' with no backward glances cast. What I am actually doing here, therefore, is reconnecting to and drawing on an educational discourse that has an important history and is still alive today, though under threat from hostile forces.

John Dewey, described by Carr and Hartnett as 'the most influential educational philosopher of the 20th century' (1996, p. 54), considered democracy to be a central value, practice and role of school education, famously asserting that '[d]emocracy has to be born anew every generation, and education is its midwife' (Dewey, 1916, p. 139). Dewey was part of a larger movement of educational progressivism, a product of the late nineteenth century that came to hold sway, according to which country we are considering, during the 40 years between 1930 and 1970, though its roots go back much further to writers like Comenius and Rousseau, and its legacy remains a significant presence today. Darling and Norbenbo (2003) suggest five recurring themes that characterise progressive approaches to schooling: criticism of traditional education, the nature of knowledge, human nature, the development of the whole person – and democracy.

Within this progressive tradition, there are many examples of individual proponents who practised democratic education, whether in schools or in work with marginalised or troubled young people. Some instances, drawn only from England and the USA, include A.S. Neill at Summerhill School, Howard Case's Epping Hill School, Tim McMullen and John Watts at Countesthorpe Community College, Lawrence Kohlberg's Just Community School movement in the USA, and Alex Bloom, the pioneer headteacher of St George's-in-the-East School. Working in one of the toughest areas of London's East End, Bloom deliberately set out to create after the end of the Second World War a 'consciously democratic community . . . without regimentation, without corporal punishment, without competition' (Bloom 1948, p. 121; for a fuller discussion of Bloom's work and other examples, see Fielding and Moss, 2011).

Nor is democracy absent from traditions of early childhood education. It was, for example, an important driving force in what has been termed the municipal school revolution that began in Northern Italy in the 1960s when a number of (mainly left-wing) local authorities (*comuni*) decided to take responsibility for the education of their young children, developing schools initially for 3–6-year-olds, then later extending their provision to children under 3 years (Catarsi, 2004). The best known example of such 'local cultural projects' is the early childhood education and municipal schools developed in the city of Reggio Emilia, in which participatory democracy was, from the start, a central value, in part at least as a reaction to many years of fascist dictatorship. But Reggio Emilia is not the only example by any means, as this excerpt illustrates, about the work of Bruno Ciari, director of education in the city of Bologna between 1966 and 1970:

[C]ontesting the traditional school model led to experimentation with new pedagogical approaches inspired by the principles of democracy, civic participation, solidarity and social justice. In many cases these highly innovative experiences were carried out by pioneer educators such as Don Milani, Bruno Ciari and Loris Malaguzzi . . . [*T*]*he collective actions undertaken to promote children's right to education were rooted in a wider political concern for the values of democracy, equality and peace.* As Malaguzzi himself stated, the commitment to the education of young children in those years was motivated by the desire to build a new society together as a reaction to fascism and to the war, through giving a new meaning to human and civil existence (Malaguzzi, 1995). It is for this reason that *democratic participation – of children, parents, teachers, educators, auxiliary staff and citizens – has become such a distinctive feature of education in the municipal schools in Reggio Emilia and, more generally, of ECE [early childhood education] in the municipal schools [in other places] that started life at that time.* The social and political roots of municipal ECE institutions, therefore, played a crucial role in shaping their pedagogical identity.

(Balducci and Lazzari, 2013, pp. 151, 152; emphasis added)

As the above quotation indicates, the tradition of democratic education is also often inscribed with the value of experimentation. Democracy provokes a desire to experiment, often because existing conservative and authoritarian forms of education are seen as unable to respond to the needs and desires of local communities and innovative educators.

Having established the pedigree of my commitment to democracy and experimentation, my intention in the rest of this chapter is twofold. First, to consider in more detail what 'democracy' and 'experimentation' might mean. Second, to examine how these values might be practised in early childhood education: what it might mean to have a democratic and experimental education.

Democracy

Today we still maintain that we like democracy and self-governance, and we also think we like freedom of speech, respect for difference, and understanding of others. We give these values lip service, but we think far too little about what we need to do to transmit them to the next generation and ensure their survival . . . We increasingly ask our schools to turn out useful profit-makers rather than thoughtful citizens . . . Education based on profitability in the global market [produces] a greedy obtuseness and a technically trained docility that threatens the very life of democracy itself.

(Nussbaum, 2010, pp. 141–2)

[Governments and major stakeholders should aspire to early childhood education and care] systems that support broad learning, participation and democracy: It is important that wider societal interests are reflected in early childhood systems, including respect for children's rights, diversity and enhanced access for children with special and additional learning needs. At centre level, touchstones of a democratic approach will be to extend the agency of the child and to support the basic right of parents to be involved in the education of their children. In this approach, the early childhood centre becomes a space where the intrinsic value of each person is recognised, where democratic participation is promoted, as well as respect for our shared environment . . . In addition to learning and the acquisition of knowledge, an abiding purpose of public education is to enhance understanding of society and encourage democratic reflexes in children. Today, societies seem to be less concerned with such ideals. Reflecting the growing marketisation of public services, consumer attitudes toward education and knowledge are increasing. Individual choice is put forward as a supreme value, without reference to social cohesion or the needs of the local community.

(OECD, 2006, pp. 219)

Despite the rich tradition of democracy as a central value and practice in education, it seems today to play little or no part in the dominant stories told about early childhood education (or indeed about any other form of education). At best, it is paid lip service, more often not mentioned at all; more generally in education, as Martha Nussbaum opines above, 'we think far too little about what we need to do to transmit [democracy and related values] to the next generation and ensure their survival'. Democracy rarely figures in policy documents or statements issued by influential international organisations, its appearance in the final report of the OECD *Starting Strong* review of early childhood policies, quoted above, being a welcome exception to the rule. But before going further, it is necessary to look more carefully at the meaning of democracy, and in particular at the different forms it may take.

Democracy is not a simple concept. It is a value expressed in diverse relationships and practices that are multidimensional and multilevelled. An education inscribed with democracy as a value needs ideally to address all dimensions and all levels. Each dimension and each level should be seen as mutually supportive and interdependent. Representative and participatory democracy, formal and informal democracy may on occasion be in conflict, but this need not always be so and they should strive to be complementary. Democratic government – federal, state or municipal – without democratic schools is a very partial idea of democracy and one with shaky foundations; while democratic schools will struggle to flourish and sustain themselves without the context of truly democratic government.

Formal democracy: government and policy-making

Liberal democracy combined with market capitalism has reinforced the tendency of individuals to act in ways that reduce our ability to make

collective choices. This is the underlying reason for the crisis in democracy
. . . Not enough people see democratic politics as part of their own personal identity to sustain the cultures and institutions through which political legitimacy is created. The result is that our preoccupation with making
individual choices is undermining our ability to make collective choices.
Our democracy is suffocating itself.

(Bentley, 2005, pp. 9, 19)

We can start our exploration of the meaning of democracy with what people
often think of when 'democracy' is mentioned, that is the formal institutions
and procedures of representative democratic government at national/federal,
regional/state and more local levels: election of representatives to governing
bodies operating at these different levels (e.g. national parliaments, local councils), the working of these bodies, and the various rules and norms associated
with such democratic forms of government (e.g. electoral procedures, an independent media, the rule of law). Such formal democracy is one of the most
important ways for making many of those 'collective choices' that Tom Bentley refers to above. It has a key role to play in education, being an important
forum for dialogue, deliberation and decision-making about the sort of critical
political questions we discussed in the previous chapters, as well as for the for-
mulation of public policy and the raising and allocation of collective resources.
As such, its health is vital.

Formal democracy, however, is in crisis. It has become a sickly institution
struggling to respond to the contemporary challenges of a complex and threat-
ened world and to retain the engagement and respect of citizens (Morin, 1999;
Bentley, 2005; Power Inquiry, 2006; Skidmore and Bound, 2008). Fewer
people vote, elected representatives are drawn from a narrowing stratum of
society and are increasingly distrusted and held in low esteem, whole sections
of the community feel estranged from mainstream politics, while many others
feel cynical or indifferent, and undemocratic political forces (from lobbyists to
extremist groups) are on the rise. As Morin observes, we are in the midst:

> of a draining and sclerosis of traditional politics, incapable of fathoming the
> new problems that appeal to it; in the midst of a politics that encompasses
> multi-faceted issues, handling them in compartmentalized, disjointed, and
> additive ways; and in the midst of a debased politics that lets itself be swal-
> lowed by experts, managers, technocrats, econocrats, and so on.
>
> (Morin, 1999, p. 112)

The weakening of democratic government is apparent in the degree to which
it has allowed politics to collapse into economics and abrogated responsibility
for decision-making and evaluative judgements to markets and technocrats:
politics has become 'reduced to technology and economics, and economics is
reduced to growth . . . the civic spirit is weakened, and people find escape and

refuge in private life' (Morin, 2001, p. 92). Symptomatic of this process has been the growing importance attached to economic calculation, 'technical research' (i.e. research as a producer of means, strategies and techniques to achieve given ends), and 'evidence-based' policy and practice, all reflecting a belief in the possibility of there being one right expert-derived answer to each and every important question: no conflicting alternatives, therefore no more political questions, only 'what works?' Major political fields, such as education, have been recast as essentially technical, handed over to managers and experts who work within unexamined and un-criticised discourses – those dominant stories I have spoken about so much, transforming what is first and foremost a political and ethical endeavour into a technical, managerial and economic exercise.

The metaphors vary – draining, sclerotic, collapse, thinning, suffocating – but all evince the same idea: a serious weakening of formal democracy. Political scientist Colin Crouch sees this current nadir as part of a cyclical process:

> [S]ocieties probably come closest to democracy in my maximal sense in the early years of achieving it or after great regime crises, when enthusiasm for democracy is widespread; when many diverse groups and organizations of ordinary people share in the task of trying to frame a political agenda which will at last respond to their concerns; when the powerful interests which dominate undemocratic societies are wrong-footed and thrown on the defensive; and when the political system has not quite discovered how to manage and manipulate the new demands
>
> (Crouch, 2004, pp. 6–7)

On this reckoning, the latest democratic moment, he contends, occurred in the mid twentieth century in most of Western Europe and North America and we have moved now into a phase of 'post-democracy' when popular democratic participation has been suborned by powerful minorities, with clear agendas:

> [B]oredom, frustration and disillusion have settled in after a democratic moment; when powerful minority interests have become far more active than the mass of ordinary people in making the political system work for them; where political elites have learned to manage and manipulate popular demands; where people have to be persuaded to vote by top-down publicity campaigns.
>
> (ibid., pp. 19–20)

Detailed consideration of the reasons for this sad state of affairs is beyond the remit of this book. What is clear is that the declining political regime being discussed here is inextricably linked to the ascendant economic regime of neoliberalism. Traditional party politics has lost its capacity to represent and pursue real alternatives, as most parties either sign up to or acquiesce in neoliberalism. Nation states seem helpless in the face of global forces beyond their power to control, reduced to doing their best to survive in an increasingly competitive, globalised market and in thrall to deterritorialised corporations and financial markets – hanging on to the juggernaut at all costs, desperate to be among the survivors of its onslaught, seeking salvation in technical practice and managerialism.

Neoliberalism itself, as I have already discussed, is at best suspicious and at worst dismissive of democracy; except, that is, for a particular understanding of democracy as the untrammelled expression of consumer preferences, an understanding that views democracy as the sum of individual choices expressed through the market. This is not a view of democracy that I hold with. Indeed I would agree with Tom Bentley, whose words start this section, that 'our preoccupation with making individual choices [is] undermining our ability to make collective choices'.

Neoliberalism is not just suspicious or dismissive of democracy; it actively corrodes and erodes. Neoliberalism undermines democracy through its onslaught on the public – whether the public domain, the public good, public spaces, public services – since democracy is about deliberating on public concerns and determining the public good, and doing so in public spaces; in stark contrast 'neoliberal market and political philosophies have sought to undermine and hollow out democracy in all spheres of public life, crowding out the public and replacing it by private non-democratic forms of organisation' (Schostak and Goodson, 2012, p. 270). Neoliberalism also undermines democracy through the growth of inequality and the concomitant concentration of wealth and power in the hands of a new dominant political and economic elite, which in the view of Colin Crouch 'is the central crisis of twenty-first-century democracy' (Crouch, 2004, p. 52).

Before getting too cast down in gloom, we should remember the good news. Mainstream democratic institutions and processes may be ailing, but there is a diverse and lively world of single cause campaign groups and movements, who manage to mobilise widespread commitment. New technologies and new ways of working politically open up possibilities for greater participation and effective resistance to powerful interests, as well as contributing to a healthy loss of deference and uncritical respect for the powerful. Democracy never has been and never will be a matter just of elections and politicians, parliaments and laws, important as such formal manifestations are. For it is also about the small-scale and the everyday, what Nikolas Rose (1999) calls 'minor engagements' in 'cramped spaces', an informal exercise of democracy to which we will return.

But, however important such everyday and participatory democracy and 'minor politics' are – and I will argue that they are very important – they cannot be a substitute for a healthy formal and representative democracy. This form of democracy is essential to the large-scale institutions of modern life, with their massive deployment of collective resources and their pervasive effects on individual and societal flourishing: institutions such as social security, transport, health – and education. These institutions, I would argue, provide many arenas for everyday democracy and they should be subject to such democratic practice: but they also require the exercise of formal democracy, the making of collective choices that are of the greatest public significance. How those choices are made, and hence how democracy is enacted, matters enormously, not least the presumptions that underpin such choices.

One presumption is rational consensus, the idea that there is one correct choice, one right answer to political questions. The task of democracy is to arrive at that choice and answer, through open deliberation or, more worryingly, by contracting the search to experts or leaving it to emerge through the play of market forces. An alternative presumption is that there cannot be one right answer to such questions, no rational consensus, only conflicting answers from which some partial accord must be sought – or, as Bill Readings puts the matter, 'to abandon consensus says nothing about limited or provisional forms of agreement and action' (1996, p. 187). This alternative presumption is what John Gray terms a democracy of *modus vivendi*:

> The ethical theory underpinning *modus vivendi* is value-pluralism. The most fundamental value-pluralist claim is that there are many conflicting kinds of human flourishing, some of which cannot be compared in value . . . To affirm that the good is plural is to allow that it harbours conflicts for which there is no one solution that is right. It is not that there can be no right solution to such conflicts. Rather there are many.
>
> (Gray, 2009, pp. 25–6)

To return to our metaphor of stories: a democracy of *modus vivendi* recognises, welcomes and encourages the telling of and listening to a variety of stories, recognising all the while that they may well conflict in important ways. Where they do and where a common position needs to be taken – for example, to decide a national policy for early childhood education on access, funding, curriculum and workforce – then choices may need to be made between stories. But that should be a collective choice involving a hearing for all stories, negotiation and compromise in search of 'limited or provisional forms of agreement and action', as well as in some instances a majority decision to favour one story line over others.

This is an agonistic idea of democratic politics, one 'that valorises dissensus, infinite openness to difference, the decentring and "tearing away" of epistemological and moral certainties', as well as offering 'the ongoing possibility of transformation in everyday life' (Amsler, 2012, p. 30), the prospect that something new, previously unknown, can emerge from an encounter with difference. In this understanding of democracy there are always differences of perspective, interest and power, which are made visible and, therefore, contestable in a continuous process, which:

should not be cause for despair because the desire to reach a final destination can only lead to the elimination of the political and the destruction of democracy. In a democratic polity, conflicts and confrontations, far from being a sign of imperfection, indicate that democracy is alive and inhabited by pluralism.

(Mouffe, 2000, p. 34)

Morin sees democracy in a similar light, where consensus is limited to respect for democratic institutions and procedures, and dissensus and conflict are positively valued:

Democracy implies and enhances diversity among interests and social groups as well as diversity between ideas, which means it should not impose majority dictatorship, but rather acknowledge the right to existence and expression of dissenting minorities and allow the expression of heretical and deviant ideas.

(Morin, 1999, p. 90)

In short, democracy so understood lives on plurality and needs the conflict of ideas and opinions as a source of vitality and productivity – but bound by respect for democratic rules that regulate antagonism (Morin, 2001). It relishes many stories and is wary of any one story presuming to dominate, claiming to have the right answer. Any such claim, which can so easily slide into the dictatorship of no alternative, should be treated with the deepest suspicion and be strongly contested.

This implies a formal democracy of governance, at whatever level, that attaches as much importance to process as to outcome (assuming the two can ever be separated, which is debatable), that welcomes and makes visible differences of view and meaning, that acknowledges the contestability and provisionality of all decisions, and that does not expect to shift responsibility for such decisions to supposedly objective and neutral experts and evidence or to the impersonal workings of the market place. Instead of reducing educational debate and decision-making through an exclusive attention to one perspective, which purports to tell the truth, an agonistic democracy of *modus vivendi* makes visible (or transparent) conflicting perspectives, for example from different paradigmatic and theoretical positions. The role of social research in such circumstances becomes to 'produce input to dialogue and praxis in social affairs, rather than to generate ultimate, unequivocally verified "knowledge"' (Flyvbjerg, 2006, p. 41), a theme we return to in Chapter 7.

Democracy as a fundamental value of early childhood education, or any other form of education, calls for a renewed and revived formal democracy, where important collective choices are made – for instance about broad policy frameworks and the allocation of resources – in a context of alternatives, well-articulated and strongly contested; a context of conflicting answers to political questions; a context where different stories, whilst critically discussed, are respectfully heard. Though not an absolute precondition for the everyday democracy I now turn to consider, which can emerge in even the most unfavourable of circumstances, a renewed and revived formal democracy of education has an important role to play in the spread, vigour and sustainability of its informal variant.

Informal democracy: democracy as a way of being in everyday life

Building everyday democracy therefore depends on applying its principles to everyday institutions through which people make their choices and develop their identities. Its basis is the idea that power and responsibility must be aligned with each other – and widely distributed – if societies are to exercise shared responsibility through social, economic and institutional diversity.

(Bentley, 2005, p. 21)

Democracy and day nursery are two terms that are not immediately associated with each other. But where and when does democracy start? In preschool? In day care? In school? Or only when people are old enough to vote? Knowledge and insights gained from the evaluation of the project 'Living democracy in day care centres' show that the basis for an everyday democratic culture can indeed already be formed in the day nursery.

(Priebe, cited in George, 2009, p. 14)

Participation in infant-toddler centres and preschools is not a function carried out by the few representatives of official bodies that have been set up, it is one of the qualities of being in a school . . . – of children, teachers (better, of all those who work in schools) and of parents: it is a system of constant communication that builds a relationship between individuals and a service not of delegating but of conversation and active protagonism, a sense of belonging, a sense of group. This protagonism everyone has, where each person is also credited and respected – their knowledge, their capacity for giving and receiving contributions in a reciprocal relationship – is one of the bases of democracy and is not a given but as we well know, a constantly evolving process and building. Once again the question is whether schools limit themselves to transmitting culture or if they are capable of being, as we aspire to being, places where culture is constructed and democracy is lived out.

(Cagliari, cited in Reggio Children, 2012, p. 195)

Formal democracy matters. But democracy also has other important dimensions, expressed in other practices, and these are as relevant, if not more so, when we claim democracy to be a fundamental value of education. In particular, democracy can be understood as a lived experience, a practice of everyday life, a mode of being in the world and 'one of the qualities of being in a school'. In the words of Dewey, democracy is 'primarily a mode of associated living embedded in the culture and social relationships of everyday life'; it is 'a personal way of individual life . . . [I]t signifies the possession and continual use of certain attitudes, forming personal character and determining desire and purpose in all the relations of life' (1939, p. 2). This is democracy understood as an approach to living and relating, an ethos and a culture, that can and should pervade all aspects of everyday living, not least in the school, where it is 'a way of being, of thinking of oneself in relation to others and the world . . . a fundamental educational value and form of educational activity' (Rinaldi, 2006, p. 156). Danish researcher Ole Langsted, writing of an early example of listening to young children about their experiences of early childhood education, also makes the point clearly, when he argues that what should precede structures and procedures for listening is the desire to listen: 'more important [than these structures and procedures] is the cultural climate which shapes the ideas that the adults in a particular society hold about children. The wish to listen to and involve children originates in this cultural climate' (Langsted, 1994, pp. 41–2).

Tom Bentley captures this idea of democracy as a way of being and acting in his term 'everyday democracy', the enactment of democratic values in the places and in the relationships where children and adults spend most of their time – 'everyday institutions'. As such, everyday democracy is seen as an antidote to the atomisation of society and the erosion of concern for the common good apparent in hyper-individualistic neoliberal societies. Bentley has argued for such everyday democracy as an urgent response to the crisis in traditional democratic politics, in which 'our preoccupation with making *individual* choices is undermining our ability to make *collective* choices' (2005, p. 19; emphasis added).

In similar vein, Paul Skidmore and Kirsten Bound emphasise how everyday democracy provides one response to the artificial separation of the collective and the individual: 'any workable approach to democracy today needs to reckon with, and be able to reconcile, our need for both a personal and a collective sense of agency' (Skidmore and Bound, 2008, p. 24). Modern democracies, they argue, must be such everyday democracies, 'rooted in a culture in which democratic values and practices shape not just the formal sphere of politics but the informal sphere of everyday life' (ibid., p. 7). This culture calls for dialogue and listening, respect for diversity and other perspectives, a readiness to contest and to negotiate, and recognition of one's own partial knowledge and particular perspective.

Such everyday democracy has its place in formal democratic institutions themselves, shaping the way politicians, administrators and others conduct themselves and their business; these formal institutions should themselves practice informal democracy in their everyday life. But it is particularly important at more local levels in more intimate settings. When Skidmore and Bound talk about everyday democracy in 'the informal spheres of everyday life', they include families, communities, workplaces – and schools. I would extend this to include all early childhood centres too; so when I speak about democracy as a fundamental value of early childhood education, I am thinking not just about formal, collective decision-making about policies and resources by elected representatives, but also about the everyday democracy that is possible in nurseries, kindergartens, preschools, nursery schools and other centres. Both types of democracy – the formal and the everyday – are about democracy, but everyday democracy is about the conduct of democracy in everyday life in everyday settings and through which democracy as a fundamental value becomes part of the lives of young children in early childhood education: democracy as lived experience.

It is important, therefore, to emphasise that democracy and democratic citizenship are not just an aspiration for a later stage of life, they are not something we prepare children to practice and become as they grow older. They are something young children can and should live here and now. It is through everyday democracy lived and practised in the early childhood centre that democracy as a fundamental value is made real. As the author of the *Demokratie Leben* project, quoted at the beginning of this section, contends, 'the basis for a democratic everyday culture can indeed already be formed in the day nursery' (Priebe, quoted in George, 2009, p. 14).

Everyday democracy in these everyday institutions is partly, as I have argued, a case of how we live with and relate to each other, children and adults alike. This is very clear in the quotation from Paula Cagliari at the start of this section, with its emphasis on 'active protagonism' – and also in the following quotation from an article by three *pedagogistas* [1] in Reggio Emilia, including Paula, writing about the meaning of a participatory educational project:

> The educational project of the nurseries and nursery schools of Reggio Emilia is by definition a participation-based project; its true educational meaning is to be found in the participation of all concerned. This means everyone – children, teachers and parents – is involved in sharing ideas, in discussion, in a sense of common purpose and with communication as a value . . . there is recognition that everyone – children, teachers and parents – is an active subject in the educational relationship, each contributing complementary and necessary knowledge
>
> [. . .]
>
> The subjects of participation then, even before the parents, are the children who are considered to be active constructors of their own learning and producers of original points of view . . . Participation, in fact, is based on the idea that reality is not objective, that culture is a constantly evolving product of society, that individual knowledge is partial; and that in order to construct a project, especially an educational project, everyone's point

of view is relevant in dialogue with others, within a framework of shared values. The idea of participation is founded on these concepts: and in our opinion, so, too, is democracy itself . . . Therefore, if we want a school based on participation, we must create spaces, contexts, and times when all subjects – children, teachers and parents – can find opportunities to speak and be listened to.

(Cagliari et al., 2004, pp. 28–9)

In both of the quotations from Reggio Emilia, certain key themes emerge that help to identify an everyday democracy in early childhood education: recognising the centre as a place for democracy, 'a social and political place'; a rich and active image of all participants, protagonists in the democratic process; the importance of communication, dialogue and listening; equal respect for the contribution of all participants, children and adults, teachers and parents; and recognition, too, that everyone's knowledge is not only valuable but also partial. Running through this is a recognition and valuing of plurality and, therefore, of (potentially conflicting) alternatives, and of the need for *modus vivendi*.

Everyday democracy in early childhood education is about the ways in which people relate to each other in everyday life. But it is also about the way certain activities are conducted, activities that involve decisions, power and responsibility, and conduct that involves:

> the practice of self-government through the choices, commitments and connections of daily life. Everyday democracy means extending democratic power and responsibility simultaneously to the settings of everyday life . . . *It means that people can actively create the world in which they live.*
> (Bentley, 2005, pp. 20–1; emphasis added)

Let me take some examples of this process of the active creation of the world through everyday democracy, and I want to emphasise these are examples and not a comprehensive listing. Everyday democracy can involve the *formal governance* of early childhood centres, for example decisions about goals and practices, personnel and resources, environments and relationships with the wider community. This may involve formal structures and procedures, such as elected governing bodies or other forums, deliberating on a regular basis and with set terms of reference; these will involve the participation of a wide range of adults – parents, staff, other local citizens – though less likely children in the case of early childhood centres (their participation increasing with age in primary and secondary schools). The system of *gestione sociale* (social management) developed in Reggio Emilia from the early years of its pedagogical project provides one example of such governance:

> management councils (*consiglio di gestione*) are made up of parents, teachers and citizens elected by other parents, teachers and citizens at public elec-

tions held every three years. The responsibility of councils is to promote participation by other families, assist teachers in decision making and realising projects, and develop relationships with the local area and with other *nidi* and *scuole dell'infanzia* in the city.

(Rinaldi, 2006, p. 44)

But everyday democracy can also involve more *ad hoc* and varied means to enable participation of children and adults alike in *decision-making*, ranging from small issues in daily life to larger matters such as designing the environment, discussed further below, and deciding about project work (see, for example, Vecchi, 2010). An example of involving very young children in decisions about their daily lives comes from the *Demokratie Leben* (Living Democracy in the Day Nursery) project, conducted in day nurseries in a town in eastern Germany, working with very young children, under 3 years of age. At the heart of this project was respecting the autonomy of 1- and 2-year-old children in everyday relationships and activities, for example feeding, changing nappies and planning activities for the day. This may involve developing negotiating skills:

> The teacher negotiates with the children what they should do in the afternoon. This shows that negotiating means more than just voting. When the vote decides, the majority is always content but in a worst case scenario almost half the group is unhappy or – like in this example – only two children. But two discontented children are already two too many. The goals of negotiation processes are that nobody is left behind or sidelined . . . Negotiation until a consensus is reached is, naturally, a perfected art. But it is always worth trying.

(Priebe, quoted in George, 2009, p. 14)

A second example is the Mosaic approach developed by Alison Clark to give voice to the perspectives of young children. This approach uses a variety of methods for working with children to generate documentation: these methods include observation, child interviewing, photography (by children themselves), centre tours, and map making. The documentation so generated is then subject to review, reflection and discussion by children and adults – a process of interpretation or meaning-making. Inspired by pedagogical documentation, discussed further below, the Mosaic approach has been used for a range of purposes, including to understand better how children experience life in the nursery (the main question being 'what does it mean to be in this place?') and to enable the participation by young children in the design of new buildings and outdoor spaces (Clark and Moss, 2005; Clark, 2005; Clark, 2010).

There is, of course, an important relationship to be explored and defined between formal democratic government and democratic decision-making in schools and early childhood centres. Strong everyday democracy calls for strong decentralisation with a presumption of local decision-making – the principle of subsidiarity, where higher levels of government only perform those tasks which cannot be performed effectively at a more immediate or local level. But (and this is a theme to which I keep returning) it does not mean doing without common and democratically determined norms. Each level of government, from nation to local, has responsibilities for democratically determining a certain normative framework that applies to the next level. National (or, occasionally, state/regional) government, for example, will determine certain common national (or regional) entitlements, structures, goals and values that may include a stated commitment to democracy as a fundamental national value.

There are a number of examples of such an explicit national commitment to democracy as a fundamental value in early childhood education, for example among the Nordic states: 'official policy documents and curriculum guidelines in the Nordic countries acknowledge a central expectation that preschools and schools will exemplify democratic principles and that children will be active participants in these democratic environments' (Wagner, 2006, p. 292). The Swedish preschool curriculum, as one example, states that '[d]emocracy forms the foundation of the preschool . . . all preschool activity should be carried out in accordance with fundamental democratic values' (Skolverket, 2010, p. 3).

Such explicit commitments are important. There needs to be what has been termed a 'proclaimed democratic vitality', an unequivocal statement that democracy is 'both the end and the means, the purpose and the practice, of education' (Fielding and Moss, 2011, p. 73), a case of nailing one's colours proudly to the mast, whilst recognising that such a commitment is a precursor to, but no guarantor of, democracy in practice. But in a democratic milieu, the framework decided democratically by one level leaves ample opportunity for democratic interpretation and decision-making by the next level, right down to the level of the individual centre and the participation there of children, educators, families and other community members. For example, a national curriculum for education should include substantial scope for local input and design, an issue to which I return in Chapter 7.

Evaluation can become another important part of a vibrant everyday democracy when participatory forms are used, which keep open the issue of outcome rather than confining evaluation to the standardised and predefined (Rinaldi, 2006): a democratic evaluation that welcomes multiple perspectives, as well as wonder and surprise. One such is pedagogical documentation, which makes learning, and other processes, visible through being documented in various ways (e.g. note-taking, video and audio recordings, the display of children's work), but then goes further by enabling the documentation to be shared and opened up to multiple perspectives, dialogue and interpretations, from both adults and children. While evaluation cannot be avoided, pedagogical documentation, with its emphasis on interpretation, prevents 'the educator from arriving at finished and closed conclusions' (Hoyuelos, 2013, p. 148) and avoids a false sense of certainty and closure.

For Loris Malaguzzi, one of the pioneers of pedagogical documentation, pedagogical documentation 'meant the possibility to discuss and to dialogue "everything with everyone"', but based on 'being able to discuss real, concrete things – not just theories or words, about which it is possible to reach easy and naïve agreement' (Hoyuelos, 2004, p. 7). It was about, too, the 'ideological and ethical concept of a transparent school and transparent education', and as such provided a powerful means for developing democratic accountability – not to be confused with the very different concept of managerial accounting (a distinction I return to in Chapter 7). It was, in other words, an effective strategy for building a public space, for creating a shared identity and history, and for opening up participatory relations.

But this profoundly democratic process, which makes public education visible to the public, can be used for much more than evaluation, indeed other purposes have a higher profile in Reggio Emilia, where pedagogical documentation was first developed. Vea Vecchi, a pioneer of this way of working, identifies three primary purposes for pedagogical documentation:

1) It is an important tool for teacher self-training, enabling reflection, comparison of ideas, interpretation, and discussion within a relatively unexplored area for pedagogy: How children learn.

2) It enables us to enter into fuller harmony with children's thinking strategies so as to support them more effectively and respectfully, i.e. without pushing our own ideas on them and thus ensuring greater levels of freedom and creativity for both individual and group thinking.

3) It enables the children to see and understand who they are and what they do, by making it possible for them to re-visit the path they have taken, their choices, pauses, and their dash towards their destination and realization of their project.

(Vecchi, 1996, p. 156)

It is, in other words, a tool not only for evaluation but for the education of teachers, for the reflection of children themselves, and for researching and supporting children's learning processes; a tool that works in ways that promote informal democracy in general and a democratic approach to learning in particular.

We can speak, therefore, about democratic *learning*, based on a pedagogy that values listening, dialogue and diversity and an understanding of learning as the co-construction of meaning whose outcome is unpredictable and therefore held open. Rinaldi epitomises democratic learning when she describes project work as evoking:

a journey that involves uncertainty and chance that always arises in relationships with others. Project work grows in many directions, with no
predefined progression, no outcomes decided before the journey begins. It
means being sensitive to the unpredictable results of children's investigation and research.

(Rinaldi, 2005, p. 19)

This is learning that is the antithesis of a learning of transmission, with its reproduction and its predefined outcomes and its 'pushing [of] our own ideas on
[children]', in favour of a learning that supports theory-building and the emergence of new thought, values uncertainty and surprise, and welcomes multiple
perspectives and unpredicted outcomes, whilst at the same time being ready
to confront and question in the process of testing and re-constructing. This
is learning enacted through a pedagogy of relationships and listening. This is
learning, too, that measures up to the democratic aspirations of the pioneers of
Reggio Emilia's early childhood education, such as Renzo Bonazzi, the Mayor
of Reggio Emilia from 1962 to 1976, who said in an interview that the city's
pedagogical project was prompted by their experience of fascism, which had
taught them 'that people who conformed and obeyed were dangerous, and that
in building a new society it was imperative . . . to nurture and maintain a vision
of children who can think and act for themselves' (Dahlberg, 2000, p. 177).

Everyday democracy can also entail creating opportunities for *contesting dominant discourses*, confronting what Foucault terms regimes of truth, which seek to
shape how we think and act, how we construct our own subjectivity and our
image of the child, what we can and cannot say through their universal truth
claims and their relationship with power. This democratic political activity
seeks to make core assumptions and values visible and contestable. Yeatman
(1994) refers to it as 'postmodern politics' and offers some examples: a *politics of
epistemology*, contesting modernity's idea of knowledge (see Chapter 2); a *politics
of representation*, about whose perspectives have legitimacy; and a *politics of difference*, which contests those groups claiming a privileged position of objectivity
on a contested subject. But the areas opened up to politics, that are repoliti-
cised as legitimate subjects for inclusive political dialogue and contestation, can
readily be extended: the *politics of childhood*, about the image of the child, the
good life and what we want for our children; the *politics of education*, about what
education can and should be; and the *politics of gender*, in the nursery, the home
and elsewhere. Pedagogical documentation can provide one means of contesting dominant discourses, through making this one of the tasks of interpreting
practice made visible.

Gunilla Dahlberg offers an example of contesting dominant discourses
through the use of pedagogical documentation. This is the Stockholm Project, which she undertook in the 1990s in Sweden, inspired by Reggio Emilia,
funded by the Swedish government and enabled by the cooperation of a
Swedish *kommun* or local authority. From that *kommun*, seven preschools were

chosen on the basis that all the staff in them wanted to participate and experiment with pedagogical documentation. That project, described in greater detail in chapters 6 and 7 of Dahlberg *et al.* (2013), started from the premise that:

> early childhood institutions and their pedagogical practices are constituted by dominant discourses in our society and embody thoughts, conceptions and ethics which prevail at a given moment in a given society. Therefore, to change a pedagogical practice, it is necessary to start by problematizing and deconstructing these discourses and to understand and demonstrate how they are related to what is going on in pedagogical practice.
>
> (Dahlberg *et al.*, 2013, pp. 138–9)

Struggling with pedagogical documentation – 'a very difficult tool to use; it needed training and new skills' – Dahlberg and the preschool teachers she worked with were able to develop a critique of dominant discourses in the preschool and their effects on pedagogical work:

> We have used documentation as a tool to understand how the child has been constructed in our early childhood institutions. It has helped us to answer the question: Do we see the child? What do we mean by saying 'to see the child'? This can be seen as a form of deconstructive work in relation to pedagogical practice – what constructions of the child are behind the way we talk about the child and what kind of constructions are behind our way of relating to the child in our practice? How have these constructions shaped how the environment has been ordered? How has the whole pedagogical space been constructed? Are there other constructions to be made? Is this a pedagogical space for the 'rich' child, pedagogue and parent?
>
> (ibid., p. 143)

From this critical work, a new construction of the child emerged, the 'rich child' discussed in the previous chapter, and a new practice that found unexpected potentialities in the child:

> It was a child that, for example, could concentrate on an activity much longer than the pedagogues' earlier constructions had said he or she should be able to, and who was not as egocentric. The children in our project more and more start saying 'look what I can do and know', and the pedagogues are becoming more and more aware of the children's potentialities – what they actually can do and do do rather than what classificatory systems say they should do. The excitement that this has generated among the pedagogues is captured in this comment by one of them: 'I have been working with preschool children for 20 years now and I never thought children know and can do that much. I now have got another child in front of me.
>
> (ibid., p. 144)

Such everyday democratic activity, through the use of pedagogical documentation to contest dominant discourses, provides an example of the possibility of confronting and resisting regimes of truth. Notice how, in this Swedish project, the pedagogues (preschool teachers) through using pedagogical documentation begin to see the children in a new light, becoming aware of their potentialities − 'what they actually can do and do do' − rather than what the dominant discourse, with its developmental norms, says they should be doing, becoming open to unpredicted outcomes not just focused on predicted outcomes. And it is through such exercises of resistance that a fifth democratic activity can emerge: *opening up for change*. For there is a close connection between contesting dominant discourses, thinking differently and pursuing change: to recall Foucault's words from Chapter 1, '[a]s soon as one can no longer think things as one formerly thought them, transformation becomes both very urgent, very difficult and quite possible'.

All forms of democracy at all levels are important and welcome; it is certainly not a case of 'either/or' but of 'and . . . and . . . and'. Traditional or formal democratic politics and institutions must be supported and revived; there is no substitute for elected parliaments and elected local assemblies − communes, municipalities, local councils − where a wide range of different interests and ideas, beliefs and perspectives can be represented, where such differences can be argued about and negotiated, where political agreements can be hammered out, and where governments can be held to account and the wings of power can be clipped. But other dimensions of democracy need to be stimulated, too, for example through developing new places and new subjects for the practice of everyday democratic living and politics − including, early childhood centres and schools and issues that are central to the everyday lives of the children and adults who participate in these institutions.

For ultimately, the different levels and forms of democracy are interrelated and interdependent. A healthy democracy needs to be healthy in all its parts, including a democratic education where children, young people and adults live democracy and can develop their democratic capacities. Which brings us back to Dewey and the importance he attached to democracy as a fundamental value of education:

> Since, in a democracy, decision-making is no longer the preserve of an aristocratic elite, schools must become embryonic societies providing all pupils with opportunities to develop the social attitudes, skills and dispositions that allow them to formulate and achieve their collective ends by confronting shared problems and common concerns. For Dewey, it is primarily by promoting the growth of social intelligence through co-operative problem-solving activities that schools can support and promote the evolution of a more democratic social order.
>
> (Carr and Hartnett, 1996, p. 63)

Democracy may be multilevel and multidimensional. But the different levels and the different dimensions add up to a 'democratic social order', a social order in which early childhood education should and can play a significant part.

Experimentation

> Learning, therefore, is a pedagogy of relationships and listening; a space open to research and continuous reflection, critique and argumentation. It is a matter of experimentation and exploration – lines of flight. Instead of universalising and totalising discourses, which often lead to exclusion, violence and injustice, experimentation and exploration lead to new becomings, to and, and, and, instead of is.
>
> (Dahlberg, cited in Reggio Children, 2012, p. 31)

> When we really think it is like being struck to the ground only to find that you are falling through it, since it does not exist anymore. It concerns a kind of vertiginous feeling of losing one's references. But at the same time it is a very joyful and affirmative affair, since it can give us access to universes we did not know anything about . . . This thought differs from the thought of recognition and representation, in that it is created, and always and continuously created, through relations and encounters. Thought, in this way, has also got the features of being experimentation, but an idea of experimentation that is something totally different from the idea of experimentation as the lifeless controlling of all parameters as well as working with an expected outcome (Deleuze, 1994). Experimentation here concerns that which is not yet known, it concerns that which comes about, that which is new and that demands more than recognizing or representing truth. Thought as experimentation concerns the new, the interesting and the remarkable:
>
> > To think is to experiment, but experimentation is always that which is in the process of coming about – the new, remarkable, and interesting that replace the appearance of truth and are more demanding than it is (Deleuze and Guattari, 1994: 111).
>
> (Olsson, 2009, pp. 26–7)

In this chapter I elaborate two values that I consider of particular importance to the story I want to tell of early childhood education. Having discussed the first, democracy, I now turn to the second, experimentation. Like democracy, experimentation is both value and practice and the two are interdependent; the value without the practice counts for little. Experimentation as a value is, as Olsson makes clear in the quotation starting this section, not about 'the lifeless controlling of all parameters as well as working with an expected outcome'; it is not about building and testing new technologies to be applied to children or adults nor about comparing intervention A against intervention B. Rather, it is about bringing something new to life, 'that which is not yet known', something that is interesting and remarkable, whether that something is a thought, knowledge, a project, a service or a tangible product. Or, in Dahlberg's words, it is about 'new becomings, to and, and, and, instead of is'. Experimentation expresses a willingness, a desire in fact, to invent, to think differently, to imagine and try out different ways of doing things. It is driven by a longing to go beyond what already exists, to venture into the not yet known, to be surprised, and not to be bound by the given, the familiar, the predetermined, the norm. Experimentation is open-ended (avoiding closure), open-minded (welcoming the unexpected) and open-hearted (valuing difference).

Without experimentation, we are locked into an endless round of reproducing, in which the same prescribed means pursue the same known ends, in a repetitive, predictable and sterile process; the story of quality and high returns in its reproductive zeal is the very antithesis of experimentation. Experimentation treats the idea of predetermined outcomes with suspicion, for its capacity to suppress or dismiss what is innovative and original. For such outcomes express our will to truth, which can be thought of 'as a will to certain outcomes, [it] sets communication along present railway tracks as pointed out by Wittgenstein, preventing alternative ways of relating to the world that are open-ended and experimental' (Roy, 2004, p. 302). Experimentation has outcomes, but welcomes those that are unexpected and surprising, that produce new understandings and meanings; it relishes emotions of wonder, amazement and excitement. Such outcomes are viewed as points on a continuous process of becoming, provisional and arbitrary and in between, not as end points marking the closure of finite and prescribed interventions.

The practice of experimentation is inscribed not only with the value of experimentation, but also with particular perspectives on epistemology and learning. We have seen these perspectives expressed by Osberg and Biesta, in the previous chapter, when they write of an 'emergentist' complexity-inspired epistemology and a pedagogy of invention, with their foregrounding of emergence and the creation of new properties. There are, too, other examples of pedagogical practice inscribed with the value of experimentation, examples which also emphasise the invention or creation of new knowledge. Dewey's approach to pedagogy has been described by a recent biographer as 'essentially experimental', expressed in his establishment of a school for testing out ideas, the 'Laboratory School' (Pring, 2007, p. 16). Biesta and Osberg also point to the example of Dewey, whose pedagogical approach is 'strongly rooted in the idea that knowledge is not a reflection of the static world but emerges as we engage with or "experience" reality' and whose goal was to make schools 'into places where children could learn directly by experiment and discovery' (Biesta and Osberg, 2007, pp. 25–6).

In another article, Biesta explores further the pedagogical ideas of Dewey and in particular his view of the centrality of experimentation:

We basically acquire our habits through processes of trial and error – or, in more theoretical language, through experimentation. In a very fundamental sense, experimentation is the only way in which we can learn anything at all: we learn because we do and subsequently undergo the consequences of doing. Yet for Dewey, there is a crucial difference between blind trial and error – experimentation without deliberation and direction – and what he calls intelligent action. The difference between the two has to do with the intervention of thinking or reflection.

(Biesta, 2007, p. 14)

Dewey contrasted this 'transactional theory of knowing' with what he called the 'spectator theory of knowledge': 'an immaterial mind looking at the material world and registering what goes on in it' (ibid., p. 13) – akin to a representational epistemology. Dewey argued, Biesta adds, that we should be experimental not only with respect to means but also with respect to ends and the interpretation of the problems we address. Viewed in this way, experimentation also includes creating new understandings and imagining innovative practices, similar perhaps to what Halpin describes as 'utopian thought experiments', which start from the question '(h)ow would social reality look if we configured it in radically different and improved terms and from different positions than is normally adopted' (Halpin, 2003, pp. 53–4). This, too, is similar to Erik Olin Wright's concept of 'real utopias', already introduced in Chapter 1.

More recently, experimentation can be seen as an important influence on the early childhood education of Reggio Emilia. Indeed, it is striking how often the words 'experiment' or 'experimentation' appear in the writings of the city's educators (e.g. Rinaldi, 2006; Vecchi, 2010). The value and practice of experimentation is central in what they term a 'pedagogy of listening', which (as we saw in the preceding chapter) requires active encouragement to children to experiment with theories and meaning-making as part of a 'community of inquirers'. To construct such a community of inquirers, with an experimental spirit, write Gunilla Dahlberg and Mimi Bloch:

requires listening and a radical dialogue. In 'real' listening children become partners in a process of experimentation and research by inventing problems and by listening to and negotiating what other children, as well as the teacher, are saying and doing. In this process the co-constructing pedagogue has to open her/him self to the unexpected and experiment together with the children – in the here and now event. S/he challenges the children by augmenting connections through enlarging the number of concepts, hypotheses and theories, as well as through new material and through challenging children's more technical work. Besides getting a responsible relation to other children by listening, they also are negotiating in between each other, enlarging the choices that can be made, instead of bringing choice down to universal trivializations.

(Dahlberg and Bloch, 2006, p. 114)

As the excerpt emphasises, there is a strong connection in this pedagogical approach between dialogue and listening, challenging and negotiation, openness and innovation – in short, between democracy and experimentation.

This way of working, inscribed with experimentation as a value, is underpinned by a strong desire to be open to new meanings and knowledges, and a corresponding reluctance to be tied by working to predetermined outcomes: 'the potential of the child is stunted when the endpoint of their learning is formulated in advance' (Rinaldi, 1993, p. 104). 'Project work' ('*progettazione*'), which plays a central role in Reggio's schools, has a strongly experimental character. It is a 'dynamic process', a 'journey that involves uncertainty and chance', with 'no predefined progression', and 'sensitive to the unpredictable results of children's investigation and research'. Consequently, a project can be 'short, medium or long, continuous or discontinuous, and is always open to modifications and changes of direction' (Rinaldi, 2005, p. 19).

Also important in this pedagogy is the theory of the hundred languages of children – by which they mean in Reggio Emilia the many communicative possibilities with which our species is genetically equipped – with particular attention given to 'poetic' or 'aesthetic languages', 'forms of expression strongly characterized by expressive or aesthetic aspects such as music, song, dance or photography' (Vecchi, 2010, p. 9). The importance of these languages is their capacity to enable children and adults to see things in new ways, to escape predefined categories and pre-existing formulas, and to develop new connections from which new knowledge can emerge – in short, multilingualism of this kind opens up for experimentation and original thinking. Vecchi emphasises the need for education and schools to create space for such thinking and asks:

> How much do we support children to have ideas different from those of other people and how do we accustom them to arguing and discussing their ideas with their classmates? I am quite convinced that greater attention to processes, rather than only the final product, would help us to feel greater respect for the independent thinking and strategies of children and teenagers.
>
> (Vecchi, 2010, p. 138)

Another example of experimentation as a value in practice in early childhood education comes from a book in this series by Liselott Marriet Olsson, *Movement and Experimentation in Young Children's Learning*. Starting from the premise that young children and learning are today often tamed, predicted, supervised, controlled and evaluated according to predetermined standards, so that '[m]ovement and experimentation in subjectivity and learning are subordinated to the outcome and to position' (Olsson, 2009, p. 9), the book argues that the challenge to practice and research is to find ways of regaining movement and experimentation in learning. Inspired by the work of Deleuze and Guattari, Olsson demonstrates the possibilities for experimentation in the classroom, leading to the emergence of new knowledge, through documenting and analysis of extensive experience in Swedish preschools:

> In many of the preschools in the city of Stockholm and its suburbs and at the Stockholm Institute of Education, 'every day magical moments' take place. Children, preschool teachers, teacher students, teacher educators and researchers come together and are literally caught up in the desire to experiment with subjectivity and learning. In these practices experimentations and intense, unpredictable events are taking place, concerning the idea of what a child is, what a teacher should do, the purpose of a preschool and its organisation, contents and forms.
>
> (Olsson, 2009, p. 11)

These 'every day magical moments' are, as Olsson says in the quotation starting this section, 'joyful and affirmative', and the new thought, the lines of flight, that define these moments are created through 'relations and encounters'. They require us to leave go of the security and constraints of known outcomes, and risk instead 'losing one's references', accessing 'universes we did not know anything about'. Or as Rinaldi puts it, losing 'absolutely the possibility of controlling the final result' (2006, p. 184).

The examples we have offered of experimentation in practice relate mainly to learning in the school: experimentation as a central process in teaching and learning. But experimentation can take many other forms. It may involve exploring the potential of working with particular paradigms or theorists. Olsson's work is just one example of an increasing body of experimentation in early childhood education that puts to work the ideas of post-structural theorists such as Deleuze, Guattari, Bakhtin, Derrida and Foucault (see, for example, MacNaughton, 2005; Edmiston, 2007; Olsson, 2009; Lenz Taguchi, 2010b; Taylor, 2013; Sellers, 2013). Such theorists have, Jo Tobin contends, provided 'a language we can use to confront the taken-for-granted assumptions of the field' (Tobin, 2007, p. 28).

Or it may involve generating new activities, stimulated by inclusion of and engagement with citizens in the local community, parents or others. Working in this way, early childhood centres can become collective laboratories for community experimentation, from which new projects emerge out of a centre's sense of solidarity with and responsibility towards its local community and a desire to try something new: 'let's see what we can do, what's possible' sums up the experimental stance. Experimentation here may involve further forms of learning, for example with adults, but also with many other purposes in mind: supporting families, building solidarities, confronting injustices, sustaining culture, generating the local economy, strengthening democracy, etc. To take instances of such experimentation from just one case, a Centre operating in a materially deprived and highly diverse area of an English city, these include: assistance with translation and interpretation; adult education; dance and other workshops; access to legal, health, housing and other services; counselling, advocacy and advice; home care and other domiciliary support workers; respite care for seriously ill parents; support for various other groups, including terminally ill children and their parents, adult survivors of child sexual abuse, domestic violence and female genital mutilation; and a range of intergenerational activities (Broadhead *et al.*, 2008).

Like democracy, therefore, experimentation can have its more formal side, involving instituting new projects in a service or community. But it also represents a way of living and relating, expressed for example in everyday pedagogical work and a resistance to reproducing the already known and pursuing the predetermined. It can be a new take on an old subject, bringing to bear new perspectives and methods; or a response to a new subject, one that has emerged from changing conditions, democratic dialogue or emergent understandings.

Democracy and experimentation

Democracy and experimentation are not inseparable; they can occur in isolation, connected to other values and practices, not to each other. Experimentation, for example, can be hidden, conducted behind a wall of secrecy, as, for example, with the development of new weapons or new drugs or new financial products. It can also play an important role in market systems 'that allow for experimentation by many economic decision-makers who can expect rich rewards for success' (Hutton and Schneider, 2008, p. 8). Markets, it is argued, are dynamic in seeking out and applying new technologies and new products, to increase efficiency and to respond to consumer demand. Here experimentation brings private gains accruing to individual entrepreneurs or businesses, with innovations geared to profit-making. Such market-based experimentation can also impose enormous costs on the public purse and the nation state – as in the case of the innovative financial derivatives, described by business investor Warren Buffet as 'financial weapons of mass destruction', whose implosion in 2008 triggered a massive financial crisis, a deep economic recession, and huge government bail-outs for corporate financial institutions paid for by ordinary tax payers.

So it matters what conditions experimentation takes place under. In choosing to link democracy and experimentation in the education system, I am inspired by Roberto Unger's advocacy of 'democratic experimentalism' in the provision of public services:

an innovative collective practice, moving forward the qualitative provision of the services themselves. That can no longer happen in our current understanding of efficiency and production by the mechanical transmission of innovation from the top. It can only happen through the organisation of a collective experimental practice from below . . . Democracy is not just one more terrain for the institutional innovation that I advocate. It is the most important terrain.

(Unger, 2005b, pp. 179, 182)

For Unger, experimentation is an essential element of what he terms 'high energy democracy', which should include 'vastly expanded opportunities to try out, in particular parts of the country or sectors of the economy, different ways of doing things' (Unger, 2005a, p. 78).

By the same token, democracy should be an essential element in educational innovation, viewing education (as I do) as a public good and responsibility. Democracy enables public deliberation from which new ideas for experimentation can be generated and prioritised; raises public understanding of experimentation in theory and practice; creates 'innovation-friendly cooperative practices' (ibid., p. 52); aids transparency; and can help share equitably the benefits of innovation. Where experimentation is a collective and democratic practice, the immaterial products to which it gives rise – Hardt and Negri's 'ideas, images, knowledge, communication, cooperation, and affective relations . . . social life itself' – accrue to the public benefit, rather than being siphoned off as private profit.

In his study of innovative schools serving disadvantaged communities in England, Charles Leadbeater draws a somewhat similar connection, in this case between innovation and collaboration ('collaboration' might be considered a quality needed for democracy, but not necessarily synonymous):

Lasting public innovations are invariably deeply collaborative undertakings, which succeed only with the mobilisation and collaboration of many different participants. In the case of changes to education these players involve at least pupils and parents, teachers and governments, politicians and policy makers, both national and local, as well as related public agencies, employers and the community around a school. Public innovation is more like mobilising a social movement . . . That process of open, collaborative innovation, is impossible unless the people involved share common goals and frames of reference.

(Leadbeater, 2008, p. 14)

Democracy can also be linked to experimentation at the level of learning, individual or group. For if learning is a process of allowing new thinking and knowledge to emerge, then this requires democratic relationships. It means combining a democratic pedagogy of listening with an experimental pedagogy of innovation:

The classroom must become a place where meanings can be responsibly negotiated and hence where the new is allowed to appear . . . To do this we must make sure within schools children have the opportunity not only to engage deeply and responsibly with curricular content, but also have the opportunity to respond to it, to make choices, take a position and be heard.

(Osberg and Biesta, 2007, p. 49)

So when Unger speaks of democracy being 'the most important terrain' for institutional innovation, I would extend that to include all educational innovation, including pedagogical work. Formal democracy can create policies and structures to stimulate and support experimentation, as I shall discuss in Chapter 7. While everyday democracy can create a milieu in which a culture of experimentation can flourish, that willingness to try something new, that desire to bring something new to life, that belief in potentiality.

Note

1 *Pedagogistas*, found in many Italian local authorities, are experienced educators, each working with a small number of municipal schools to help, inter alia, develop understanding of learning processes and pedagogical work through, for example, pedagogical documentation. Their role is discussed further in Chapter 7.

Chapter 6

The Crow Project

A local enactment of the story of democracy, experimentation and potentiality

The last two chapters have told another story about early childhood education, a story of democracy, experimentation and potentiality, a story very different to the more widely told stories of quality and high returns and of markets. I must admit, though, that my telling of this story of democracy, experimentation and potentiality has been somewhat abstract and academic, foregrounding principles, concepts and theories. I certainly don't denigrate principles, concepts and theories; they matter, indeed they are essential. But something is missing: children and educators enacting the story locally, in their everyday lives, in their actual experience of doing early childhood education. To fill this important gap, an example is needed that makes the abstract far more concrete and that demonstrates how the story can translate into actual practice.

The Crow Project can provide that example. It tells the story of the pedagogical work undertaken in a Swedish preschool by a group of children and preschool teachers (referred to mostly as 'pedagogues'). The story teller in this case is one of the teachers, Ann Åberg. The case, the story of the Crow Project, is told by her in her own words, interspersed by short quotations from other sources that she has selected to deepen the reader's understanding of the work she is recounting. I am very grateful to Ann for allowing her story to be included, with its vivid account of pedagogical work inscribed with democracy and experimentation and a strong belief in the unlimited potentiality of children. The story is inspired and influenced also by the early childhood education of Reggio Emilia, in particular in the use made of pedagogical documentation, the importance attached to children as individual and group learners, and the adoption of an open-ended approach to project work with a strong emphasis on listening. Ann is the co-author of a widely read book in Sweden on a pedagogy of listening (Åberg and Lenz Taguchi, 2005).

Today, Ann Åberg is a pedagogical consultant for the Swedish Reggio Emilia Institute based in Stockholm,[1] as well as a *pedagogista* (see note 1, page 138) in a preschool called Äppelviken situated in Bromma, a suburb of Stockholm. But when she wrote about the Crow Project, in 2005, she was a preschool teacher in another preschool in the same neighbourhood, located in a residential area near to open space. The preschool was for 58 children, organised into three age groups; the Crow Project tells of project work with the group of 4- and 5-year-old children, as it developed over the course of a year.

I now offer the reader another voice, the early childhood educator, telling the story of democracy, experimentation and potentiality in a particular place and a distinctive register, and joined by the voices of a group of children, all protagonists in 'the year of the crow'.

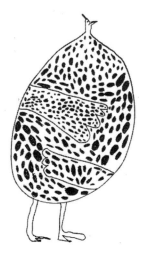

CROW: a knowledge-building project about birds
Narrated by Ann Åberg

I am sitting in a mini-meeting with some children (ages 4 to 5), taking stock of what occurred in our Crow Project. The project has been under way for one year now and the time has come to wrap it up before the summer holidays. We are all curious to hear what the children think about what we learned and discovered together over the course of the year and, more importantly, *how* we learned what we learned. We also hope the children's input will give us, as pedagogues, ideas as to how we might conclude the project.

On the floor in front of us lies all our respective documentation. It consists of the children's drawings and paintings, our own notes, many of which include photographs from our bird watching expeditions in the forest, and research conducted by the children at the actual preschool. Other documentation includes birds the children fashioned out of plaster and clay. Overhead hangs a huge crow which the children constructed as part of a team effort during the spring semester. Initially, only two children were involved in the project. The two eagerly set out to build the crow's body out of chicken wire, but, in no time, they realised this was both a bigger and more complex task than they had imagined. That being the case, they recruited the help of other children in the group. At the end of the day, all the children were involved, in some way or another, in the creation of the giant crow. Some worked at covering the wire mesh body with plaster of Paris; others either painted it or decorated it with feathers.

The floor is also covered with imaginative drawings and hand carved birdhouses executed by the children. They have spent long hours constructing and discussing different theories about what colours birds like best for their homes.

> **William**: I painted my birdhouse with a little bit of green, but mostly blue, because I think it's meant for a blue tit. I think blue tits prefer living in something blue.

The 'year of the crow' was outrageously entertaining and the kids have lots of memories they are more than willing to share. '*It was Jesper who figured out how to make a plaster bird*' says Gustav gazing at his own plaster blue tit. '*I got almost everyone excited about making plaster birds*' boasts Jesper with pride. The children talk at length about 'plaster fever' and recall and marvel at the many small details of their days around the work table where the entire group became totally engrossed in building birds out of plaster.

The children also tried making birds out of other materials. When Linnea looks at her bird she remembers how 'super hard' it was to stick the wings on the soft clay body. Jenny listens and looks surprised when she hears Linnea describe the difficulties she encountered:

> **Jenny**: I think that was the easiest thing in the world!
> **Linnea**: So how did you do it then?
> **Jenny**: I asked Emelie how she did it and I just watched.

The children inspect both their own and each others' bird drawings produced over the past year. They readily distinguish the differences when we exchange drawings. The children's earlier drawings were distinctly different from the ones they produced later on in the project. In the very first drawings you can actually see how difficult it was for them to draw a bird. The drawings are lacking in detail and you can sense how many of the children were hurrying to complete a seemingly difficult, if not unpleasant task. In their later drawings we witness something entirely different. They communicate new knowledge, marked enthusiasm, imagination and growing involvement. They are remarkably rich in fanciful detail. The variety is infinite. The differences in the children's work confirm how they continuously acquire new knowledge, which they later apply to their drawings (examples of early and later drawings can be found on page 166).

The children's drawings on the floor look almost like a film which, frame by frame, depicts how their curiosity shapes an ever more powerful relationship with the birds. The birds are no longer unknown entities flying overhead. They become the children's friends. And the children become extremely pleased with themselves when they discover the differences in their pictures over time:

> **Pontus**: Look, my first crow looks like a paper bag! But the second one has striped legs and a hairy beak. At first I didn't know that crows had striped legs and hair, so I couldn't draw that.

Pontus' first bird

Pontus' later bird, with hair and stripes

> **Maja**: I remember I was really pleased with my first crow, but now I can draw what a bird looks like even better. I also know a lot more, of course.

Maja's first bird

Maya's later bird, a blue tit

By reviewing the earliest documentation together with the children we can observe the child's individual learning process. What is most interesting, however, is how apparent the importance of the group is to the individual in the learning process. We repeatedly hear the children give examples of how they use each other's diverse knowledge and skill sets to enhance their own understanding and learn something new. I'd like to quote Vea Vecchi [an *atelierista* from Reggio Emilia] who, in an article in Modern Childhood [a magazine published by the Swedish Reggio Emilia Institute] on both individual and group learning, maintains: '*The group becomes something which drives each child further, further than he or she could travel as an individual*'. Joint reflection (evaluation) of the documentation gives both us and the children an opportunity to look at our experiences in a new and different light. Our common vision of project work expands and becomes increasingly richer each time we reflect together. By listening to both the children's ideas and our own, we, as pedagogues, continuously discover new ways of understanding and relating to the subject we are working on. The children's diverse ways of understanding and thinking constitute a very important and powerful driving force in our teaching process.

Documentation becomes pedagogical as soon as we, after individual and/ or collective (adults or adults and children together) evaluation thereof, make that choice to continue the work with the group (of children). For children and adults alike, the focus of such work is the learning process rather than the actual goal/result. The objective is to challenge both the children's questions and modes of expression and the adults' uncontested way of understanding the world around them. All too clear goal-oriented content can counteract other pedagogical objectives such as participation, dialogue, confidence-building, imagination and creativity.

(Elfström, 2003, p. 15)

Pondering diversity

This last year's work with pedagogical documentation has challenged my traditional understanding of my role as preschool teacher. The documentation process has enabled a new and different understanding of children and children's learning processes, which changes both my way of relating to the children and my vision of the role and responsibility of the preschool. As a result of the experiences I shared with children and colleagues in the pedagogical documentation process, we abandoned our old way of looking at preschool as a vicarious home and started appreciating the preschool as a common ground for learning – as a democratic meeting place that celebrates diversity and listening. With pedagogical documentation as a working tool, we slowly but surely acquired greater ethical awareness that led to a more democratic work method. A work method that does *not* entail inscribing both oneself and the children in a deadlocked method, but aims at keeping the pedagogical practice in constant flux.

When we were working on the Crow Project, I often wondered *how* pedagogical documentation impacted on the way we worked this time compared to past projects. When I think back on other bird-related projects over the years, I recall that we, as pedagogues, focused primarily on teaching the children basic bird facts. We were, for example, teaching the children the names of the most common birds. In retrospect I ask myself: To whom were these names so important? And I wonder how meaningful it was for the children. Did they actually learn something that they thought was exciting to know about birds? I don't recall choosing bird themes because the children actually demonstrated an interest in or curiosity about birds. Birds were simply one of many important 'categories' that we were supposed to look at with the children.

In the Crow Project, however, we wanted to listen to the children more consciously and proceed in a fashion other than our conventional way of thinking about and understanding a science project. Our aim was not to impart to the children any scientific truths about birds. Instead, we wanted to understand how we might shape a meaningful context for the children's keen interest in crows that we had observed. This time, with documentation as a work tool, it became feasible for us to make the children's own natural science-building process visible and focus on their questions. As a result, we discovered that the children learned many things about birds we had not considered. For example, the majority learned the names of the most common birds that visited our bird table. It was also evident, by the end of the project, that the children, at their own doing, had learned the names of the most unusual birds and any other number of facts by either looking them up in a book or in some other way.

Once we decided to strive to make the children's thoughts and questions visible, it became self-evident to begin with what the children already knew. We were curious to understand the different ways children perceive nature/crows. Proceeding from what children already know in a pedagogical project is not only democratic. It is highly ethical in nature. It suggests I am interested in what you think and know; I respect what you think and I take that into account when I challenge you. This is, as I suggested earlier, a different approach from the one we normally take as pedagogues, built on what we think is important for children to learn about a subject and then proceeding on the basis of what we know and understand about that subject – our own context and our own meaning-making process.

Let me give you an example. In several instances in the Crow Project the children were given the opportunity to meet so-called 'bird experts' who had come to pay us a visit. Several of our bird-loving guests had prepared themselves to reply to questions they normally had answers to. For example: What are our most common birds? Which birds spend the winter in Sweden? But we, as pedagogues, wanted to build on the children's own curiosity and therefore decided to ask the children to prepare themselves for the meeting with the 'expert' by thinking through the questions they were keen on pursuing. When the focus is the child's own curiosity or sense of wonder, the questions become something far from the ordinary. Here below are some examples of questions posed by the children.

How do birds kiss?
Can birds fart?
Do birds think?

KRÅKA

ousTA

Even experts have difficulty answering these questions with certainty. Not even an ornithologist can be one hundred per cent certain as to whether or not birds 'think'. I cannot help but wonder what would have happened if we had asked our guests to share their knowledge of birds, rather than listening to the children's questions. Perhaps that would have been exciting for the children too, but the content of the conversation would not have been anywhere near what the children were most interested in. In fact, the children did not get many answers to their questions. Instead, a series of new questions were sparked, setting in motion an animated discussion between the children and our guests. The children listened attentively to all the different theories about birds and they were not always convinced that the expert necessarily had the right answer. On that occasion Philip (age 5) posed a question to the expert and when he heard the answer he looked so doubtful and responded: '*But that's not necessarily so; it can also be the other way round*'. Our efforts to value children's thoughts and to consistently take their theories seriously, in my opinion, explain how Philip, so naturally, could dare to question the expert's answer to his question. As a result of this stance, the children, in practice, feel they have the same right as adults to think differently. Philip was confident about his own theories and was convinced that they were no less exciting than those of the expert.

> Another aim of pedagogical documentation is to attempt to understand and render visible the social and societal constructions we have created that govern how we see children . . . And to do so in order for the teacher to open up to new constructions. It is all about changing practice.
>
> (Elfström, 2003, p. 15)

Documenting in smaller groups to breed curiosity

Our decision to dig a little deeper and focus on the children's own questions proved to be what planted the real seeds of our work. From the very outset, the children's questions did not deal with any old crow, but rather our own crow. That plump crow with white-speckled tail feathers we used to encounter every week in the forest when we picnicked on the rock. A personal and meaningful context was obvious. The question was how we could go further. We started the project by compiling the children's own questions and thoughts about crows. We listened carefully and documented their prior experiences and knowledge. A little further down the road, the very first documentation exercises provided an extremely valuable source of material with interesting questions from which we drew ideas throughout the project period.

Our 'own crow' in the forest – the protagonist of our project – had disappeared by the time we returned to preschool after summer vacation. Fortunately, we eventually found other crows in a neighbouring park. Our task as pedagogues, during our first crow watching expedition, was to determine which children appeared the most curious about the crows. Our objective was to start a project with a small group of children clearly exhibiting great interest. Our experience from past projects taught us that focusing on a small interest group from the start would make it possible, in a fascinating way, to inspire other children later on. We identified five to six children who were particularly keen on studying the crows in the park. The following day we invited this small group of children to return to the park on a second crow expedition. But before we set out, we had a little meeting with the children and asked them to think of questions about crows they hoped to solve. Here are some examples of the questions we documented:

> I wonder how they fly?
> I want to see what their feet look like.
> I wonder what their eyes look like?

When we arrived at the park the children swiftly proceeded with their research. Since their questions required seeing the crows at close range, we enticed the crows to come closer by feeding them bread crumbs we had taken along. We documented what occurred on camera and in note form. When we returned to preschool, we gathered the children together again to address their questions and reflect on our discoveries. Did anyone find the answer to his/her question?

> **Maja**: I saw that their feet were a little black and a little grey, almost like baby birds.
> They had long small claws, I replied.
> **Philip:** You know what I saw? That they could glide. They didn't need to flap their wings all the time. Sometimes their wings were perfectly still.

The children talked at length about their crow investigation in the park. And since our intention was to spread the discoveries of the little group, we asked the children to decide what discovery they wanted to talk about with the other kids. After a brief discussion, they chose to show the others how they discovered that crows can glide. Later that same day we invited the rest of the children to an altogether different air show. This was where our conscious 'contagion' began. We returned to the park, on several occasions, with all the children (in smaller groups) to watch the crows. We chose to focus our documentation process on the little group, but that is not to suggest that we ignored the other children's discoveries. Quite the contrary. We documented the little group's discoveries to give the others the opportunity to be infected by their enthusiasm. The children in the little group were given the task of inviting some of the other children to a meeting after each time they met, in order to share documentation and talk about their exciting discoveries. As there was already much interest in the crows among the majority of the children, the little group's inquisitiveness spread with relative ease. Our mini-meeting (with the larger group) was a fantastic place for spreading joy and curiosity. After each such meeting we could observe at once how the invited children showed great interest in either testing something they had heard or conducting their own research.

On one such occasion, at the beginning of the term, when the little group had drawn crows together, Moa lingered a moment at the table. She wanted to do another drawing. She bends forward to take a close look at the stuffed crow standing on the table. Suddenly she discovers something new:

Moa: But, hello, now I see something odd. The crow has striped legs!

She becomes totally enthralled with her new discovery and straight away wants to attempt drawing a crow with striped legs.

Moa had made an exciting discovery – the type of discovery we hoped many of the other children would experience. The following day we asked Moa to open the meeting of the little group by showing her picture and describing her discovery to the other children. That made for a thrilling start. Her story inspired the others in the group and infected them with much enthusiasm, joy and curiosity to investigate and draw crows with striped legs. Curiosity spread like wildfire throughout the group when Moa also got the chance to address the other children in a mini-meeting. Later that same afternoon, we could see traces of contagion at the large drawing table. There were countless drawings of crows with striped legs. Here, for example, are Moa's drawing that infected several children with curiosity and delight.

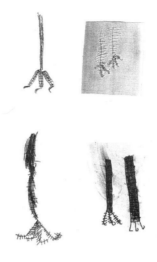

Listening for meaning

This development influenced how we subsequently organised our meeting in the little group. We decided to introduce each one by revisiting the previous outing. We focused on something each child had said or done and the child had the opportunity to reflect one more time, together, on his/her experience. As a result of this joint reflection process, both the children (and the pedagogues) continuously gained insight into both their own and others' ways of thinking and acting which, in turn, sparked new ideas and exciting questions. We laid the children's pictures, our notes and photographs from the previous day on the table and we saw how the children's curiosity and interest grew each and every time.

There was a major difference compared to our earlier project work where we often encountered problems trying to sustain the children's interest in the subject we had chosen. So now, after the fact, I can understand what occurred. We, as adults, had been obsessed with playing knowledge brokers. It was our own ideas about what was interesting that dictated how we planned the content of our work. We failed to listen to which questions the children were most interested in exploring and, as a result, I believe it was hard for us to sustain the children's interest.

But when we use documentation as a point of departure in our conversation with the children we are always able to understand what fascinates them most and that enables us to persevere and delve deeper like engaged children. This time the children were the protagonists, not the category. We adults did not become centred on brokering our knowledge to the children. Instead, we became absorbed in attempting to understand what they were trying to understand and then, as a next step, to use their questions as a driving force in the project. We focused on the children's questions. That does not mean that we stuck exclusively to the children's questions. Naturally, we were forced to continuously think how we, as pedagogues, might challenge the children when they could not recall. We listened to the children, but it was our ongoing responsibility to consider what we, as pedagogues, could add, and how to shape a meaningful setting which challenged the children's thoughts and actions.

> Drawing on the children's reflections helps the teacher understand things in a light other than the obvious. More specifically it enhances the children's participation in the group learning process by building on and tapping into their thoughts and actions . . . [T]eachers read [pedagogical documentation] alongside children, colleagues, even parents on occasion. This paves the way for any number of different routes the learning process can take. But it is the teachers who are ultimately responsible for adhering to the subject they have chosen to work with. This is vital if the learning process is to become more profound and not dissipate.
>
> (Åberg and Lenz Taguchi, 2005, p. 87)

Interest in the birds continued to grow stronger throughout the entire group of children each time the little interest group was invited to the mini-meeting and shared its experiences. After one half autumn semester it was impossible to say that some of the children were more interested than others. We thus decided to make the little group a flexible group. We wanted to have an open group for all the children, but we also wanted to maintain a certain structure. We felt it was important to stick to our idea of a little group and, above all, it was vital that one or more of the children who had participated previously be present as motors in the process to 'retell' or 'revisit' what had occurred. Retelling was important for many reasons. Largely because we wanted to avoid the risk of our group work becoming a series of disjointed events. With the help of these storytellers we hoped to create a meaningful context in which the children could explore a little deeper and weave together and develop their own experiences by reflecting as a group on their respective experiences. In these sessions we managed to capture several ideas about new challenges. The sessions further served as an ongoing evaluation of the project work together with the children. In conversation with and among the children, both our own picture of the project and that of the children changed, enabling us to discover new and exciting stepping stones in our work.

In the beginning we worked on the project three mornings a week with a little group of children, but occasionally, in the middle of the term, the project consumed our entire day and, to the greatest possible degree, all the children in the larger group were both involved and engaged in a variety of ways. Furthermore, over the course of the year, the parents became more involved in our work with birds.

A sense of exploration, curiosity and desire to learn should form the foundations for the preschool activities. These should be based on the child's experiences, interests, needs and views. The flow of the child's thoughts and ideas should be used to create variety in learning.

(Skolverket, 2010, p. 9)

Striped legs, hairy beaks and back claws

The children were fascinated by several different aspects of the project work. But there was something they continuously revisited throughout the year. That was discussing and testing several different theories and possible explanations as to why crows have hairy beaks and the function their back claw serves. Here below are some of their observations about back claws:

> **Question**: Do you ever wonder why crows have back claws?
> **Johan**: I think they're like brakes. I think crows like to brake on the ground.
> **Moa**: I think it helps them walk.
> **Sofia**: Hmm, if they didn't have back claws they would fall backwards.

Pontus: Nah. I think it gives them that extra push when then fly.
Jonathan: I see it like this. That back claw is for sitting still in the woods when they don't want to fly.
William: It's to scoop up food.

The discussions were never about who was right or wrong. On the contrary. The children seemingly enjoyed listening to each other's interpretations. They drew both their own and each other's theories and tested their different theories on the entire body. They were not at all interested in finding out whether or not there was a scientific explanation. They simply derived pleasure from listening to and testing each other's theories.

Here is a picture of one child's theory about why crows have back claws. We asked Philip to draw his theory.

Can you draw your theory . . . on how the
crow uses its back claw?

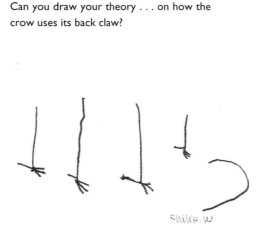

Philip. W

Under the drawing, I have added what Philip says: 'Perhaps to scoop up their food just in case they miss with their beak. But the back claw is also like the heel we have on our feet'.

Question: Ever wonder why crows have striped legs?
Jenny: They like to dress up too from time to time.
Jonathan: It's like this. The stripes shine in the dark at night. One night when I was out I saw a crow with shiny legs.

To find out what it looks like when the crow's stripes light up at night, the children taped reflectors on their legs, switched off the lights and then lit up each other's legs with flashlights. It was a thrilling experiment, which the children loved testing over and over again. Here below are two different theories about why crows have hair on their beaks:

> **Danielle**: They have hair so they won't freeze.
> **Pontus:** Naa. The hair is like feelers. If they can't see something, they can feel it.

By listening to the children's conversations, we, as pedagogues, naturally picked up many new ideas we could draw on to challenge the children in exciting and different ways.

When, at the end of the project year, we looked back at this very part of the documentation, the following reasoning took place:

> **Elsa**: Do you remember how we ran around with the flashlights and lit up everybody's legs? That was so much fun.
> **William**: It was a little scary, because it was so bloody dark in there.
> **Moa**: Maybe not so many people know that crows have striped legs. Imagine we're the only ones in the world who know that!
> **Jonathan**: Yeah. And we even know that crows can use the hair on their beaks as landing gear.
> **Johan:** I remember thinking that crows use their back claws like brakes.
> **Emma**: Yeah, they hold onto the ground with that claw too; otherwise they would be flying up in the air all the time.

When their learning is documented, children can revisit and thereby interpret their learning experiences and also reflect on how to develop their experiences further . . . Documentation is not limited to making visible what already exists; it also makes things exist precisely because it makes them visible and therefore possible.

(Giudici *et al.*, 2001, p. 17)

Winding down and gearing up together

At the start of the project we documented the children's own questions and ideas about crows. When we set to compiling the year's discoveries just before summer, naturally we were curious about revisiting these same questions to see if we could detect any differences in the way children think. When we read the documentation the children became visibly surprised:

Jesper: I knew so little then!
Linnea: Oy, oy, oy. Now we know tons more.

The children's revisiting of the documentation material made visible the differences that fascinated them and sparked many new and exciting questions. Moreover, we pedagogues got a clear picture of how the children's own questions drove the project forward. At the beginning of the project the children found it difficult to formulate questions. Now, suddenly, the entire room was swimming with new and engaging questions:

Emma: I actually wonder how they protect themselves from dangerous animals.
Philip: Yeah, and I wonder why they lose their feathers.
Sofia: I wonder how they find food in the forest. How do they know where the food is in the summertime, because no one puts out any food in the bird feeder? I've thought a lot about that.

Upon revisiting the documentation the majority of the children discovered that over the course of the past year they indeed got the answers they sought to their first questions. But the children also realised that there was so much more left to explore. Indeed the more they discovered, the more questions they wanted to explore. When Philip at the beginning of the project was asked what more he would like to know about crows, he replied: '*One doesn't really know what one wants to know. Maybe what they look like when they fly?*' At a mini-meeting, a half year later, Philip said: '*I want to know more and more all the time. Now I wonder how birds can see their prey on the ground when they fly so fast. I also wonder how hair can grow on a crow's beak*'. And, upon revisiting the documentation at the end of the project, Philip said: '*It's crazy how much we know about birds now. But I still wonder why they have feathers and whether birds can talk to each other. Maybe crows can only talk to crows. Maybe blue tits can't talk crow talk*'.

As Philip developed a closer relationship with the birds, his interest in them also grew and his questions increased in number. When we listened to the children's reflections while revisiting the documentation, it also became apparent to us how we might end the semester. When the children described their experiences we heard a lot of new questions come up. Accordingly, we decided to add the children's new ideas and questions as the conclusion to the existing documentation. We ended our project work by documenting the children's answers to the question: What have you become curious about now? In that way the project did not actually come to an end. Our thinking was that documentation of this kind could inspire the children to continue their investigation.

> Preschool teachers are responsible for all children having real influence over working methods and contents of the preschool.
>
> (Skolverket, 2010, p. 12)

Learning for life and for later

In addition to gaining new insight into how we, as pedagogues, created a more democratic work methodology, we also discovered that we became more curious about nature in a more intimate manner than before. I personally remember reading articles that might not have caught my eye in the past. I even saved an article from a newspaper that I could use later in our Crow Project. The article looks at the fact that we, in Sweden, are less and less interested in knowledge about nature. According to biologist Fredrik Sjoberg:

> [i]n Sweden we often talk about our feelings and sensitivity for nature. About how we Swedes have a particularly warm relationship with nature. I believe that the power of seeing a redstart again has a lot of bearing on how that love story has unfolded. When biological illiteracy spreads, those feelings fade. Nature becomes a green curtain. Incomprehensible and, therefore, difficult to relate to on the whole. This can make it more difficult to make headway with questions concerning nature conservation.

In our Crow Project I feel that together we built an inquisitive and loving relationship with nature which, in all likelihood, will shape how the children identify with animals and nature in the future.

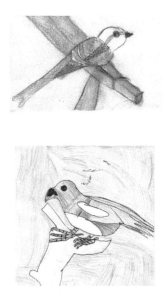

The adults' 'take' on the project

When we adults evaluated the Crow Project, we could see that we gained new insight into how we created a more democratic work methodology. With the children's questions as a driving force, we succeeded in creating a meaningful context which enabled both children and adults to learn from and with each other. We had an exciting and entertaining year and felt satisfied with the project, but not so satisfied that we ignored thinking about how we might have proceeded differently.

During the course of the year the children demonstrated great enthusiasm in reproducing both the crow's calls and movements. From these observations we could choose to work with the crow in an entirely different way. We had also wanted to focus on light, dance and drama. We saw and heard the children's interest, but we chose not to do so on this occasion. We also wanted to try working with the younger children in the adjacent section. We noticed that the very youngest children were infected by the older children's interest in birds. This clearly led to exciting cooperation between the youngest and the oldest preschoolers.

Naturally, there were many routes we could have pursued. When we revisited the documentation it was interesting to attempt to interpret together what we did, but it was equally interesting to examine what we chose not to do. What ideas did we discard and why, and which of all the discarded ideas might we use the next time round?

We called this project Crow, but naturally the project didn't only deal with crows. If it had it would have become terribly tedious. For children and teachers alike the project dealt with so much more – discovering the joy of learning together and the dialogue with other investigators, thinkers and researchers. It was about experimenting with several different languages. About listening, discussing, imagining and asking ourselves questions. About examining and calling into question conceptions of the pedagogue's role not only in enabling children to partake more in their own learning process but in giving parents the opportunity to participate in the pedagogical process. It dealt with learning to feel and shape an intimate relation with animals and nature and challenge and question scientific truths. With the help of our documentation work concerning the children's own curiosity, we could create a meaningful context and exciting exchange amongst the children where both children and pedagogues were able to discover each other's differences as a valuable resource and a driving force in our group learning process.

> Pedagogical documentation is intended as much for teachers as it is for children. As teachers we can equally ask ourselves: Where do I stand now? What is the next step? We can also follow our own learning curve or process. Pedagogical documentation constitutes a type of relationship and communication in itself. It is an active meaning-making process and not only a cognitive one. The aim of pedagogical documentation is to use several different theories to understand children's behaviour and challenge not only the children but ourselves, and even the scientific concepts of the content children work with . . . as well as children's development and learning.
>
> (Lenz Taguchi, 1997)

And the group hugs the individual

In some way each new project is invariably connected to a project which already exists in the child's memory and experience. The child deposits each new project in his/her knowledge bank, which he/she can access and naturally relate each new problem to. In the Crow Project we saw how the children were interested in differences in size. That led us the following year to a project on how children understand and approach mathematics in their everyday life. A maths project, with a major dose of birds, for obvious reasons. We had no doubts about the importance of giving the children the opportunity to reflect together on the Crow Project. But the following [project] gave us an even more convincing opportunity to recognize the importance of enabling children to understand the value of learning from and with each other.

In the maths project the children were inordinately interested in different ways of measuring. In one case, Alva (age 5) had a question which she shared with my colleague Carina. Her solution to how she should go about finding the answer astonished us:

> **Alva**: I wonder how far it is to all the children's homes?
> **Carina:** Yeah, how can we find out?
> **Alva**: Well, we can get a bunch of children in a little group and see what we learn.

'We can get a bunch of children together in a little group and see what we learn' says Alva. That speaks volumes about how she perceives the importance of the group in her own learning process. Alva (and naturally her classmates) has experienced thinking together with others and believes, to a large extent, that ideas multiply if there are several persons thinking together. She has become curious about how others think and is perfectly aware that others contribute to her happiness because she learns or understands in new and different ways.

Learning should be based, not only on the interaction between adults and children, but also on what children learn from each other. The group of children should be regarded as an important and active part in development and learning.

(Skolverket, 2010, p. 6)

Making children visible beyond preschool walls

A little more than two years after we concluded our bird project we had the opportunity to gather together our old 'crow kids' (who by now had started school) and their parents to attend an extraordinary event. We were invited to the opening of a permanent art exhibition of a different ilk. In a huge office building, right in the heart of central Stockholm, there is a dizzying, dazzling light well. In the midst of that light well is a glass elevator. On both sides of its glass walls, on several levels, were hung 37 original drawings of birds created by children in our bird project.

It all began when the drawings ended up in the hands of architect Harald Zetterstrom who became terribly fascinated with the children's pictures. To quote Harald: '*I was looking for a special motif. Something that could add a human dimension to this huge chequered building. When I saw the children's drawings I knew immediately that I had found it*'. At his initiative the children's drawings eventually came to be used as decorative art in a part of the building that Harald had designed. At a meeting, which took place before the construction was under way, I had the opportunity to describe how the children worked with birds to some of the office management. The fact that they knew about the work behind the children's pictures, in my opinion largely accounted for the highly respectful way in which they welcomed and thanked the children at the inauguration.

When this was complete, a large party was organised at the office for the children and their families, and all those who had been involved in the Crow Project were invited. The guests constituted a large gathering of interested parents, siblings and pedagogues. Some took the opportunity to take along both a grandfather and a grandmother. We were some 60 to 70 persons, running up and down the stairs in this twelve-storey office building to see all the birds on the glass walls. Even though much time had passed since the drawings were made, the children could still recognise and identify both their own and each others' pictures. The children recounted with much enthusiasm memories from the project period. We were then invited into a room with a long, beautifully set table with juice, cakes and candy for the children. Two directors delivered fantastic thank you speeches to the children and each child received a diploma as a souvenir and token of appreciation. I am convinced that the children will always remember that special day. It was a day ripe with respect for the children, in all sincerity, from adults far beyond the preschool walls.

Learning with and from each other – co-constructing new knowledge

Documentation is one way of understanding the world in a different light and making listening visible. Where there is both the desire and the will to listen to the children, I, as their teacher, have the opportunity to practise, together with the children and my colleagues, an ongoing process of knowledge-building, not only about what child and teacher can be and become, but what pre-school and I as a pedagogue can become. But in order for this to occur, we, as pedagogues, must naturally be aware of the value that underlies what we are proposing to the children. Those of us fortunate enough to work closely with children have the opportunity to discover both the children, ourselves and the world in a new and different light over and over again. That is a great, great privilege. It follows that we must also recognise the tremendous responsibility we have for how we interact with and relate to the children, how we relate to our task as pedagogues, and how we perceive the role of preschool today and tomorrow.

> We must continuously try to understand the meaning of our curricula in relation to our changing times and possibilities. Just like laws, the language of goals in the curriculum should not be insensitive to the changes taking place in people's understanding of things.
>
> (Åberg and Lenz Taguchi, 2005, p. 147)

Observations by the book's author

It is not my intention to offer a comprehensive analysis of Ann Åberg's story of the Crow Project, which can in any case be no more than one person's reading, one person's take on the story. Each reader will be able to offer their own reading of this case, finding many possibilities and meanings in such a rich narrative. I will instead confine myself to three observations about how the Crow Project seems to me to enact the story of democracy, experimentation and possibility, but also adds further depth and nuance to it. Why, in short, I find it both inspirational and illuminating.

First, there is the insight it offers into the potential of pedagogical documentation, a method of working that plays a central role in the Crow Project: as a tool to enable reflection, to challenge existing understandings and to construct new ones, for researching and learning, and also as a means of fostering participation by and dialogue between children, parents and pedagogues:

> Joint reflection (evaluation) of the documentation gives both us and the children an opportunity to look at our experiences in a new and different

light. Our common vision of project work expands and becomes increasingly richer each time we reflect together. By listening to both the children's ideas and our own, we, as pedagogues, continuously discover new ways of understanding and relating to the subject we are working on. The children's diverse ways of understanding and thinking constitute a very important and powerful driving force in our teaching process.

Documentation in this case plays an important part in ensuring a pedagogy of movement, a process we might term, recalling the discussion in Chapter 1, transformative change. It was, Ann writes, a work method 'that does *not* entail inscribing both oneself and the children in a deadlocked method, but aims at keeping the pedagogical practice in constant flux'.

Pedagogical documentation contributes to a second observation: the new understandings or images that Ann and her colleagues constructed – of the children, of the preschool and of themselves as teachers. The children emerge from the Crow Project as protagonists and researchers, active meaning makers and co-constructors of knowledge, constantly asking questions, forming, testing and reforming theories, engaged in complex and creative relationships with other children, both in the smaller and larger group, and with the pedagogues. The perception of the preschool moves from 'a vicarious home' to a 'common ground for learning . . . a democratic meeting place that celebrates diversity and listening'.

The teachers in this 'democratic meeting place' no longer act, as before, as 'knowledge brokers', imposing their own ideas about what is interesting, asking their own questions and dictating the content of the work – summed up by Ann as 'teaching the children basic bird facts . . . the names of the most common birds', which leaves her wondering 'To whom were these names so important?' Instead the teachers also assume a new image: as researchers, active meaning makers and co-constructors of knowledge. They become listeners, realising their past failure to listen to children and now wanting to do so. Their role changes, to create a fruitful environment for learning and to understand and work with what the children are bringing to the preschool, including their learning strategies, their interests and their questions:

> Our aim was not to impart to the children any scientific truths about birds. Instead, we wanted to understand how we might shape a meaningful context for the children's keen interest in crows that we had observed. This time, with documentation as a work tool, it became feasible for us to make the children's own natural science-building process visible and focus on their questions.

This does not mean, though, that the teacher's job is simply to elicit and document children's theories. They are there also to ensure rigorous subjectivity, creating 'a meaningful setting which challenged the children's thoughts and actions', a place of 'listening to and testing each other's theories'.

Third, explicit references to democracy recur throughout this case – and remember this account precedes the current book by some years, so it was not written specially to fit with or echo the story of democracy, experimentation and potentiality as propounded in earlier chapters. Here are pedagogues in an ordinary Swedish preschool talking about their practice in terms of democracy in a quite matter of fact way. Not only is the preschool a 'democratic meeting place', but pedagogical documentation led to 'a more democratic work method', while 'proceeding from what children know is democratic and ethical'. When the pedagogues evaluated the project, 'we could see that we gained new insight into how we created a more democratic work methodology'. All this within the context of a national curriculum that states 'all preschool activity should be carried out in accordance with fundamental democratic values'

However, it seems to me that the democracy of the project goes well beyond these specific references to being 'democratic'. It is pervasive, the project vividly exemplifying democracy as a way of being and relating – from the emphasis on listening, through the deep respect shown for children's questions and theories and the discovery of 'each other's differences as a valuable resource', to the constant dialogue and openness to new perspectives and ideas. And alongside democracy, there is experimentation: with different languages, with new ideas and exciting questions, with new methods of working and new understandings.

I cannot end without commenting on the language. There are no words here from the vocabulary of the story of quality and high returns or the story of markets: no mention, for instance, of 'evidence-based', 'programmes', 'quality', 'learning goals', or 'outcomes'. Instead we hear the language of pleasure and potential: the project was 'outrageously entertaining'; the children 'marvel' and display 'a sense of wonder' and conduct a 'thrilling experiment'; 'curiosity spread like wildfire' through the group as did 'joy'. Here, indeed, is cause to believe in the world again.

The children's first bird drawings

The children's later bird drawings

Note

1 Started in 1992, to develop the relationship between Reggio Emilia and Sweden and to deepen understanding of and support working with Reggio Emilian pedagogical ideas and practices, the Swedish Reggio Emilia Institute organises regular seminars and other meetings with leading educators from Reggio Emilia. It is much in demand in Sweden for consultancy work, mostly commissioned by *kommuner* (local authorities), involving work with groups of preschool teachers over a period to make change happen, though always starting from a dialogue to discuss what the Institute and preschools can do together. It holds a regular summer symposium, first begun in 1996 with some 60 participants and now hosting over 400. These week-long events include lectures from leading researchers and innovative preschool teachers who are working with new theoretical perspectives (such as Deleuzian ideas) and experimenting with change.

Chapter 7

What conditions to enact the story of democracy, experimentation and potentiality?

The story of democracy, experimentation and potentiality has been enacted – the Crow Project has provided one example – though admittedly not widely, largely in isolated cases that are often precarious, struggling to survive. It could, though, be enacted on a larger and more sustainable scale, though never universally, perfectly and permanently: no story ever can. But like any story enacted on a larger and more sustainable scale, attention must be given to the conditions needed for such change. Wishing and hoping for transformation are not enough, though the desire for transformation is certainly important; thought and resources need to be given to structure and organisation.

Another way of thinking about the enactment of a story is, in Erik Olin Wright's terms, as the implementation of a real utopian project, involving in this case the transformation of the institution of early childhood education through redesigning it on the basis, inter alia, of democracy and experimentation as fundamental values. I outlined in Chapter 1 how Wright proposes three criteria for real utopias: desirability, viability and achievability. If the story as told in Chapters 3 and 4 corresponds to the desirability criterion, paying particular attention to values, ethics and goals, the focus in this chapter is on the viability part of the project, offering 'systemic *theoretical models* of how particular social structures and institutions would work'.

The third element, of achievability, 'what it would take to actually implement' my proposals, is addressed in the final chapter. There I will look more into the likelihood of achieving transformative change in early childhood education, confronting the apparently insuperable barrier of neoliberalism as the dominant political economy. I will put forward reasons why such change is not unthinkable, why the story of democracy, experimentation and potentiality should not be written off as just pie in the sky, as well as what that process of change might entail.

For now though I will focus on viability: the conditions for enactment of my story, the major features in the design of an early childhood education of democracy, experimentation and potentiality. I set out these conditions under seven main headings: early childhood centres; early childhood workforce; the educative commune; academia; national (or state) government; evaluation and accountability; and time. None of these structural and organisational conditions guarantees an early childhood education of democracy, experimentation and potentiality; but each can contribute to both creating and sustaining an environment that is conducive to such an educational project, giving it a good chance not only to embed but also to grow. The importance attached to such structural and organisational conditions has been crucial to the ability of Reggio Emilia's educational project to survive over 50 years, an unparalleled achievement in the history of progressive education, and not just to survive but to sustain continuous experimentation and movement:

> Many experiences or reforms have failed or are failing as a consequence of organizational adaptation to the [pedagogical] idea itself. Malaguzzi was able to seamlessly unite the ideas of a project with a strong organization that made its evolution possible. This organization is not neutral, but already the result of the selection of content and educational goals . . . *The organization is a determining factor for the success of a project. Malaguzzi knew this very well.*
>
> (Hoyuelos, 2013, p. 216; emphasis added)

By focusing here and in the next chapter on more structural and organisational conditions, I do not intend to reduce transformation to a matter of grand designs and machinery, of levers and technologies. What matters, just as much, is the longing and the capacity to think differently, to listen to and work with different stories; and the passion, commitment, collaboration and sheer hard work of individuals and groups of individuals who want to tell a different story and who desire to gain and maintain movement to achieve transformative change. What matters, too, is that the conditions are inscribed with and at the service of the values, beliefs and goals that drive the project of change, so that, as Carlina Rinaldi says 'organisation expresses a value and is not an end in itself' (2006, p. 159) – technical practice in the service of political practice. Structural and organisational conditions, including technical practices, have their place in early childhood education, indeed are indispensible: but always as resources, not substitutes, for democracy and experimentation.

Much can be achieved by a committed early childhood centre and even more by a committed local authority through the exercise of prefigurative practice. This is a concept discussed further in the next chapter. But for the moment it can be said to express the idea that change need not wait until everyone, in every place and at every level are fully signed up; it has to start somewhere, even as a few isolated cases, such prefigurative practice offering an instance of possibility. I agree with the feminist writer Sheila Rowbotham about the importance of 'making something which might become the means to making something more' and that 'some changes have to start now else there is no beginning for us' (Rowbotham, 1979, p. 140).

So I do not want to imply that nothing can happen until all three levels – early childhood centre, local authority and national government – are aligned. That is not the case and is a recipe for inaction. But the fullest and widest implementation calls for coherent action at all levels, including a national policy framework that defines and enables certain common entitlements, structures, values and goals backed up by a common and secure funding system. The greater the alignment, the broader and more sustained the process of transformative change is likely to be.

Early childhood centres

> Our criteria suggest that the basic form of service should be through multi-purpose children's centres offering part and full-time care with medical and other services, to a very local catchment area, but there is much room for experimentation.
>
> (Tizard *et al.*, 1976, p. 220)

> What was once viewed as either a privilege of the wealthy for a few hours a day, or an institution for needy children and single mothers, has become, after 70 years of political vision and policy-making, an unquestionable right of children and families. Furthermore, parents now expect a holistic pedagogy that includes health care, nurturing and education for their pre-schoolers.
>
> (Lenz Taguchi and Munkammar, 2003, p. 27)

One of the main features of a viable re-designed early childhood education, in which democracy and experimentation serve as fundamental values, is a ubiquitous network of early childhood centres that are:

- available as an entitlement or 'unquestionable right' of citizenship to all young children and families in their local catchment areas;
- age integrated, welcoming children from birth to compulsory school age – though some might be combined with 'extended' (or 'full-service') schools for older children;
- open all day and all year;
- multi-purpose, offering education-in-its-broadest-sense, 'a holistic pedagogy', but also many other projects for children, families and their local communities, 'with much room for experimentation';
- democratically managed and democratically accountable to their immediate local community and their 'educative commune';
- directly funded from taxation (i.e. supply funded) and free to users.

What is proposed here is a hybrid centre in the sense that it combines the best features of Nordic preschools or kindergartens, with their entitlement to access,[1] their age-integration and their 'holistic pedagogy' where, as the Swedish preschool curriculum puts it, 'care, socialisation and learning form a coherent whole' (Skolverket, 2010, p. 4); with some of the features of English Children's Centres at their best, in particular their commitment to and capacity for a wide range of purposes and projects. But unlike the current crop of English Children's Centres, which though widespread remain essentially marginal to a mainstream that consists of a marketised and fragmented system of private nurseries, playgroups and state schools, the early childhood centres I envisage are (like Nordic preschools and kindergartens) the sole, or at least the main, providers of early childhood education. Each centre would serve 'a very local catchment area', the early childhood equivalent of the 'common school': a public space for *all* citizens living locally – children, young people and adults – without admission criteria except residence.

These centres are connected to form local collaborative networks – in sharp contrast to local markets of competing businesses – with a universal (though non-compulsory) offer that complements other universal services, such as health and compulsory schooling. Like these other universal services, all early childhood centres are not only universally available as of right but also available without charge, the argument made nearly 40 years ago still holding good today:

> One of the most discriminatory anomalies of the present service [in 1970s England] is that nursery education is free while parental contributions are expected of playgroup and day nursery users . . . For a society which provides free education [and] a free public health service, a free preschool service is a logical corollary.
>
> (Tizard *et al.*, 1976, p. 214)

This system of 'common' early childhood centres, public spaces open to all citizens providing a public education, is committed to democracy as a fundamental value, with all centres not only democratically managed but also striving to practice democracy in their everyday life and work. Some are provided as cooperatives or by non-profit private organisations; others directly by local authorities – municipal centres. In many countries, this statement – that local authorities should act as providers – may seem a statement of the obvious. Yet in a country like England, where neoliberalism and the story of markets have taken such strong hold, local authorities have been increasingly excluded by central government from assuming such a role.

I see no inherent reason why such public bodies cannot provide services themselves, and do so well, indeed there are many examples where they have done this and continue to do so. Moreover, if these democratically elected bodies have a responsibility for a public early childhood education, if they are to be truly 'educative communes', it is difficult to see how they can meet this responsibility without being directly involved in its practice. For if they are reduced to contracting services to others to provide or acting as a 'market manager', local authorities will lose 'touch with the knowledge necessary to understand certain activities . . . [becoming] a kind of institutional idiot, [their] every ill-informed move being anticipated in advance and therefore discounted by smart market actors' (Crouch, 2004, p. 41). Put another way, they will be akin to a private householder paying others to undertake plumbing and electrical work, having no idea what these contractors are doing or what constitutes good work. Roberto Unger, the advocate of 'democratic experimentalism' as an important strategy for bringing about transformative change, whilst arguing the need for 'new social agents' to develop innovative services, also argues for a provider role for government in 'those services which are too innovative, too difficult or too unrewarded by the market to be provided directly' (Unger, 2005b, p. 179).

While envisaging a public early childhood education with a public–private mix of providers, all committed to and enacting democracy as a fundamental value, I see no place in that mix for early childhood centres run as private businesses for profit, whose main purpose is to secure return on capital and which cannot be expected or required to adopt democratic practice. Businesses could, of course, still offer early childhood education, but would receive no public funding or other support. Nor in my story of early childhood education, with the value it places on solidarity and collaboration, do I see any place for markets, where competition is a fundamental value. Where early childhood education has fallen into the market domain and become subject to capitalist relationships, it will be necessary to reclaim it for the public domain and inscribe it with democratic and solidaristic relationships.

The early childhood workforce

> TARGET 25: All qualified staff employed in [early childhood] services should be paid at not less than a nationally or locally agreed wage rate, which for staff who are fully trained should be comparable to that of [school] teachers.

> TARGET 26: A minimum of 60% of staff working directly with children in collective [early childhood] services should have a grant eligible basic training of at least three years at a post-18 level . . .

> TARGET 29: 20% of staff employed in collective services should be men.
> (European Commission Childcare Network, 1996, p. 24)

If the early childhood centre is one of the main foundations of a re-designed early childhood education, another is a core early childhood profession to work in these centres. That profession may be an early childhood 'teacher' or 'pedagogue',[2] different countries opting for different professional traditions and identities. But whatever the choice, the profession is distinguished by specialisation in working with children below compulsory school age and their families. It is, in other words, a 0 to 6 profession,[3] which is not premised on younger being lesser in any sense: so it is a profession that has parity with all other teachers or pedagogues, in line with the recommendation of the European-funded CoRe (Competence Requirements in Early Childhood Education and Care) project that '[t]here can, in principle, be no justification for applying different (lower) standards to the early childhood profession' (Competence Requirements in Early Childhood Education and Care, 2011, p. 50). This means a comparable level of initial education, at present mostly at Bachelor level but increasingly moving to Masters level; comparable opportunities for professional development including access to higher degrees (discussed further below); and comparable pay and conditions.

The last point may seem rather prosaic, amidst a discussion of utopian transformation suffused with lofty values. But it is in fact vital and radical. For far too long, large swathes of the early childhood workforce have consisted of poorly educated and lowly paid 'childcare workers' (OECD, 2006), while even graduate professional workers have often not had parity of pay and other employment conditions with their peers in compulsory schooling. Take the situation in England, where in 2011 the average pay of childcare workers, the bulk of the early childhood workforce, was just under £8 an hour, with more for heads (£9.80 per hour in playgroups, £10.60 in full-day childcare), but much less for non-supervisory staff working directly with children (£6.80 and £6.60 respectively). This can be compared, for 2011, with the national minimum wage of £6.08 an hour (for workers aged 21 and over), the London Living Wage (intended to provide for 'a minimally acceptable quality of life' in London) of £8.30 an hour, and the average national hourly wage of £14.76 (Brand et al., 2012, Tables 5.16–19). In other words, 'childcare workers' in direct everyday contact with children earn just above the legal minimum and less than half of average earnings.

This state of affairs (which is not, it should be emphasised, confined to England) is a scandal, symptomatic of societies trying to get important work done on the cheap by exploiting women workers. But it is not just wrong, it is also short-sighted, a blatant false economy. Low pay and education cannot provide a basis for the complex and demanding work required for good early childhood education and are totally incompatible with the image of the educator outlined in Chapter 4 or the creative pedagogical work of educators exemplified in the Crow Project. It devalues the work itself, the people who do it and young children themselves, treating them all by implication as lesser than what follows in the education hierarchy. It contributes to the growth of debased low-paid employment and an economy of 'crappy jobs', ignoring the opportunity provided by expanding early childhood education to increase good employment. It cannot have any part in a story of democracy, experimentation and potentiality.

The early childhood teacher or pedagogue will be the core of the workforce, but not the whole workforce. There will also be a group of other educators working alongside the professional group, but with a lower level of initial qualification, though what proportion of the educator workforce they should be is still uncertain: somewhere, probably, between the 40 per cent implied in the EC Childcare Network's target quoted at the start of this section and the 20 per cent implied by the New Zealand target of an 80 per cent graduate workforce (Mitchell, 2011). Furthermore, multi-purpose centres will have need of other types of worker – from health, social work, community and other backgrounds – to enable those purposes and projects that fall outside the immediate domain of the teacher or pedagogue.

One final point about the early childhood workforce in a re-designed early childhood education concerns its composition. It is important, I believe, for it to be representative of the wider population, in terms of age, ethnicity, disability, sexuality and, above all, gender. I say 'above all' because it is on gender that current early childhood workforces everywhere are least representative of the population at large, with an overwhelmingly female composition, and because it is gender that has proven most stubbornly resistant to change. My argument for the importance of a representative workforce is not because I believe in some simplified and essentialist concept of gender (as in 'boys need a male role model') that denies the complexity and fluidity of identities; but because it creates more diverse pedagogical communities, broadens the experiences and perspectives of the workforce, and undermines stereotypical thinking that has so adversely affected understandings of early childhood work (as in 'young children are women's work' and 'any woman can naturally do the work').

It is not the remit of this book to discuss in detail how to achieve this re-composition of the workforce, a re-composition leading to diversity becoming 'the norm not the exception'.[4] I am, however, convinced it is feasible, even the most intractable challenge of moving towards a mixed gendered workforce. But for this to happen, there must be a strong and sustained political commitment; and this must be backed by carefully researched and constructed strategies covering recruitment, education and everyday work, and underpinned by careful use of targets and monitoring.

The educative commune

While the educational reforms promoted by the [Italian] central government in those years [1960s and 1970s] remained anchored to conservative positions and, in practice, failed to fully realise the right to education for all children through compulsory schooling, innovative educational practices were being initiated at the local level, in schools run by progressive local authorities, through the commitment of educators, parents and municipal administrators. The experience of municipal early childhood services initiated by Loris Malaguzzi in Reggio Emilia and the experience of scuola a tempo pieno promoted by Bruno Ciari in Bologna are only two of many examples that attest to how local experimentalism made a significant contribution to the debate on educational continuity in Italy.

(Balducci and Lazzari, 2013, pp. 151–2)

I have already introduced the notion of the 'educative commune', in Chapter 4, a democratically elected and accountable local body, usually a commune, municipality or local authority, though in some cases the role might be played by a more specialist 'education board'. I call this body 'educative' to recognise its important role in local public education, representing the local citizenry's interest in and responsibility for that education. Early childhood centres should be democratically accountable to such bodies; but educative communes, in turn, should be responsible and accountable for early childhood education in their areas, making an important contribution to the enactment of the story of democracy, experimentation and potentiality.

How might the educative commune exercise this responsibility for a public early childhood education? First and foremost, the educative commune, representing and accountable to its citizenry, *proclaims the public responsibility for and the public interest in education*, insisting education is a matter for all citizens and not just those who are parents of young children or professional educators; it also *proclaims the centrality of democracy in this public education*. We gave an example of this in Chapter 4, when we quoted from the 2009 regulations of the *comune* of Reggio Emilia, which included the unequivocal statement that '[e]ducation is the right of all, of all children, and as such is a responsibility of the community' and that this education 'is a meeting place where freedom, democracy and solidarity are practiced and where the value of peace is promoted' (Comune di Reggio Emilia, 2009, p. 5).

The educative commune *acts as an a dvocate, mediator and interpreter* between the very local early childhood centre and the more distant nation state. Where the nation state is highly centralised, then this is more difficult; the local authority can be reduced, as happens for example in England, to an agent of central government power, to be dictated to, overridden or tossed aside when central government no longer feels the need for it or sees it as a hindrance to its own exercise of power. But in a decentralised democracy, founded on the principle of subsidiarity, then the 'educative commune' can play this vital and creative role of intermediary. National frameworks, such as curricula, should allow scope not only for local interpretation, but also for local supplementation, and the educative commune can coordinate and incorporate local responses. While, equally important, the educative commune can represent local views to, and share local experiences with, central government, which recognises its own limitations, including its inability to understand fully the complexity and diverse contexts of the nation's many constituent parts.

The educative commune *plays a direct, active role in a local and democratic public education*: it is one of the main protagonists. As already mentioned, it is a direct provider of some services. But another aspect of this role is playing an active role in creating and implementing a local educational project: 'a shared and democratic exploration of the meaning and practice of education and the potential of the school . . . [providing] an educational context and ethos, as well as a forum for exchange, confrontation, dialogue and learning between schools' (Fielding and Moss, 2011, p. 125). Such projects – exemplified by Reggio Emilia's 50-year-long local educational project with its distinctive pedagogical identity constituted by particular understandings, theories and practices – provide one means of initiating and sustaining 'democratic experimentalism' and pedagogical movement. Their starting point can, indeed should, be the political questions we discussed in earlier chapters, following the example of Reggio Emilia whose municipal project derives from its answer to the question 'what is our image of the child?' It may well be, as in Reggio Emilia, that not all schools choose to participate in such a local project, but it provides one possibility for collective experimentation and for linking democracy and experimentation.

The educative commune provides *support for the implementation and evaluation of the local educational project.* It actively fosters collaboration between centres, encouraging the creation of networks to enhance cooperation both for specific, shorter-term projects and in the longer term; and it builds an infrastructure to support democratic experimentalism and pedagogical movement. This infrastructure can include various shared resources and activities, for example: seminars, conferences and study groups; environmental services; archive and documentation centres; and access to a wide range of publications and other sources of information and inspiration. Of particular importance, this infrastructure includes teams of *pedagogistas*, pedagogical coordinators or counsellors, each working with a few centres, offering educators opportunities for exchange, reflection and discussion, introducing them to new thinking and practices, and facilitating contact between centres, local communities and the commune itself.

Carlina Rinaldi, Reggio Emilia's first *pedagogista* in 1970, describes the crucial role played by the local authority team of *pedagogistas* in the educative commune, within the city's 'municipal schools'. The team acts, she says, as:

a sort of metaphorical 'place' which fosters dialogue between schools and within the schools themselves, a place which gives direction, which has to have a sense and a role of cultural and pedagogical responsibility, but also a political responsibility toward the schools and the city. This is why it should be 'a place not only of words but also of listening'. It is a link, yet again, between theory and practice. But where should it take its inspiration from? From the schools! From the schools and from the culture, indeed from the cultures and the most advanced research in all the disciplines. The great ability of the team is to keep abreast of things because of its ability to be attentive to the voices of all. It has to be able to listen to the voices of the auxiliary staff, of the parents, of the teachers, and has to be able to talk with them.

(Rinaldi, 2006, p. 160)

So the *pedagogistas* listen, they dialogue, and they foster reflection, professional development and the relationship between theory and practice. They make links, they cultivate collaboration and they strengthen networks: between schools, between schools and their communities and the city itself, and between schools and the educational project of the educative commune. They facilitate the sharing of experiences and knowledge, the dissemination of research and experimentation through networks of centres. They are, Rinaldi says, 'responsible for the relationship between the inside and the outside world' (ibid., p. 167), making connections, crossing borders, improving flows, offering new perspectives. By doing so, they can foster active participation in the local educational project and cultivate a shared educational identity.

Annalia Galardini, the head of early childhood education in Pistoia, another Italian city which has created its own local educational project (for more on this project, see Galardini and Giovannini, 2001; Musatti *et al.*, 2014), describes the team of *pedagogistas* in that local authority as 'a decisive factor in the quality of local networks of services' and develops Rinaldi's discussion of the *pedagogista* role:

> [The *pedagogista's* role] is to nurture and improve the quality of educational policies for children . . . One of the *pedagogista's* strategic functions has been to guarantee a link between the various services in order to develop a unified educational identity and a shared perception of children's needs. This coordination function emphasises dialogue and collaboration between educators, schools and families . . . [The role] has meant giving visibility to good practices, guiding individual services away from a self-referential educational style, and, above all, the opportunity to project the identity of the nurseries and nursery schools to the outside community . . . This has been the *pedagogista's* task: to ensure that there are links between the services in order to create networks and to set down roots in the local area; and to foster a spirit of collaboration and open-mindedness in order to raise awareness and sensitivity in the local community about children's rights and the function of nurseries and nursery school.
>
> (Galardini, 2008, p. 18)

Pedagogistas are widely used in areas of Northern Italy, not just in Reggio Emilia and Pistoia, and are to be found also today in some other countries, such as Sweden. But there are other examples of local authorities that have built up infrastructural support to early childhood centres, including the German institution of *Fachberatung* (pedagogical counselling) and the Pedagogical Advisory Centre in the Belgian city of Ghent (Kaga *et al.*, 2010). The importance of such backing for enacting a story of democracy, experimentation and potentiality cannot be overestimated.

There will be many other possible roles for an educative commune, but four more will suffice for now. The educative commune has a duty *to develop a democratic public education*; it needs a passionate and proclaimed commitment to democracy, but it has to go beyond the rhetoric of democracy, beyond insisting on its importance, to engage actively with the hard work of implementation. The educative commune has a *commitment to local experimentalism*, both initiating experimentation and supporting centres who wish to experiment. The educative commune is *politically accountable for public education* provided in its community, as well as being a public body to which centres themselves are accountable. And the educative commune manages *certain administrative tasks* in a democratic and transparent way, such as planning, admissions and data collection.

The educative commune may be a leading player in a local, democratic and public education project. But it need not be the only player operating on a larger scale than the individual centre and acting to link these centres with a wider community. Richard Hatcher (2012) proposes Local Education Forums, open to all with an interest in education, their purpose being 'to take positions on all key policy issues' and its mode of operating 'based on participative deliberative democracy'. Such Forums could play an important role in creating, implementing and evaluating local educational projects, offering additional spaces for participatory democracy and helping better connect local authority, communities and schools. The educative commune, as part of its duty to develop a democratic public education, could take responsibility for creating and supporting this instance of 'mass deliberation in the public realm . . . an absolutely crucial process in a democratic and open society' (Power Inquiry, 2006, p. 11).

Such public meeting places could be further supplemented by other opportunities for encounter between educators and fellow citizens, for example summer schools (still found today in Barcelona and other towns in Spain); or the 'Pedagogical Februaries' that took place for some years in Bologna in the 1960s, which were open seminars initiated by the city and organised by educational experts, but aimed at involving all members of civil society:

> The purpose of these initiatives – that took place every year in February – was to bring the debate on education [to] the centre of society . . . The idea underpinning [these initiatives] was that education should be considered an issue concerning the whole society and, as such, it needs to be debated within meetings in public spaces.
>
> (Lazzari, 2011, pp. 53–4)

Such forums, summer schools and seminars can be conceptualised as 'pedagogical meeting places', a concept that could be extended to include other encounters that might be initiated by an educative commune. One such meeting place, envisaged by Gunilla Dahlberg and Hillevi Lenz Taguchi in a paper written in 1994 for a Swedish government commission, is between early childhood and compulsory education. In their 1994 paper, *Preschool and School – Two Different*

Traditions and the Vision of a Meeting Place, Dahlberg and Lenz Taguchi note a general tendency in the relationship between early childhood and compulsory education: 'that the education system tends to go further down in age'. This downward pressure on early childhood education, or 'schoolification', has already been discussed in Chapter 2, including the potentially serious consequences that can follow from the subordinating of early childhood education to the demands and perspectives of compulsory schooling.

But how to get a more equal relationship? The core of the problem, as these two Swedish authors see it, is that the two forms of education in Sweden have different traditions, leading to quite different understandings of education and learning. In particular, they have two separate understandings or images of the child – 'the child as nature' and 'the child as a re-producer of culture and knowledge' – so that 'the preschool has taken a position opposite to that of the school'.

In a later book, Dahlberg describes this image of the child as nature, prevalent in the Swedish preschool, as 'an essential being of universal properties and inherent capabilities whose development is viewed as an innate "natural" process – biologically determined, following general laws . . . [in] a standard sequence of biological stages that constitute a path to full realization' (Dahlberg *et al.*, 2013, p. 49). This tradition and image values a holistic view of the child; free play and creativity, giving rise to free and self-confident people; free expression of ideas and feelings; fun; and the here and now.

By contrast, the Swedish school is 'dominated by the reproduction of the prevailing culture and knowledge', and hence an understanding of the child as a 're-producer of culture and knowledge'. This child is understood as starting life 'as an empty vessel or tabula rasa . . . [needing] to be filled with knowledge, skills and dominant cultural values which are already determined, socially determined and ready to administer – a process of reproduction or transmission' (ibid., p. 48). With this image of the child in mind, there is a far greater emphasis in the school, compared with the preschool, on the future and economic life. The school is subject centred, meaning that 'the basis for all activities is linked to the learning of concrete subject knowledge . . . with the transfer of concrete and assessable knowledge as the goal'. These subjects are mostly decided and organised by others, and not the children, in contrast to the 'preschool's tradition of child-centredness, where the ideal is that the child, as much as possible, should choose the contents and forms of expression'.

What is to be done given such very different understandings in the preschool and the school? Not one sector colonising the other; nor each sector simply taking on the better bits of the other. Instead Dahlberg and Lenz Taguchi propose early childhood and compulsory education coming together in pedagogical 'meeting places' to create a new and shared 'common view' about education. This, the authors suggest, might be based on a new and shared image or understanding of the child not as nature, not as reproducer – but as a constructor of culture and knowledge and an investigative child:

The idea that the child is a constructor of culture and knowledge builds a respect for the child as competent and curious – a child who is filled with a desire to learn, to research and develop as a human being in an interactive relationship with other people. It is a rich child. A child who takes an active part in the process of constructing knowledge.

I argued in Chapter 2 that the idea that early childhood education's role is to ready or prepare children for compulsory school is contestable, based on a hierarchical motion of education in which each stage is subservient to the next. The concept of a meeting place offers a very different set of relationships between each part of the education system, equal in status and dialogic and democratic in process. And the educative commune could, in my view, play an important part in fostering such relationships, not least by creating actual pedagogical meeting places.

What all these examples of meeting places have in common is the possibility for the educative commune to adopt an important role: to stimulate and sustain a democratic politics of education in its home area, nurturing the concept of public education and contributing to the re-politicisation and democratisation of education. In short, the educative commune playing a key role in the renewal of a democratic public education.

National government

A systematic approach entails developing a common policy framework with consistent goals across the system (e.g. with regard to staffing, financing, programmes etc.) and clearly defined roles and responsibilities at both central and decentralised levels of governance . . . Coherence and co-ordination is facilitated by integrated administrative responsibility.

(OECD, 2001, p. 127)

The task of national government (shared, in some federal countries, with state governments) in the design of a transformed early childhood education is, first and foremost and alongside local educative communes, to *proclaim the public responsibility for and the public interest in education*, insisting education is a matter for all citizens; as well as to *affirm the centrality of democracy in this public education*. Its second task is to create *a coherent and consistent national policy framework* for early childhood education that is supportive of the story of democracy, experimentation and potentiality. Such a framework calls for integrated policy-making and administrative responsibility for early childhood education: this requires responsibility to be located within one government department – not two departments (education and welfare), as is still the case in the split systems of early childhood education that continue to predominate in the world today and create inequalities, discontinuities and other dysfunctionalities (for a fuller discussion, see Kaga *et al.*, 2010). That one department is most likely to be education, as it is today in nearly all of those countries that have adopted integrated responsibility (these include all five Nordic countries, the Baltic states, Slovenia, Croatia, Brazil, New Zealand and England).

The national policy framework is built on a political statement, which sets out democratically determined answers to political questions, including the fundamental values of early childhood education. From there, it continues to cover five main structural areas that, between them, support a common and seamless approach across the whole system, not one approach for 'childcare' services and another one for 'early education' services, nor one approach for children under 3 years and another for children over 3 years:

- entitlement: all children and families to have access, as of right, to early childhood centres from birth (bearing in mind that these are multi-purpose services, so that access for very young children, under a year or so, may mainly mean to projects for child and parent or even just to support parents);[5]
- funding and resources: a common system of supply side funding, involving tax-based financing of centres themselves, ensuring either free or low cost attendance;
- curriculum: a broad statement of concepts, values, purposes and goals for early childhood education, including an integrative concept of education-in-its-broadest sense, in which care is viewed as inseparable from learning, and democracy and experimentation as fundamental values;
- workforce: defining the structure, roles, education and status of the workforce, as well as goals for a representative composition, and assuring parity with comparable professionals such as school teachers or other pedagogues;
- type of provision: setting out the main characteristics of the preferred type of provision for the public system of early childhood education, and conditions to be met for the receipt of public funding.

This framework provides a clear statement of intent and structure for a system that is uniform in certain important respects. But, to return to a recurrent theme, it should also enable diversity of projects and practices. I have already touched on one way in which this can be done, through a broadly defined 'framework' curriculum, which leaves plenty of scope for local interpretation and for local supplementation, to express local conditions and traditions and locally determined values and objectives. Such an early childhood curriculum can be found in the Nordic countries and New Zealand. Other examples include what the Royal Society of Arts in London has termed an 'Area Based Curriculum', which uses 'the local area to illustrate curriculum content, and [uses] local stakeholders (including young people) to co-design the curriculum . . . supporting schools to partner with organisations or groups from the local area to design aspects of the curriculum utilising the local area as a resource' (Thomas, 2011, p. 298); or the proposal of the Cambridge Primary Review (2009) for a curriculum divided between nationally determined and local determined components, to account for 70 and 30 per cent of teaching time respectively.

Another way to enable such diversity is by a national policy framework that actively encourages experimentation, both in pedagogical work and in other projects (for example, with parents or with other members of local communities) undertaken by early childhood centres. What is being proposed is the state assuming a new purpose and ethos, becoming a social agent for experimentation, something envisaged by de Sousa Santos:

> Rather than impose one form of sociability, the state must be made to create the conditions for social experimentation, that is, the conditions necessary so that alternative sociabilities may be credibly experimented with in each of the six structural spaces [household, work, market, community, citizenship, world]. This implies a profound transformation of the welfare state. In the paradigmatic transition, the welfare state is the state form that guarantees social experimentation.
>
> (Santos, 1995, p. 483)

Unger's concept of democratic experimentalism refers to 'the organisation of collective experimental practice from below'. But he, too, envisages a role for the state. This role includes helping 'to produce new social agents who can provide [new] services . . . in a form which is both customised and innovative'; and helping to 'propagate the most successful practices, accelerating the process of experimental winnowing out of what does not work' (Unger, 2005b, p. 179).

A third and more concrete example of the state actively promoting experimentation, specifically in the field of early childhood education, is the Centres of Innovation action research programme launched in 2002 by the New Zealand government as part of its ten-year strategic plan for early childhood education, *Pathways to the Future: Nga-Huarahi Arataki*. Funded by the New Zealand Department of Education, the aim of the initiative was to challenge teachers' practice and foster their research development by building innovative approaches, facilitating local action research and sharing the resulting knowledge, understanding and practice with others in the early childhood sector. Before being closed down at short notice in May 2009, by a newly elected right wing government as a cost-cutting measure, there were five rounds of this programme, each focused on innovation in specified areas: for example, improved links between services developing as 'learning communities'; infants' and toddlers' care and education; and inclusive Early Childhood Education for diverse children and families. The successive rounds involved practitioner teams in 20 early childhood services, each team working with a research associate to 'promote a deeper exploration of innovative teaching and learning processes', as well as developing dissemination strategies to share their experiences with other centres.[6]

New Zealand is unusual, though not unique, in the minor role played in early childhood education by local authorities; national government is essentially the only level of government significantly involved. In most countries, though, local authorities – communes, municipalities, local councils – are protagonists alongside national government. Any design for early childhood education, therefore, has to specify a relationship between local and national; nor can this relationship be treated in isolation from the wider issue of how local and national government relate across the main fields in which they are both involved.

My assumption is that national governments set frameworks, as already described, and that local authorities work within those frameworks, but with substantial scope for interpretation, supplementation and experimentation. This is a model of decentralised government and subsidiarity, benefiting from and sometimes troubled by, the inherent tension between the local and the national. Local authorities are accountable to national government for their implementation of the national framework; but both are also engaged in a learning relationship, in which national government benefits from local knowledge generated by local authorities and distributes new knowledge so created to other local areas. There is a national story shared by all; but this is continuously enriched by hearing local stories with their accounts of local innovations.

The academy

> Two scenarios may be outlined for the future of social science. In the first – and today, dominant – scenario, it is scientism, the belief that science holds a reliable method of reaching the truth about the nature of things, which continues to dominate social science . . . The second scenario replaces scientism with phrenosis. Here the purpose of social science is not to develop epistemic theory, but to contribute to society's practical rationality by elucidating where we are, where we want to go, and what is desirable according to different sets of values and interests.
>
> (Flyvbjerg, 2006, p. 43)

> The University is where thought takes place besides thought, where thinking is a shared process without identity or unity . . . 'thinking together' is a dissensual process.
>
> (Readings, 1996, p. 192)

I should make it clear from the beginning that I do not view the academy – institutions of higher education and research – as the sole fount of knowledge and research. Through pedagogical documentation and collaboration between educators and *pedagogistas*, the early childhood centre can be 'one of the most privileged places for the building of professional competence and knowledge' (Rinaldi, 2006, p. 58). I note the comments of Jerome Bruner on visiting centres in Reggio Emilia that 'it is like a seminar at the graduate department of the university, with the same kind of respect, of exchange in talking about what you have just said, and about your former thinking' (ibid.). I note, too, a strong belief among Reggio Emilia's educators in the importance of research as part of their work, research 'ceasing to be a privilege of the few [in universities and other designated places]' and understood instead as 'the stance, the attitude with which teachers approach the sense and meaning of life' (ibid., p. 148). Furthermore, we hear Rinaldi's frustration when she speaks of what she perceives as a dismissive attitude by universities towards teachers as researchers:

> [I]t's not that we don't recognise your [academic] research, but we want our research, as teachers, to be recognised. And to recognise research as a way of thinking, of approaching life, of negotiating, of documenting. It's all research. It's also a context that allows dialogue. Dialogue generates research, research generates dialogue . . . Can you find a university teacher who can learn from a practitioner? Very rarely! That is why Malaguzzi was never recognised and I think will never be recognised as a researcher. But to do good practice means to continue to do research, to continue the theory . . . [So] we [in Reggio] are, first of all, researchers.
>
> (ibid., p. 192)

This is very salutary and should give cause to those of us working in the academy to think very carefully and very humbly about its contribution to a re-designed early childhood education. It has an important part to play. But only if it can build a respectful, dialogic and collaborative relationship, a democratic relationship, with educators in early childhood centres and with educative communes; taking part, indeed, in a process of dismantling hierarchical thinking about different parts of the education system, a thinking reflected when people refer to one part 'preparing' children or young people for the next part.

One basis for such a democratic relationship is the adoption of what economic geographer Bent Flyvbjerg calls a 'phronetic' position in research, in contrast to an 'epistemic' position that seeks to discover and apply objective and universal theories and laws and is suited to the natural but not the social sciences. Phronetic social science recognises such certainties are impossible in the social sciences 'because the phenomena modelled are social, and thus "answer back" in ways natural phenomena do not' (Flyvbjerg, 2006, p. 39). Phronetic social scientists are aware, too, of the importance of perspective and context and the inescapability of interpretation, and thus adopt a democratic approach of *modus vivendi*, which acknowledges that their interpretation is only one of many that are possible and should as such be considered along with others in democratic processes of public deliberation. Flyvbjerg, a proponent of a phronetic role for the social sciences, concludes that:

> [t]hough imperfect, no better device than public deliberation following the rules of constitutional democracy has been arrived at for settling social issues . . . Social science must therefore play into this device if it is to be useful . . . No one voice, including that of the researcher, may claim final authority . . . [P]hronetic social science explicitly sees itself as not having a privileged position from which the final truth can be told and further discussion arrested . . . To the phronetic researcher, this is the reality of social science, in contrast to researchers who act as if validity claims can and should be given final grounding (and with it, total acceptance). By substituting phronesis for episteme, phronetic social scientists avoid trying to lift this impossible burden.
>
> (ibid., pp. 39, 41)

Assuming then this phronetic sensibility and the laying aside of claims by academic social science to a privileged position, claims founded on a false belief that such science 'holds a reliable method of reaching the truth about the nature of things', I would identify three roles for the academy in the enactment of a story of democracy, experimentalism and potentiality. First, the *provision of initial education* for the 0 to 6 early childhood profession, either to a Bachelor's or Master's level, together with opportunities for post-graduate studies, up to and including doctoral level. While believing that the place for such education is in academia, rather than some workplace-based system of apprenticeship or learning on the job, I also believe that this education must be based on a strong relationship between theory and practice, and therefore between academia and early childhood centres: such 'close collaboration guarantees a reciprocal interaction between theory and practice in both learning environments, and supports the development of critical reflection as a core professional competence during initial professional preparation' (Competence Requirements in Early Childhood Education and Care, 2011, p. 50).

Second, *working with new theoretical perspectives* and supporting their introduction into early childhood education so as to stimulate experimentation and a dialogue between theory and practice. These theoretical perspectives can and should be diverse and wide-ranging, drawing on many disciplines and different paradigms. The story of quality and high returns suffers from being confined to one paradigmatic position (ignoring or unaware of others) and overly dependent on just a few disciplines, notably developmental psychology and economics. As I hope this book has demonstrated from the range of authors cited, early childhood education has much to gain from listening to other disciplinary narrators – sociologists, political theorists, geographers, philosophers, historians, to name but a few – and exploring other paradigmatic positions.

Bearing in mind this plea for diversity in this role of working with new theoretical perspectives, the academy can be a space for the initial work of reading into and deepening understanding of such new perspectives; as well as initiating the task of putting them to work, seeing how they could offer early childhood education new thought and practices, providing stimuli for experimentation. One way the academy can do this innovative and applied work is through close relationships with early childhood educators, via degree or other courses, professional development and collaborative action research.

The book *Doing Foucault in Early Childhood Studies*, published in this series, provides an example. The author, Glenda MacNaughton, an Australian academic with a deep interest in post-structural theories and their application in early childhood education, includes vignettes from 'early childhood educator-researchers', who are 'using the ideas of Foucault and poststructuralists to create and sustain critical reflection and activism in their everyday life in early childhood studies' (2005, p. 3). Here one of these educator-researchers, Sally Barnes, an experienced teacher and centre director describes the impact of new theoretical perspectives, introduced to her by Glenda, on her and her work:

> In the initial stages of looking at my work through a poststructural lens, I was shocked and unsettled by what I saw (although I realise now that what I was seeing was always there) . . . As a teacher, developmentalism no longer drives my understandings of the child or my curriculum decisions, nor does it justify practices that discriminate, disadvantage or exclude. Instead, I see the kindergarten as a space where power and desire . . . [go] to the heart of our experience as human beings and seems far more important than whether a child can hold a pencil with a mature pencil grip. Without hesitation I would say that engaging with poststructural ideas has enriched my teaching. I am more articulate and confident about my work, my understandings of the child are deeper and richer and my educational work is more intellectually stimulating than I ever imagined it could be or would be.
>
> (cited in MacNaughton, 2005, p. 16)

The book *Movement and Experimentation in Early Childhood Education* by Liselott Mariett Olsson (2009), also published in this series, presents a second example from the opposite side of the world. It shows Swedish preschool teachers and Liselott working together with inspiration both from Reggio Emilia and from the theories of Deleuze and Guattari, as part of professional development work undertaken by the Stockholm Institute of Education (now subsumed into the University of Stockholm). At the time, Liselott was a doctoral student at the Institute, one of Gunilla Dahlberg's research group, members of whom were working not only with Deleuzian theory and its application to pedagogical work, but also with: pedagogical documentation from the perspective of Foucauldian and Derridean theories; the preschool environment read from a Foucauldian perspective; and post-structural theories and aesthetics. Here can be seen the mingling of ideas and perspectives, not just the educational project of Reggio Emilia, but also French philosophical theorists, which has been a feature of the most innovative work in Sweden. As well as being a doctoral student herself, Liselott was a teacher educator at the Institute who, through in-service training courses, worked closely with many preschools and *kommuner*. Prior to that, she had worked as a preschool teacher for nearly a decade, during which time she was herself introduced to new theoretical perspectives via the Institute of Education, another example of the academy's role in disseminating new thinking to early childhood teachers and pedagogues.

Here Liselott describes the emerging process of dialogue and engagement between teachers and academics in the 1990s, of which she was a part as a preschool teacher prior to becoming a doctoral student and university educator; and some of the consequences for the ways teachers approached and thought about their work. It shows how the process worked with, and put to work, new theoretical perspectives as well as concepts and practices from Reggio Emilia. This Swedish experience resonates with the experience taking place in Australia, not least in a critical stance both take towards developmental psychology as a dominant discourse:

> In 1993 a government funded project [the Stockholm Project led by Gunilla Dahlberg and discussed in Chapter 5] was started up in some preschools in Skarpnäck, a commune in Stockholm, where ideas about children, teachers, and preschool environments, content and form were questioned and experimented with (Barsotti, Dahlberg, Göthson and Åsén, 1993). The research group 'The Ethics and Aesthetics of Learning', at the Stockholm Institute of Education, led by Professor Gunilla Dahlberg, worked with the preschools, using poststructural and Foucault-inspired discourse analysis, to challenge the dominant discourse of developmental psychology, in which the child already has got its position and predetermined development, and where learning is seen as a question of transmission and reproductive imitation. Taken for granted images of the child were deconstructed. The image of the child as a rich child capable of constructing knowledge, presented in the preschools in the Italian city of Reggio Emilia, was offered to the Swedish preschools as an alternative image of the child . . .
>
> All this was done as a way of inspiring and giving tools to these preschools to be able to begin a process of changing their practices (Dahlberg and Moss, 2005). Many other Swedish communes followed up the efforts being made in Skarpnäck, for instance Trångsund, south of Stockholm, and Bromma, west of Stockholm. The research group served as a meeting place for practice and research. In the mid 1990s, a network was created called 'Pedagogical and Theoretical Spaces'. In this context teachers, teacher students, teacher educators and researchers have met together to work with questioning preschool practices and making room for them to change. The Swedish preschools involved in these efforts have now many

years of experience of how to question and deconstruct one's own practice, and they have produced alternative ways of thinking of the child, the teacher and the preschool's environment, content and form.

(Olsson, 2009, p. 7)

In a more recent research project about language, reading and writing, 'The Magic of Language', funded by the Swedish Research Council, Olsson again shows the rich possibilities for invention arising from collaboration between academics and practitioners working with new philosophical perspectives, taking further earlier work with the theoretical perspectives of Deleuze and Guattari. The project involves a group of researchers, PhD students, principals and teachers from four preschools, an *atelierista* and *pedagogistas* and student teachers, and creates knowledge through experimentation and documentation:

> Data collection and analysis was conducted through children, teachers and researchers collectively experimenting with literacy in practice, departing from a problem-based approach and working with documentation (observations, film sequences, interviews and children's artefacts) as events . . . Theoretical concepts are used pragmatically and in order to broaden the domains for the experimental work, and practical experimentations are used so as to intensify theoretical concepts . . . [This context] is still very much a context in progress; we are constantly struggling to keep a balance between theory and practice. This relation between theory and practice, or concepts and practical experimentations, seems to us to not be something you can make into standardised method.
>
> (Olsson, 2013, pp. 232–3)

Third, with the important provisos already introduced of the need for a phronetic sensibility and acknowledgement of the contribution of educator-researchers, the academy has an important role to play in *research* about early childhood education. In the current climate, dominated by the story of quality and high returns, much academic research has been in a technical role, acting as 'a producer of means, strategies, and techniques to achieve given ends' (Biesta, 2007, p. 18); in particular seeking more effective technologies to maximise return on investment. It has frequently been highly positivistic and reductive, adopting the presumptions of epistemic science in its claims to offer universal and certain results uncluttered by context or complexity; results that not only claim to hold good anywhere, but do not question the given ends, results that are taken to be firm evidential foundations on which to build policy and practice (like the 'iconic' US studies discussed in Chapter 2).

There will always be a role for technical research. But that role must be understood as producing evidence that requires interpretation, not least to take account of context and perspective: no evidence, by and of itself, can tell us what we must do. Moreover that role must not be at the expense of other roles and approaches. Research, for example, has an important role to play in developing a democratic politics of education, by applying critical thought and alternative perspectives. As Biesta comments, drawing on work by De Vries:

> [The technical role for research] is only one of the ways in which research can be practically relevant . . . [Another is] by providing a different way of understanding and imagining social reality . . . the *cultural role* of research. The first thing that is important about de Vries's distinction [between a technical and a cultural role for research] is that it allows us to see that the provision of instrumental knowledge is not the only way in which educational research can inform and be beneficial for educational practice. While there is an important task for educational research in finding, testing, and evaluating different forms of educational action, research can also play a valuable role in helping educational practitioners to acquire a different understanding of their practice, in helping them to see and imagine their practice differently.
>
> (ibid., p. 19)

Research built around pedagogical documentation – a good meeting place for educators and academics – is one way of pursuing the cultural role of research; the use of pedagogical documentation in the Crow Project and the new understandings it enabled provides an example. Another way is for research to be built around critical case studies, strategically chosen with the aim of fostering understanding, reflection and action, and which 'stay close to the complexities and contradictions of existence' (Lather, 2006, p. 788); for example, studies of innovative early childhood centres or of experimentation with new ways of working.

This brings the discussion back again to the importance of a close relationship between theory and practice, and between the academy and early childhood education, with a thick network of connections built up through degree and other courses, continuous professional development and the creation of various forums for dialogue and mutual learning – early childhood educators gaining access to new theoretical perspectives and research emanating from the academy; academics accessing the results generated by educators from working with these new theoretical perspectives and from research into learning processes and other subjects, in particular emanating from pedagogical documentation.

In sum, the academy can make an important contribution to an early childhood education of democracy, experimentation and potentiality. But not by assuming a privileged position that claims unique access to truth. Rather the academy should be what Bill Readings calls a 'community of dissensus' (1996, p. 180): a place that enables people, both within and outwith, to think; a place 'where thought takes place besides thought'; a place that welcomes diverse thinking and alternative stories; a place where critical thinking contests dominant narratives and makes the familiar strange; a place that fuels democracy by helping society deliberate on political questions; and a place that can stimulate experimentation by also helping society to formulate and implement answers to these questions.

Evaluation and accountability

> The question, then, is how we can raise the question of accountability as something that exceeds the logic of accounting.
>
> (Readings, 1996, p. 164)

> Achievement grows out of the internal goods of motivation to improve (that follows recognition and the mutual deliberation of purpose) rather than the external imposition of quantifiable targets, while public trust follows deliberation of common purpose out of difference and discord, rather than forces of competition that only create a hierarchy of class advantage and exclusion. Trust and achievement can only emerge in a framework of public accountability that enables different accounts of public purpose and practice to be deliberated in a democratic public sphere: constituted to include difference, enable participation, voice and dissent, through to collective judgement and decision, that is in turn accountable to the public.
>
> (Ransom, 2003, p. 476)

Whatever the story enacted, whatever the institutional design created, evaluation and accountability must play an important part. On that, most story tellers can agree. But how do we understand evaluation and accountability? For what purposes are they undertaken? Given answers to these questions, what types of organisation and what processes are involved?

There are, of course, various forms of accountability, each calling for a particular form of evaluation. Professional accountability leaves the field to professional review and self-discipline; professionals are accountable to professional codes and bodies that set standards for behaviour, evaluate their peers to keep them up to the mark, and determine what constitutes misconduct. Bureaucratic accountability calls on services to follow certain specified procedures, evaluating them according to whether or not they act by the rule book. While consumer accountability, prominent in the story of markets, views evaluation as a matter for the individual consumer, the service provider striving to keep the confidence and custom of the consumer, who is free to transfer that custom to another provider if they lose confidence in the original provider.

The story of quality and high returns takes us into the field of managerial accountability, which is about performativity: the incessant measurement of individual or service performance in relation to explicit, predetermined standards, targets or other outcomes, with goal-setting and measurement assumed to be objective, technical, transparent. To further control performance, practitioners and services may be required to use selected strategies or programmes chosen for their apparent effectiveness as evidenced in previous research studies. Such processes enable effective governing through the enforcement of quasi-contractual obligations, ranging from the goals set in appraisals to the performance indicators that will trigger payment by results. This is 'the logic of accounting', accounting being adopted as 'a powerful technology for acting at a distance on the actions of others . . . a control mechanism for governing at a distance' (Rose, 1999, pp. 152, 154), a defining feature of what has been termed an audit society.

Evaluation in this instance requires making ourselves or our services calculable and comparable through predefined and quantifiable outcomes: evaluation as a statement of fact based on accurate measurement of performance. Has individual A achieved agreed goal B? Has service C delivered outcome D? Following through to its logical conclusion, the evaluation is reduced to whether service C produces the pre-specified results it has been contracted to achieve using an also pre-specified 'evidence-based' programme: if it 'delivers', if the evaluation of performance passes muster, if the numbers add up, then everyone gets paid; if it doesn't, then payments and returns are forfeit. In this case, evaluation is reduced to determining delivery of contracted performance, determining compliance with or conformity to an agreed specification; it is the exercise of a technical practice of managerial accounting performed by technicians – whether inspectors, professional evaluators or some other group of auditors – to the specification of experts. For individuals and services subject to such a regime, all activity is focused on what will impact on measurable performance outcomes, what Stephen Ball calls 'the tyranny of metrics' (2012b, p. 20). Immeasurable outcomes, unexpected consequences, surprise and wonder have no part in such accountability; nor have plural values and multiple perspectives; nor have context and complexity; nor have professional judgement or local knowledge; nor has the idea of practice as a process of research and learning. All that counts and is counted is delivery of contracted performance.

The story of democracy, experimentation and potentiality seeks democratic public accountability of a public early childhood education. This is about the exercise of democratic responsibility – of centres to citizens and citizens to centres – through 'different accounts of public purpose and practice [being] deliberated in a democratic public sphere'. Evaluation involves a judgement of value of the early childhood centre, understood to be a complex and multipurpose institution, with the potential for many possible projects and outcomes only some of which may be pre-specified, an institution whose complexity and potentiality cannot be reduced to the measurement of predetermined outcomes. The 'value' part of 'judgement of value' implies evaluation always occurs in a political context, in relation to the answers given to political questions, which define (at least provisionally) public understandings of a good early childhood education and a good early childhood centre; it is 'an act of judgement embedded in a discursive . . . context' (Readings, 1996, p. 132). While the 'judgement' part implies that the evidence, or documentation, brought to the evaluation process is not self-evident: it requires reflection, interpretation and meaning-making, with no guarantee whatsoever that all involved will arrive at a similar meaning and judgement. Dialogue, contestation and possibly dissensus will be part and parcel of this evaluative process, which at the same time does not preclude 'limited or provisional forms of agreement and action' (ibid., p. 197).

This understanding of evaluation – as part and parcel of the exercise of a democratic form of public accountability – opens out the process. It can include a wide range of evidence, for example the documentation or other research conducted by educators, as well as the documentation or other research conducted by academics, and the views of children and of parents. It can include the participation of a wide range of citizens, who participate because they have an interest in and responsibility for education. If public early childhood education is responsible to the citizens who have willed its existence, then those citizens are responsible for the public early childhood education and should exercise that responsibility, in part, through active engagement in evaluation. That citizen responsibility cannot be delegated to experts, though their views on the subject, their documentation and their interpretations, have their place in the deliberative process, provided they, the experts, come to it with a phronetic sensibility, rather than asserting an innately privileged position.

We are dealing, too, with an inherently messy and uncertain business, with many protagonists and different contexts and perspectives in play, a situation in which '[a]ny linear, hierarchical and regulatory concept of accountability is misplaced' (Ransom, 2003, p. 473). Rather than the no-nonsense managerial approach of determining a statement of fact, with precise criteria defined and measurement technologies tried and tested, the democratic judgement of value calls for qualities of reflection, dialogue and practical wisdom, as well as taking 'responsibility for the judgement delivered rather than hiding behind a statistical pretension of objectivity' (Readings, 1996, p. 132). While judgements must be made, they are recognised as unavoidably partial and provisional. As Bill Readings so rightly puts it, the 'question of evaluation is finally both unanswerable and essential' (ibid., p. 133): we must attempt evaluation but we can never arrive at a final, correct answer.

Evaluation as a judgement of value, understood as a democratic, public and participatory exercise, can be: of the individual centre; of the network of centres in a neighbourhood; of the early childhood education of a commune; and of the early childhood system across the whole nation or state. It can be thought of as a process of pedagogical documentation, involving a wide range of potential documentation, ranging from children's learning processes made visible in a wide variety of ways through to statistical information on attendance at early childhood education or the composition of the workforce – and it should be emphasised that reliable statistical information has a role in making a judgement of value, numbers do have a part to play, but always remembering that statistics like all documentation need to be interpreted and deliberated upon.

The purpose of such evaluation also needs consideration. Evaluation as managerial accounting is essentially a means of discipline, one of a variety of tools for governing early childhood education and educators and ensuring they conform and deliver; it is about performance and effectiveness, understood as the cost of delivering pre-arranged results. Evaluation as a crucial part of democratic accountability is very different. It helps extend and renew democracy, by inviting the participation of active citizens in matters of central concern to the public good. It provides an important opportunity to deliberate upon the public good 'through democratic participation, contestation and judgement in the public sphere' (Ransom, 2003, p. 470). It also offers opportunities for learning among all those involved in education – politicians and parents, policy-makers and *pedagogistas*, educators and managers, children and other citizens – about processes and effects, projects and possibilities. It opens up discussion about future directions: pedagogical improvements and experimentation. It makes education more transparent for the citizenry, revealing both its potentialities and its difficulties, its successes and its shortfalls. Rather than a thin account of performance against predetermined outcomes, evaluation in democratic accountability offers a thick understanding of potentiality – both realised and still to come.

Time

> Today there is too little talk about schools and time. For me it is important that for a school to be a place of life, then it needs the time of life and the time of life is different, for example, to the time of production. In production, the most important element is the product. But, as we said already, in a school what is important is the process, the path we develop. The education relation needs to be able to make time, it needs to be slow, it needs empty time . . . In any formative relationship, time is the necessary element for creating the relationship. So a school that forms is a school that gives time – time to children, time to teachers, time for their being together.
> (Rinaldi, 2006, p. 207)

> When asked how the early childhood institutions in Reggio Emilia had time to work so rigorously with pedagogical documentation, Loris Malaguzzi answered, 'We prioritise'.
> (Dahlberg *et al.*, 2013, p. 18)

It is undeniable that the story of democracy, experimentation and potentiality requires time if it is to be enacted. Time for the educators for thought, for listening, for dialogue, for reading, for research, for professional development. Time for pedagogical documentation and for other practices of everyday democracy and experimentation. When a colleague of Malaguzzi was asked why early childhood institutions in Reggio had such a reflective and exciting atmosphere, she replied, 'We discuss, and we discuss, and we discuss, and we discuss, and we discuss' (ibid.). How to make time for all of this?

One answer is that it is a matter of organisation and employment conditions. Time in the working week must be allocated for pedagogical documentation and for other practices of everyday democracy and experimentation. Such as the 10 per cent non-contact time proposed as a target by the EC Childcare Network (1996), three or four hours a week to read, reflect, research and discuss; or the time actually set aside each week in Reggio's municipal schools for meetings to work together with documentation:

> Every week the school staff meets to dialogue their hypotheses on the work in progress in each class by viewing the documentation together . . . The only requirement is that of interaction, as this time is designed for being together: with a co-teacher, with all the school colleagues, with personnel of other schools, and the primary feature is communication.
>
> (Rinaldi, 2006, p. 135)

Another answer is also about organisation, but again organisation driven by values and goals. Activities such as pedagogical documentation, as Malaguzzi made clear, can be prioritised and work organised accordingly, not left precariously dependent on occasional spare moments squeezed from a busy schedule. No doubt, too, where an educational project motivates and excites educators, some non-work time is used in the interests of work, whether to read, talk or just to think. This is not advocacy of compulsory overtime nor ignoring the importance of having a life beyond work; but it is a recognition that people who love what they do and believe that it matters greatly cannot simply leave that work behind them when they walk out of the workplace.

But if we are serious about a democratic education, built on wide participation across many areas, then time is not an issue simply confined to professional educators. It is an issue for children, who should have time to 'meditate and to experiment on their own, but above all with their peers' (ibid., p. 136); time to pursue investigations and research, time to develop and test theories, time to create connections and relationships, time just to be. This requires a curriculum and a pedagogy that is not time constrained, driven by the need to tick off predefined goals and finish pre-timed projects, but that instead allows learning to grow in many directions in the 'course of a project [that] can thus be short, medium or long, continuous or discontinuous, and is always open to modifications and changes of direction' (Rinaldi, 2005, p. 19). The importance of giving time to project work is vividly illustrated in the account of the Crow Project in the preceding chapter.

Last but not least, there is a need for time for parents and other citizens who wish to participate in the democratic life and projects of the early childhood centre. This is, of course, part of a much larger issue. Participation in democracy of whatever kind and in whatever institutions, and in all forms of what Ulrich Beck terms 'public work', what might be labelled 'civic or community engagement', activities outside the market, all this participation requires time. And for those in the labour market, this means greater decommodification of work, freeing more time up from the demands of the market. The active citizen needs time to participate, dialogue, contest and reflect; and preferably without risk of stress and exhaustion from trying to make time in an over-crowded schedule dominated by the demands of an increasingly intensified employment in an increasingly competitive and performative labour market. In current conditions, the concern expressed by Stuart White is easy to understand:

> When thinking about the limits of the market we usually think about the appropriateness of allowing specific goods and services to be produced on a market basis . . . I want to consider a second issue. This is more to do with the aggregate amount of social energy and time that is devoted to market activity as opposed to non-market activity. My thought is that one way in which the market can be 'invasive' (to borrow a term from Steven Lukes) is that market activity – by which I primarily mean paid employment – can come to command an excessive share of people's overall energy and time . . . My worry simply stated is that there is some level of engagement with the market which crowds out the time and energy needed to develop, maintain and exercise the capacities of competent democratic citizenship.
>
> (White, 2008, pp. 124–5)

Furthermore, as Shah and Goss argue, the need for civic engagement has never been greater. For our societies today face 'challenges where we need to act collaboratively more than ever. We need to deepen democracy through more deliberative and participative democratic mechanisms which spread democracy into the "everyday" of our lives' (2007, p. 26).

I am talking here about how to enable a more participant and a more flourishing way of life, one which includes participation in the public domain as well as in the private and market domains, one which gives people more control and therefore choice over the use of their own time, one which makes real the concepts of everyday democracy and democratic experimentalism, one which recognises there is more to life than paid work. This is a very big issue and not one I have space or competence to adequately address, though some potentially interesting ideas can be flagged up, for example:

- a *universal Basic or Citizen's Income*, an unconditional and non-withdrawable payment made by government at a uniform level and regular intervals to every adult[7] as a right of citizenship, one argument for which is that it 'gives everyone some real freedom – as opposed to a sheer right – to withdraw from paid employment in order to perform autonomous activities, such as grass-roots militancy or unpaid care work' (Parijs, 2004, p. 20; for a fuller discussion, see Ackerman *et al.*, 2005);

- a *time credit system*, providing all citizens with an allocation of paid leave that can be drawn down for use across the life-course and for a wide variety of purposes, an example being the Belgian Time Credit (*Tijdskrediet/ Crédit temps*) system (Fusulier, 2009); and
- a *new norm for employment and care careers*, no longer based on the model of a male breadwinner working with an unbroken record of full-time employment and no presumed care responsibilities, but on what Nancy Fraser (1997) terms the 'universal caregiver model', in which all jobs would be designed for workers who combine paid work and care-giving – and, I would add, other personally and socially important commitments.

In her exercise in 'thought experiment', Fraser adds her voice to those who insist on the importance of utopian thinking as a precursor to transformative change:

> [T]he trick is to imagine a social world in which citizens' lives integrate wage earning, caregiving, community activism, political participation, and involvement in the associational life of civil society – while also leaving time for some fun. This world is not likely to come into being in the immediate future, but it is the only imaginable postindustrial world that promises true gender equity. And unless we are guided by this vision now, we will never get any closer to achieving it.
>
> (ibid., p. 62)

Without such transformative change in the use of time, we are stuck in the situation we find ourselves in today, where most of the talk in early childhood education about 'parental' involvement implicitly assumes participation by mothers who are not employed or else work part-time hours and who are further assumed to be primarily responsible for the care and upbringing of young children. Once again, the possibility of rethinking time and its use in a democratic, egalitarian and sustainable society is passed up on; rather the powers-that-be try and get by on the cheap, piling costs on a minority, with minimum inconvenience to themselves and to normative (albeit increasingly dysfunctional) patterns of employment. Here, surely, is fertile territory for experimentation.

Concluding in solidarity

In cases where the story of democracy, experimentation and potentiality have been enacted – in instances such as the early childhood education of Reggio Emilia or the Crow Project in Sweden – human agency has played an important part. People have wanted to bring about transformative change, they have desired to work with new understandings, new relationships and new practices. No doubt in some instances, such agency may be sufficient, at least for a short time.

But my contention would be that such agency is not enough, at least if the story of democracy, experimentation and potentiality is not only to be enacted but to be sustained. For that, attention needs to be given to creating nurturant and stimulating conditions. Without them, transformative change in education has too often failed or fizzled after a few years, leaving an important memory but no lasting presence. For that reason I have devoted a chapter to trying to think about what these nurturant and stimulating conditions might be, what design features might make an early childhood system inscribed with democracy, experimentation and potentiality viable.

In doing so, I have drawn to some extent on cases where we can see elements of such a system – parts of Italy, parts of Sweden. The Crow Project, for example, was arguably enabled by a national framework that has provided a well-funded and universal system of preschools, a curriculum that leaves space for local initiative and explicitly proclaims democracy as a fundamental value, a well-educated workforce and many examples of creative partnership between academics and preschool teachers. None of these conditions determined the Crow Project would happen, but they created an environment where it could happen. And this project is not the only example of Swedish experimentation referred to in this book.

The experience both of Sweden and Reggio suggest one final condition for enacting and sustaining a story of democracy, experimentation and potentiality: the building of solidarities At a time when the prevailing economic regime and dominant narratives in early childhood education place such stress on autonomy and competition, I want to suggest the importance of solidarity and collaboration: within and between educators, centres, educative communes and nations working with shared values and telling similar stories, within and across borders. In Sweden, such solidarities have been fostered inter alia by the Reggio Emilia Institute, with its networks of associated preschools and its annual summer symposiums (see note 1 on page 167). While one reason for the long-running and continuing success of the transformative educational project in Reggio Emilia has been the building of and support received from solidarities: between the municipal schools in the city; between the schools and the commune; between educative communes in that part of Italy with similar hopes and aspirations; and between Reggio Emilia itself and its global network of fellow travellers, not least in Sweden. Such solidarity makes us better able to resist the DONA and create alternatives.

Notes

1 As an example, in Sweden all children are entitled to a place in a 'preschool' from 12 months of age, coinciding with the end of well-paid parental leave. In autumn 2010 458,000 1-to-5-year-olds attended these age-integrated and public funded centres, 83 per cent of the age group, with attendance ranging from just under half

(47 per cent) of 1-to-2-year-olds up to nearly all (94 per cent) of 4- and 5-year-olds (Skolverket, 2012). A small number of children attended family day care.

2 'Pedagogue' is a profession found in many continental European countries, working across a range of services for children and adults, including in some countries (e.g. Denmark, Germany) early childhood education. The pedagogue and the social pedagogy she or he practises are different from the profession of teacher and the school-based concept of education that many teachers practise. In particular, the pedagogue adopts a holistic approach to working with children (or adults) in which learning, care, health, general well-being and development are viewed as totally inseparable (for a fuller discussion of pedagogues and pedagogy, see Cameron and Moss, 2011).

3 It could be a profession with a slightly broader age remit, including the widely recog-nised definition of early childhood as stretching from birth to 8 years.

4 This term comes from a report prepared by children, parents and staff for an evalua-tion of Sheffield Children's Centre (referred to in Chapter 5, page 136). The Centre is possibly unique in having successfully pursued a gender mixed workforce reflect-ing its 'view that men working with children need to become an accepted norm in society'; though they have also emphasised that diversity covers many other areas: 'socio-economic groups and political affiliations; religious faiths and belief forms; age, race, ethnicity and nationality; sexuality; family composition; health status and physical and mental abilities' (Meleady and Broadhead, 2002, pp. 14–15).

5 An important complement to the early childhood education envisaged here is a system of well-paid parental leave designed to promote more equal sharing of child upbringing between mothers and fathers, an entitlement coordinated with an entitle-ment to early childhood education. In Sweden, for example, parental leave paid at 80 per cent of earnings, including a period exclusively for fathers, runs for just over a year, with access to preschools as a right for all children from 12 months irrespective of parental employment (Duvander and Haas, 2013).

6 For more information, see www.educate.ece.govt.nz/Programmes/CentresOfInno-vation.aspx; and the series of publications on the Centres of Innovation programme available at www.nzcer.org.nz/default.php?products_id = 2445.

7 Confining the Basic or Citizen's Income to 'every adult' not only raises the issue of definition, when is adulthood deemed to start, but begs the question of why only adults, why not children, especially if they are deemed to be citizens.

Chapter 8

Real utopia – or
pie in the sky?

The absence of hope is not the 'normal' way to be human, [but] a distortion.
(Freire, 1998, p. 69)

The revolutionary agenda of neoliberalism has accomplished a lot in the way of physical and institutional change these last twenty years. So why, then, can we not envision equally dramatic changes (though pointing in a different direction) as we seek for alternatives?
(Harvey, 2000)

In the preceding chapters, I have explained my dislike for today's dominant stories about early childhood education: the story of quality and high returns and the story of markets. I have also told an other story that I do like, the story of democracy, experimentation and potentiality, and have discussed some of the design features or structural conditions that might be supportive of the enactment of this story. I have, in Erik Olin's Wright's terms, set out two of the three criteria for evaluating this real utopia, desirability and viability, going as far as reconceptualising and redesigning the institution of early childhood education. But, some might think, this is still a long way from achieving transformational change, offering instead mere pie in the sky – an appealing prospect, but not going to happen!

This chapter deals with Wright's third criterion for evaluating real utopias: achievability – what would it take to actually implement the proposals. Reviewing his three criteria, Wright concludes that desirability is too easy: 'it is too easy to elaborate the moral principles and values we want to see embodied in alternatives' (Wright, 2007, p. 31). Viability he considers 'the most pressing intellectual task' of the three, 'because there is so much scepticism among people who are convinced of desirability and willing to participate in the political work to make alternatives achievable, but have lost confidence in the workability of visions beyond the existing social order' (ibid., p. 32). So where does this leave achievability? This involves the political and economic conditions and strategies necessary to bring about widespread and sustained transformative change, to move from the design stage to widespread application. This criterion, Wright says, is 'too hard', since there are too many 'contingencies and uncertainties for us to assign meaningful possibilities to the achievability of a given viable alternative very far into the future'. In other words, it is too hard because we cannot tell what the future might bring.

But before getting to future contingencies and uncertainties, there seems a more fundamental obstacle to achieving the story of democracy, experimentation and potentiality, and one I have already emphasised. Indeed it might seem I have painted myself into a corner. For having argued the profound influence on early childhood education of a dominant political economy – a regime of neoliberalism – how can I talk about achieving change without simply ignoring this looming presence or else naively wishing it away? I seek to do neither.

In considering the obstacle posed by neoliberalism, a sense of contemporary proportion is helpful. Without ignoring or underestimating the significance of neoliberalism, it is also important to resist the image of an all-powerful neoliberalism, wholly determining what is possible and what is impossible. This dystopian image can easily lead to despair and hopelessness. But while we need to take seriously capitalism in general and neoliberal capitalism in particular, we should not go over the top, confusing current dominance with immutability, self-confident assertiveness with infallibility. I have already argued in Chapter 3 that neoliberalism is not 'some monolithic entity, with a definition and practice that is homogeneous, universal and static'. It is also increasingly revealed to have feet of clay, its faith in the magic of markets cast into grave doubt by the 2008 financial crash and by an accumulation of other experience, leading Nobel Prize-winner Joseph Stiglitz to argue that:

> [n]eo-liberal market fundamentalism was always a political doctrine serving certain interests. It was never supported by economic theory. Nor, it should now be clear, is it supported by historical experience. Learning this lesson may be the silver lining in the cloud now hanging over the global economy.
>
> (2013b, p. 2)

Though it must also be acknowledged, some years on from the collapse of Lehmann Brothers, that 'it now looks as though neoliberalism has come through the crisis unscathed' (Mirowski, 2013a, p. 8), indeed emerging if anything stronger, its insatiable appetite for marketisation and privatisation unaffected. Historian and philosopher of economic thought Philip Mirowski puts this down to several causes including 'cognitive dissonance', in which true believers have not allowed contradictory evidence to dent their worldview, 'the prior decades of "everyday neoliberalism" that had taken root in the culture', and 'industrial-scale manufacture of ignorance about the crisis' (2013a, pp. 336–8). This does not mean, of course, that the sighting of clay feet was illusory nor that the fault line revealed has now healed over. It does suggest, however, that neoliberalism is deeply embedded and highly resilient, and that reports of its imminent death were premature.

A sense of proportion also means to recognise that neoliberalism is not the only show in town. Gibson-Clarke (two economic geographers who present one authorial identity) caution against 'capitalocentric' discourses that render invisible or minimise alternatives, those other forms of economic production that exist in the here and now, and that 'serve both to disable our imagination of different possibilities and to undermine our motivation for struggle' (Maroney, nd). In the introduction to the second edition of their book *The End of Capitalism (As We Knew It)*, Gibson-Clarke discuss their strategy of resistance to the political economy of capitalism:

> Determined as we were to reinvigorate our economic imaginations and also to enact alternative economies, we have ended up (so far) with a collaboratively designed project that has four distinct yet overlapping phases . . . [The first] involves *deconstructing the hegemony of capitalism* to open up a discursive space for the prevalence and diversity of noncapitalist economic activity worldwide. The second requires *producing a language of economic difference* to enlarge the economic imaginary, rendering visible and intelligible the diverse and proliferating practices that the preoccupation with capitalism has obscured; we see this language as a necessary contribution to a politics of economic innovation. The third is the difficult process of *cultivating subjects* (ourselves and others) who can desire and inhabit noncapitalist spaces . . . developing a vision of the 'community economy' as an ethical and political space of becoming . . . Finally, there is the actual practice of *building community economies* in place.
>
> (Gibson-Clarke, 2006, p. x; emphasis added)

It is a fourfold strategy of interest to all those who wish to resist the dominant stories in early childhood education (or any other field) and elements of which, at least, are present in this book, for example deconstructing the hegemony of these stories, by pointing to alternatives, and producing a language of educational difference. I also hope the book has made some contribution to reinvigorating pedagogical imaginations.

So things are never as bleak as they might seem: the will to hegemony, such as we see with neoliberalism, never does blot out all alternatives and the dictatorship of no alternative fails to eradicate imagination and hope or dissent and resistance. Foucault, indeed, argues that power relations, whether positive or negative in their effect, always allow resistance: 'where there is power there is resistance'. Put another way, if there is no resistance, the relationship is not one of power but of slavery, and we are not reduced to that relationship, certainly not in education. Developing this theme, Stephen Ball adds that '[l]ike power itself, resistance is manifold and operates at a multiplicity of points in different forms, in many small acts and passing moments' (Ball, 2013, p. 32).

Neoliberalism, when all is said and done, is only one story. Despite the persistence and fervour of its true believers, it is not a true and final account of how we are and how we must be for ever and ever – we are not at the end of history. We are not confronting a natural phenomenon or a necessity. Neoliberalism's values and assumptions – such as an essentially selfish and calculating subject, *homo economicus*, and the infallibility of markets – are contestable and have proven in practice to be fallible. Neoliberalism may be a hegemonic story for the moment, but that does not mean it is either a good or a satisfying story. Arguably, increasing numbers of people are coming to this conclusion as they see the unpleasant consequences of the rapacious and atomising regime it instigates.

We must also regain a sense of historical perspective. Instead of taking time for granted and being fixated on the here and now, a longer-term perspective is needed, one that recognises change as an inevitable part of the human story, with economic regimes, and therefore social arrangements and institutions, appearing as transient phenomena. Neoliberalism may be a powerful and widespread force today, but it was not ever so. It was for many years an economic doctrine with little following, before being 'plucked from relative obscurity and transformed into the central guiding principle of economic thought and management' (Harvey, 2005, p. 2). Indeed, as political scientist Susan George reminds us, and as anyone who grew up immediately after the Second World War can attest:

> [i]n 1945 or 1950, if you had seriously proposed any of the ideas and policies in today's standard neoliberal toolkit, you would have been laughed off the stage or sent off to the insane asylum. At least in the Western countries, at that time, everyone was a Keynesian, a social democrat or a social-Christian democrat or some shade of Marxist. The idea that the market should be allowed to make major social and political decisions; the idea that the State should voluntarily reduce its role in the economy, or that corporations should be given total freedom, that trade unions should be curbed and citizens given much less rather than more social protection – such ideas were utterly foreign to the spirit of the time. Even if someone actually agreed with these ideas, he or she would have hesitated to take such a position in public and would have had a hard time finding an audience.
>
> (George, 1999, p. 1)

Now, in the second decade of the twenty-first century, any serious alternative to the neoliberal toolkit can seem equally laughable, even insane. We have again fallen into the ahistorical trap of assuming that the present will be with us for ever, with more of the same as the only possibility for the future. Unsurprising, therefore, that at times we can end up actually believing there is no alternative. But in doing so, we overlook the existence of cyclical (medium-term) and epochal (long-term) change (Schostak and Goodson, 2012).

If, however, we recall history and the changes that constantly happen in it, we can see the present as just another period of history, and remind ourselves that history itself has not suddenly ended by lapsing into a condition of stasis, a sort of infinite Groundhog Day. Indeed we are now, many would argue, in a critical phase of change, politically, economically and environmentally. As John Schostak and Ivor Goodson argue 'something momentous is going on . . . [b]ut what emerges is as yet unpredictable'. The urgent challenge and struggle, they conclude, that:

> arises from such anticipated re-ordering of the 'world order' of economic and political powers is to find the new models through which research and education can enhance the powers of people. Where is such struggle to take place? It can only take place in the key spheres, institutions and organisations of everyday life involving work, education, community and government . . . Education may play its part, as when adults work with the young to re-imagine the future.
>
> (Schostak and Goodson, 2012, p. 270)

This reference to new models for education that 'can enhance the powers of people' and 'enable adults [to] work with the young to re-imagine the future' resonates with Keri Facer's argument (in Chapter 4) for the potential of education and schools for 'future building', providing spaces for imagining, discussing and contesting alternative futures, places where struggle can take place. From this perspective, the mantra that says education is about preparing children for the global race, a future proofing function premised on more of the same, is not only devoid of democracy and experimentation, and wasteful of potentiality, but hopelessly short-sighted.

The neoliberal story tellers knew all this in the 1950s and 1960s, when a very different economic regime predominated and the 'neoliberal toolkit' seemed laughable or insane. They retained a sense of history. They did not give up. They did not assume their day had passed never to re-appear. No: they treated neoliberalism as a real utopian project; they developed their stories and sought new listeners; and they worked together behind the scenes on designing what were in their terms desirable and viable alternatives (see note 1 on page 74 and Mirowski, 2013). They expected change to come with the faltering of the dominant post-war Keynesian regime; and when it did, they had to be ready to take the opportunity, to put forward their stories, to achieve their real utopia. Their strategy was outlined back in 1962 by economist Milton Friedman (1912–2006), the arch priest of the neoliberal resurgence:

> Only a crisis – actual or perceived – produces real change. When that crisis occurs the actions that are taken depend on the ideas that are lying around. That, I believe, is our basic function: to develop alternatives to existing

policies, to keep them alive and available until the politically impossible becomes politically inevitable.

(Friedman, 1982, p. ix)

So we must all tread a careful path between taking the current political and economic regime seriously, and recognising its oppressive bearing on how we talk and practice early childhood education, and much else besides; whilst at the same time not allowing it to lead to a sense of powerlessness and despair. There are cracks and tensions in the edifice of neoliberalism, making it neither seamless nor stable nor permanent. These weaknesses allow some scope here and now for resistance and alternatives, for thinking and acting differently; and while the uncertainties about the future can in some ways make achievability hard to plan for in any great detail, they also make achievability seem a more likely prospect. We may not know exactly how the future will unfold, we may not be able to prepare any grand strategies for achieving total transformation, for there are too many contingencies and uncertainties: but we can expect with some confidence that more of the same is not on the cards. All of which should encourage us to harken to Friedman's words and 'develop alternatives to existing policies, to keep them alive and available until the politically impossible becomes politically inevitable'.

Wright himself also sees uncertainties and contingencies about the future not just as a problem for developing practical strategies for social change, but also as a source of possibility and hope:

> The further we look into the future, the less certain we can be about the limits on what is achievable. Achievability is often determined by historically contingent windows of opportunity that open up unexpectedly rather than anticipated strategies understood well in advance. No one, for example, would have thought in 1985 that a destruction of the Soviet Union and the shock therapy transition to some form of capitalism was achievable within a decade. So to let our firm knowledge of achievability constrain our analysis of viability would necessarily exclude discussions of some alternatives that do eventually become achievable.
>
> (Wright, 2007, p. 32)

Here then is a reason for telling new stories and designing viable new institutions. Far worse than appearing a laughing stock or seeming to cook up pie in the sky is to be caught out devoid of ideas and designs when one of those windows of opportunity opens up. We should not, Wright argues, let the immediate difficulties of achievability constrain us from addressing desirability and viability; just because we can't see our way to the end does not mean we should abandon planning our journey.

So with David Harvey, I 'envision equally dramatic changes [to those brought about by neoliberalism] (though pointing in a different direction) as we seek for alternatives'. And I have attempted to address, in part at least, Tony Judt's *cri de coeur* in Chapter 2, that:

> we have such difficulty even *imagining* a different sort of society from the one whose dysfunctions and inequalities trouble us so . . . We appear to have lost the capacity to question the present, much less offer alternatives to it. Why is it so beyond us to conceive of a different set of arrangements to our common advantage? Our shortcomings – excuse the academic jargon – is *discursive*. We simply do not know how to talk about these things.
>
> (Judt, 2009, p. 86)

I have offered a different discourse about early childhood education, a different way of talking about things, a different story. Admittedly, this may be easier than the larger task of talking differently about the whole political economy. But perhaps we have to work at different levels and from different perspectives, trying to build new stories for many fields and gaining mutual support from so doing – putting up a variety of new buildings around and opposite to the crumbling neoliberal edifice.

So what I have sought to do is work to overturn one barrier to achievability of a real utopian early childhood education, by telling a story about an alternative and creating viable designs for that story, remembering Foucault's belief that once we can think differently, change becomes both urgent and possible. Or, as Wright puts it:

> the actual limits of what is achievable depend in part on the beliefs people hold about what sorts of alternatives are viable . . . Developing systematic, compelling accounts of viable alternatives to existing social structures and institutions of power and privilege, therefore, is one component of the social process through which the social limits on achievable alternatives can themselves be changed.
>
> (Wright, 2007, pp. 32–3)

By adding to the alternatives, I have also sought to contribute to the renewal of a democratic politics of education. DONA – the repressive hold of an insistent 'dictatorship of no alternative' – 'reinforces an erosion of democracy in all matters, since democracy is the politics of difference, of alternatives' (Schostak and Goodson, 2012, p. 263). Every alternative contributes to a melting of the icy grip of DONA, and the re-emergence not only of democracy but of movement also.

Step-by-step change and the importance of prefigurative practice

The question of achievability is also bound up with the process envisaged for bringing about transformative change. Should we envisage sweeping, rapid and widespread change, bringing about a sudden and complete rupture with the past? Does transformative change mean waiting until we are certain that the road ahead is totally clear, with no obstacles remaining? Or do we envisage the process as something more halting, piecemeal, cumulative and uneven, rather akin to Unger's concept of 'radical reform' that I touched on in Chapter 1?

The latter is closer to my view of how transformative change might take place, as it is to Wright's, who suggests that:

> central to the problem of envisioning real utopias concerns the viability of institutional alternatives that embody emancipatory values, but the practical achievability of such institutional designs [real utopian alternatives that embody emancipatory values] often depends upon *the existence of smaller steps, intermediate institutional innovations that move us in the right direction but only partially embody those values.*
>
> (Wright, 2007, p. 38; emphasis added)

In developing this notion of intermediate institutional innovation, Wright coins the term 'waystations' or intermediate reforms that have two main characteristics:

> First, they concretely demonstrate the virtues of the fuller programme of transformation, so they contribute to the ideological battle of convincing people that the alternative is credible and desirable; and second, they enhance the capacity of action for people, increasing their ability to push further in the future.
>
> Waystations that increase popular participation and bring people together in problem-solving deliberations are particularly salient in this regard. This is what in the 1970s was called 'non-reformist reforms': reforms that are possible within existing institutions and that pragmatically solve real problems while at the same time empowering people in ways which enlarge their scope for action.
>
> (ibid., p. 38)

Even though we cannot achieve transformative change immediately or even immanently, it does not mean there is no point in starting, no value in moving towards waystations that demonstrate viability, that increase confidence that another future may be possible. The journey is not some tiresome procedure that must be endured to reach the end. Rather it is an exhilarating and pleasurable experience, an opportunity to build participatory democracy, to experiment with new ways of thinking, relating and acting, to arouse curiosity and desire, and to broaden interest and support by demonstrating viability. Good things happen from starting on the journey, not only when the journey is finished. Examples, cases, waystations inspire and encourage.

This thinking, which attaches great importance to the process of change, is very similar to the concept of 'prefigurative practice', prefigured in the last chapter: the anticipation of future modes of being through processes and relations that exemplify and embody the viability and desirability of radical alternatives. In short, demonstrating what is possible. Prefigurative practice is, in the words of the Gramscian scholar Carl Boggs 'the embodiment within the ongoing political practice of a movement, of those forms of social relations, decision-making, culture and human experience that are the ultimate goal' (Boggs, 1977/78, p. 100). Nearer to home, in the field of education, the importance of this concept is captured in Roger Dale's argument that:

> rather than waiting until all the necessary social engineering has been done, and the planned widespread social change brought about, this approach to social change suggests that education through its processes, the experiences it offers, and the expectations it makes, should prefigure, in microcosm, the more equal, just and fulfilling society that the originations of comprehensivism aimed to bring about. *Schools should not merely reflect the world of which they are a part, but be critical of it, and show in their own processes that its shortcomings are not inevitable, but can be changed.* They aim to show that society can be characterized by communal as well as individual values, that all people merit equal treatment and equal dignity, that academic ability is not the only measure of a person, that racism and sexism are neither inevitable not acceptable.
>
> (Dale, 1988, p. 17; emphasis added)

All the example I have given in this book, such as the pedagogy of listening in municipal schools in Reggio Emilia or the experimentation in Swedish preschools, are instances of 'prefigurative practice', instances of possibility showing that the world's shortcomings are not inevitable, showing that there are alternatives, showing the virtues of a transformative change that is still to come.

At the start of this book, I put forward an understanding of transformative change as moving into a state of movement, not transiting from one static point to another. This does not mean movement that is directionless; the movement I want to see is inscribed with certain values and ethics, certain understandings and purposes, for example those proposed in Chapters 4 and 5, points of reference against which to check our bearings. But having a sense of direction does not mean knowing for certain, here and now, where you want to get to in the future, your final destination. Just as I reject an education concerned with securing high returns by achieving fixed and predefined goals, so too I reject the idea of a journey with a known final end point, a 'quality' early childhood education that once achieved we can tick off, then sit back to enjoy the ringing of cash registers.

So my notion of the process of transformative change is one of continuous movement, endless waystations, practice that prefigures future practice that prefigures . . . It is a process of emergence, constantly bringing the new into being, continually realising potentialities, embracing diversity and dissensus and welcoming wonder and amazement. I end this book, therefore, on a note of hope. That there are always alternatives; that we cannot know what a body can do; that another world is possible; that schools and education can play a part in imagining and prefiguring that world; that the absence of hope is not the 'normal' way to be human. And that I am not alone in wanting something different, in being attracted towards other stories, and (ending where I started with the words of the Dark Mountain Project) in wanting to 'reassert the role of story-telling as more than mere entertainment'.

References

Åberg, A. and Lenz Taguchi, H. (2005) *Lyssnandets pedagogic: etik och demokrati i pedagogiskt arbete.* Stockholm: Liber.

Ackerman, B., Alstott, A. and Van Parijs, P. (2005) *Redesigning Redistribution: Income and Stakeholder Grants as Alternative Cornerstones for a More Egalitarian Capitalism.* London: Verso.

Aldrich, R. (2010) 'Education for survival: An historical perspective', *History of Education*, 39 (1), 1–14.

Alexander, R. (2012a) 'Entitlement, freedom, minimalism and essential knowledge: Can the curriculum circle be squared?' Paper given at *CPPS Westminster Seminar*, London, 23 April 2012. (www.newvisionsforeducation.org.uk/2012/05/10/entitlement-freedom-minimalism-and-essential-knowledge-can-the-curriculum-circle-be-squared/).

Alexander, R. (2012b) 'Moral panic, miracle cures and education policy: What can we really learn from international comparisons? *Scottish Education Review*, 44 (1), 4–21.

Allen, G. (2011a) *Early Intervention: Smart Investment, Massive Savings.* London: Cabinet Office. (https://www.gov.uk/government/publications/early-intervention-smart-investment-massive-savings).

Allen, G. (2011b) *Early Intervention: The Next Steps.* London: HM Government. (www.dwp.gov.uk/docs/early-intervention-next-steps.pdf).

Amsler, S. (2012) 'Taking great pains: Critical theory, affective pedagogies and radical democracy'. Paper given at *Real Utopias, American Sociological Association Annual Conference*, Denver, CO, 17–21 August 2012.

Anderson, B. (2006) '"Transcending without transcendence": Utopianism and an ethos of hope', *Antipode*, 38 (4), 691–710.

Anyon, J. (2005) *Radical Possibilities: Public Policy, Urban Education and a New Social Movement.* London: Routledge.

Apple, M. (2004) 'Creating differences: Neo-liberalism, neo-conservativism and the politics of educational reform', *Educational Policy*, 18 (1), 12–44.

Apple, M. (2005) 'Education, markets and an audit culture', *Critical Quarterly*, 47 (1–2), 11–29.

Archer, M. (2008) 'Childcare and early years provision in a diverse market: The government's approach'. Paper given at a seminar organised by the *International Centre for the Study of the Mixed Economy of Childcare*, London, 12 May 2008. (www.uel.ac.uk/icmec/seminar/index.htm).

Arendt, H. (1993) 'The crisis in education', in *Between Past and Future: Eight Exercises in Political Thought*. New York: The Viking Press.

Balducci, L. and Lazzari, A. (2013) 'Bruno Ciari and "educational community": The relationship from an Italian perspective', in P. Moss (ed.) *Early Childhood and Compulsory Education: Reconceptualising the Relationship*. London: Routledge.

Ball, S. (2003) *Class Strategies and the Education Market*. London: Routledge.

Ball, S. (2007) *Education plc: Understanding Private Sector Participation in Public Sector Education*. London: Routledge.

Ball, S. (2012a) *Global Education Inc.: New Policy Networks and the Neo-Liberal Imaginary*. London: Routledge.

Ball, S. (2012b) 'Performativity, commodification and commitment: An I-Spy guide to the neoliberal university', *British Journal of Educational Studies*, 60 (1), 17–28.

Ball, S. (2013) *Foucault, Power and Education*. London: Routledge.

Ball, S. and Vincent, C. (2006) *Childcare, Choice and Class Practices: Middle-Class Parents and Their Children*. London: Routledge.

Ball, S., Bowe, R. and Gewirtz, S. (1994) 'Market forces and parental choice', in S. Tomlinson (ed.) *Educational Reform and Its Consequences*. London: Institute for Public Policy Research.

Barad, K. (2007) *Meeting the Universe Halfway: Quantum Physics and the Entanglement of Matter and Meaning*. Durham, NC: Duke University Press.

Barsotti, A., Dahlberg, G., Göthson, H. and Åsén, G. (1993) *Pedagogik i en föränderlig omvärld – ett samarbetsprojekt med Reggio Emilia* [Education in a Changing World – a project in cooperation with Reggio Emilia]. *Forskningsprogram*. Stockholm: HLS, Institutionen för barn- och ungdomsvetenskap, Avdelningen för barnpedagogisk forskning i Solna.

Bauman, Z. (1993) *Postmodern Ethics*. Oxford: Blackwell.

Bauman, Z. (1995) *Life in Fragments: Essays in Postmodern Morality*. Oxford: Blackwell.

Beck, U. (1998) *Democracy without Enemies*. Cambridge: Polity Press.

Becker, G.S. (1976) *The Economic Approach to Human Behaviour*. Chicago, IL: University of Chicago Press.

Bennett, P. (2009) *The Last Romances and the Kelmscott Press*. London: William Morris Society.

Bentley, A. (2008) 'Nursery trade secrets', *Nursery World*, 17 July 2008. (www.nursery-world.co.uk/news/login/832086).

Bentley, T. (2005) *Everyday Democracy: Why We Get the Politicians We Deserve*. London: Demos.

Berners-Lee, M. and Clark, D. (2013) *The Burning Question: We Can't Burn Half the World's Oil, Coal and Gas, So How Do We Quit?* London: Profile.

Biesta, G. (2007) 'Why "what works" won't work: Evidence-based practice and the democratic deficit in educational research', *Educational Theory*, 57 (1), 1–22.

Biesta, G. (2010) *Good Education in an Age of Measurement: Ethics, Politics, Democracy*. Boulder, CO: Paradigm Publishers.

Biesta, G. (2013) 'Interrupting the politics of learning', *Power and Education*, 5 (1), 4–15.

Biesta, G. and Osberg, D. (2007) 'Beyond re/presentation: A case for updating the epistemology of schooling', *Interchange*, 38 (1), 15–29.

Blackburn, P. (2012) 'Future directions for a mature UK childcare market', in E. Lloyd and H. Penn (eds) *Childcare Markets: Can They Deliver an Equitable Service?* Bristol: Policy Press.

Blakemore, S.-J. and Frith, U. (2005) *The Learning Brain: Lessons for Education.* Oxford: Blackwell.

Bloom, A.A. (1948) 'Notes on a school community', *New Era*, 29 (6), 120–21.

Boddy, J., Cameron, C., Mooney, A., Moss, P., Petrie, P. and Statham, P. (2005) *Introducing Pedagogy into the Children's Workforce: Children's Workforce Strategy, Response to the Consultation Paper.* London: Thomas Coram Research Unit

Boggs, C. (1977/78) 'Marxism, prefigurative communism, and the problem of workers' control', *Radical America*, 11.6–12.1, 99–122.

Bourdieu, P. and Passeron, J.-C. (1990, 2nd edn) *Reproduction in Education, Society and Culture.* London: Sage.

Brewer, M. (2012) 'Labour's child poverty effort was exceptional', *The Guardian*, 12 June 2012. (www.guardian.co.uk/society/2012/jun /12/labours-effort-cut-child-poverty-exceptional?newsfeed=true).

Brind, R., Norden, O., McGinigal, S., Oseman, D., Simon, A. and La Valle, A. (2012) *Childcare and Early Years Providers Survey 2011. Research Report DfE RR240.* London: Department for Education.

Broadhead, P., Meleady, C. and Delgado, M.A. (2008) *Children, Families and Communities: Creating and Sustaining Integrated Services.* Maidenhead: Open University Press.

Bruer, J. (2011) *Revisiting 'The Myth of the First Three Years'.* Canterbury: Centre for Parenting Culture Studies, University of Kent. (http://blogs.kent.ac.uk/parenting-culturestudies/files/2011/09/Special-briefing-on-The-Myth.pdf).

Buber, M. (1947/2002) *Between Man and Man.* London: Routledge.

Burman, E. (1994, 1st edn) *Deconstructing Developmental Psychology.* London: Routledge.

Burn, G (2006) *The Re-Emergence of Global Finance.* Basingstoke: Palgrave Macmillan.

Butler-Jones, D. (2008). *Report of the State of Public Health in Canada.* Ottawa, ON: Public Health Agency of Canada.

Cagliari, P., Barozzi, A. and Giudici, C. (2004) 'Thoughts, theories and experiences: For an educational project with participation', *Children in Europe*, 6, 28–30.

Cambridge Primary Review (2009) *Introducing the Cambridge Primary Review.* Cambridge: University of Cambridge (http://www.primaryreview.org.uk/downloads/CPR_revised_booklet.pdf).

Cameron, C. and Moss, P. (eds) (2011) *Social Pedagogy and Working with Children and Young People.* London: Jessica Kingsley Publishing.

Carr, W. and Hartnett, A. (1996) *Education and the Struggle for Democracy: The Politics of Educational Ideas.* Buckingham: Open University Press.

Catarsi, E. (2004) 'Loris Malaguzzi and the municipal school revolution', *Children in Europe*, 4, 8–9.

Chakrabortty, A. (2013) 'Swedish riots: If instability can happen here, what might unfold elsewhere? *The Guardian*, 28 May 2013. (www.guardian.co.uk/commentisfree/2013/may/27/swedish-riots-inequality-stockholm).

Chia, R. (1999) 'A "rhizomic" model of organizational change and transformation: Perspective from a metaphysics of change', *British Journal of Management*, 10 (3), 209–27.

Clark, A. (2005) 'Ways of seeing: Using the Mosaic approach to listen to young children's perspectives', in A. Clark, A.T. Kjørholt and P. Moss (eds) *Beyond Listening: Children's Perspectives on Early Childhood Services.* Bristol: Policy Press.

Clark, A. (2010) *Transforming Children's Spaces: Children's and Adults' Participation in Designing Learning Environments*. London: Routledge.

Clark, A. and Moss, P. (2005) *Spaces to Play: More Listening to Young Children Using the Mosaic Approach*. London: National Children's Bureau.

Cleveland, G. and Krashinksy, M. (2002) *Financing ECEC Services in OECD Countries*. (www.oecd.org/dataoecd/55/59/28123665.pdf).

Cleveland, G. and Krashinsky, M. (2004) 'Financing early learning and child care in Canada'. Discussion paper prepared for the Canadian Council on Social Development's *National Conference on Child Care in Canada*, Winnipeg, 12–14 November 2004. (www.ccsd.ca/pubs/2004/cc/cleveland-krashinsky.pdf).

Coffield, F. and Williamson, B. (2011) *From Exam Factories to Communities of Discovery: The Democratic Route*. London: Institute of Education University of London.

Competence Requirements in Early Childhood Education and Care (2011) *Final Report*. London and Ghent: University of East London, Cass School of Education and University of Ghent, Department for Social Welfare Studies. (http://ec.europa.eu/education/more-information/doc/2011/core_en.pdf)

Comune di Reggio Emilia (2009) *Regolamento Scuole e Nidi d'infanzia del Comune di Reggio Emilia*. (www.scuolenidi.re.it/allegati/Regolamentonidiscuolinfanzia%20.pdf).

Credit Suisse (2013) *Global Wealth Report 2012*. (http://economics.uwo.ca/news/Davies_CreditSuisse_Oct12.pdf.).

Cribb, J., Joyce, R. and Phillip, D. (2012) *Living Standards, Poverty and Inequality in the UK: 2012*. London: Institute for Fiscal Studies. (www.ifs.org.uk/comms/comm124.pdf).

Crouch, C. (2003) *Commercialisation or Citizenship: Education Policy and the Future of Public Services*. London: Fabian Society.

Crouch, C. (2004) *Post-Democracy*. Cambridge: Polity Press.

Dahlberg, G. (2000) 'Everything is a beginning and everything is dangerous: Some reflections on the Reggio Emilia experience', in H. Penn (ed.) *Early Childhood Services: Theory, Policy and Practice*. Buckingham: Open University Press

Dahlberg, G. (2003) 'Pedagogy as a loci of an ethics of an encounter', in M. Bloch, K. Holmlund, I. Moqvist and T. Popkewitz (eds) *Governing Children, Families and Education: Restructuring the Welfare State*. New York: Palgrave.

Dahlberg, G. (2012) 'Contextualising the Reggio Emilia experience', in *One City, Many Children: Reggio Emilia, a History of the Present*. Reggio Emilia: Reggio Children.

Dahlberg, G. (2013) 'A dialogue with the co-author of "the vision of a meeting place"', in P. Moss (ed.) *Early Childhood and Compulsory Education: Reconceptualising the Relationship*. London: Routledge.

Dahlberg, G. and Lenz Taguchi, H. (1994) *Förskola och skola – om två skilda traditioner och om visionen om en mötesplats* [Preschool and school – two different traditions and the vision of a meeting place]. Stockholm: HLS Förlag.

Dahlberg, G. and Moss, P. (2005) *Ethics and Politics in Early Childhood Education*. London: Routledge.

Dahlberg, G. and Bloch, M. (2006) 'Is the power to see and visualize always the power to control?', in T. Popkewitz, K. Pettersson, U. Olsson and J. Kowalczyk (eds) *The Future Is Not What It Appears to Be: Pedagogy, Genealogy and Political Epistemology. In Honour and in Memory of Kenneth Hultqvist*. Stockholm: HLS Förlag.

Dahlberg, G., Moss, P. and Pence, A. (2013, 3rd edn) *Beyond Quality in Early Childhood Education and Care: Languages of Evaluation*. London: Routledge.

Daily Telegraph (2012) 'Privately educated MPs, actors and sports stars dominate society, says Gove', *Daily Telegraph*, 10 May 2012.

Dale, R. (1988) 'Comprehensive education'. Talk given to Madrid Conference, April, unpublished.

Dark Mountain Project (2009a) *Uncivilisation: The Dark Mountain Manifesto*. (http:// dark-mountain.net/about/manifesto/uncivilisation-manifesto).

Dark Mountain Project (2009b) *FAQs*. (http://dark-mountain.net/about/faqs).

Darling, J. and Norbenbo, S.E. (2003) 'Progressivism', in N. Blake, P. Smeyers, R. Smith and P. Standish (eds) *The Blackwell Guide to Philosophy of Education*. Oxford: Blackwell.

Deleuze, G. (1994) *Difference and Repetition*, trans. Paul Patton. London: Athlone Press.

Deleuze, G. and Parnet, C. (1987) *Dialogues*, trans. Hugh Tomlinson and Barbara Habberjam. London: Athlone Press.

Deleuze, G. and Guattari, F. (1999) *A Thousand Plateaus: Capitalism & Schizophrenia*, trans. Brian Massumi. London: Athlone Press.

Denavas-Walt, C., Proctor, B.D. and Smith, J.C. (2013) *Income, Poverty, and Health Insurance Coverage in the US 2012*. Washington, DC: United States Census Bureau. (www.census.gov/prod/2013pubs/p60–245.pdf).

Department for Education and Skills (England) and other government departments (2002) *Delivering for Children and Families: Inter-departmental Childcare Review*. (http:// dera.ioe.ac.uk/8814/2/su%20children.pdf).

Department for Education (England) (2013) *More Great Childcare: Raising Quality and Giving Parents More Choice*. London: Department for Education. (https://www.gov. uk/government/uploads/system/uploads/attachment_data/file/170552/More_ 20Great_20Childcare_20v2.pdf.pdf).

Dewey, J. (1916/1980) 'The need of an industrial education in an industrial democracy', in J. Boydston (ed.) *The middle Works of John Dewey, 1899–1924*. Carbondale: Southern Illinois University Press.

Dewey, J. (1938/1988) *Experience & Education* (in The Later Works, 1925–1953, vol. 13, ed. Jo Ann Boydston). Carbondale, IL: Southern Illinois University Press.

Dewey, J. (1939) 'Creative democracy – The task before us', address given at a dinner in honour of John Dewey, New York, 20 October 1939. (http://chipbruce.files. wordpress.com/2008/11/dewey_creative_dem.pdf#)

Dickens, C. (2012) *A Tale of Two Cities*. (www.gutenberg.org/files/98/98-h/98-h.htm).

Diedrich, W.W., Burggraeve, R. and Gastmans, C. (2003) 'Towards a Levinasian care ethic: A dialogue between the thoughts of Joan Tronto and Emmanuel Levinas', *Ethical Perspectives*, 13 (1), 33–61.

Dorling, D. (2010) *Injustice: Why Social Inequality Persists*. Bristol: Policy Press.

Dumas, C., and Lefranc, A. (2012) 'Early schooling and later outcomes: Evidence from pre-school extension in Franc', in J. Ermisch, M. Jantti, and T. Smeeding (eds) *Inequality from Childhood to Adulthood: A Cross-National Perspective on the Transmission of Advantage*. New York: Russell Sage Foundation.

Duvander, A.-Z. and Haas, L. (2013) 'Sweden country note', in P. Moss (ed.) *International Review of Leave Policies and Research 2013*. (www.leavenetwork.org/lp_and_r_ reports/).

Early Childhood Education Taskforce (New Zealand) (2011) *An Agenda for Amazing Children: Final Report*. (www.taskforce.ece.govt.nz/wp-content/uploads/2011/06/ Final_Report_ECE_Taskforce.pdf).

Edmiston, B. (2007) *Forming Ethical Identities in Early Childhood Play*. London: Routledge.

Eisenstadt, N. (2011) *Providing a Sure Start: How Government Discovered Early Childhood*. Bristol: Policy Press.

Elfström, I. (2003) 'Portfolie, individuella handlingsplaner och pedagogisk dokumentation, vad är skillnaden?' [Portfolios, individual action plans and pedagogical documentation, what is the difference?], *Modern barndom*, 7, 12–15.

Emmott, S. (2013) *10 Billion*. London: Penguin Books.

European Commission (2006) *Efficiency and Equity in European Education and Training Systems* (COM(2006) 481 final). Brussels: European Commission. (http://ec.europa.eu/education/policies/2010/doc/comm481_en.pdf).

European Commission (2011) *Early Childhood Education and Care: Providing All Our Children with the Best Start for the World of Tomorrow* (COM(2011) 66 final). Brussels: European Commission. (http://eur-lex.europa.eu/LexUriServ/LexUriServ.do?uri=COM:2011:0066:FIN:EN:PDF).

European Commission (2013a) *Towards Social Investment for Growth and Cohesion* (COM(2013) 83 final). Brussels: European Commission. (ec.europa.eu/social/BlobServlet?docId=9761&langId=en).

European Commission (2013b) *Barcelona Objectives: The development of childcare facilities for young children in Europe with a view to sustainable and inclusive growth*. (http://ec.europa.eu/justice/gender-quality/files/documents/130531_barcelona_en.pdf).

European Commission Childcare Network (1996) *Quality Targets in Services for Young Children*. Brussels: Equal Opportunities Unit.

Facer, K. (2011) *Learning Futures*. London: Routledge.

Fendler, L. (2001) 'Educating flexible souls: The construction of subjectivity through developmentality and interaction', in K. Hultqvist and G. Dahlberg (eds) *Governing the Child in the New Millennium*. London: RoutledgeFalmer.

Fielding, M. and Moss, P. (2011) *Radical Education and the Common School: A Democratic Alternative*. London: Routledge.

Fisher, B. and Tronto, J. (1990) 'Toward a feminist theory of caring', in E. Abel and M. Nelson (eds) *Circles of Care, Work and Identity in Women's Lives*. New York: State University of New York Press.

Flax, J. (1990) *Thinking Fragments: Psychoanalysis, Feminism and Postmodernism in the Contemporary West*. Berkeley and Los Angeles, CA: University of California Press.

Flyvbjerg, B. (2006) 'Social science that matters', *Foresight Europe* (October 2005–March 2006), 38–42.

Fortunati, A. (2006) *The Education of Young Children as a Community Project: The Experience of San Miniato*. Azzano San Paolo: Edizioni Junior.

Foucault, M. (1983) 'On the genealogy of ethics: An overview of work in progress', in H. Dreyfus and P. Rabinow (eds) *Michel Foucault: Beyond Structuralism and Hermeneutics*. Chicago, IL: University of Chicago Press.

Foucault, M. (1984) 'What is enlightenment?', in P. Rabinow (ed.) *The Foucault Reader*. New York: Pantheon Books.

Foucault, M. (1987) 'The ethic of care for the self as a practice of freedom', in J. Bernauer and D. Rasmussen (eds) *The Final Foucault*. Cambridge, MA: MIT Press.

Foucault, M. (1988) *Politics, Philosophy, Culture: Interviews and Other Writings 1977–1984*, trans. Ala Sheridan and others. London: Routledge.

Fraser, N. (1997) 'After the family wage: A postindustrial thought experiment', in *Justice Interruptus: Critical Reflections on the 'Postsocialist' Condition*. New York: Routledge.

Freire, P. (1996 edn) *Pedagogy of the Oppressed*. London: Penguin Books.

Freire, P. (1998) *Pedagogy of Freedom: Ethics, Democracy and Civic Courage*. Lanham, MD: Rowan and Littlefield.

Freire, P. (2004 edn.) *Pedagogy of Hope*. London: Continuum.

Friedman, M. (1962/1982) *Capitalism and Freedom* (1982 edn). Chicago, IL: University of Chicago Press.

Fusulier, B. (2009) 'Belgium: Articulating work and family: The gendered use of institutional measures', in P. Moss (ed.) *International Review of Leave Policies and Related Research 2009* (Employment Relations Research Series No. 102). London: Department for Business, Innovations and Skills (www.berr.gov.uk/files/file52778.pdf.

Galardini, A. (2008) 'Pedagogistas in Italy', *Children in Europe*, 8, 18.

Galardini, A.L. and Giovannini, D. (2001) 'Pistoia: Creating a dynamic, open system to serve children, families and community', in L. Gandini and C. Pope Edwards (eds) *Bambini: The Italian Approach to Infant/Toddler Care*. New York: Teachers College Press.

Gaudin, T. (2008) *The World in 2025: A Challenge to Reason*. Brussels: European Commission DG Research (ftp://ftp.cordis.europa.eu/pub/fp7/ssh/docs/the_world_in_2025_en.pdf).

Gillies, D. (2011) 'State education as high-yield investment: Human capital theory in European policy discourse', *Journal of Pedagogy*, 2 (2), 224–45.

George, S. (1999) 'A short history of neoliberalism: Twenty years of elite economics and emerging opportunities for change'. Paper presented at conference *Economic Sovereignty in a Globalising World*, Bangkok, Thailand, 24–6 March 1999. (www.globalexchange.org/campaigns/econ101/neoliberalism.html).

George, S. (2009) *Too Young for Respect? Realising Respect for Young Children in Their Everyday Environments*. Den Haag: Bernard van Leer Foundation.

Gibbons, A. (2011) 'Are we in the middle of a sixth mass extinction', *Science Now*, 2 March 2011. (http://news.sciencemag.org/sciencenow/2011/03/are-we-in-the-middle-of-a-sixth-.html).

Gibson-Clarke, J.-K. (2006, 2nd edn.) *The End of Capitalism (As We Knew It): A Feminist Critique of Political Economy*. Minneapolis, MN: University of Minnesota Press.

Giroux, H. (2004) 'Neoliberalism and the demise of democracy: Resurrecting hope in dark times', *Dissident Voice*, 7 August 2004 (www.dissidentvoice.org/Aug04/Giroux0807.htm).

Giudici, C., Rinaldi, C. and Krechevsky, M. (eds) (2001) *Making Learning Visible: Children as Individual and Group Learners*. Reggio Emilia: Reggio Children.

Gray, J. (2007) *Black Mass: Apocalyptic Religion and the Death of Utopia*. London: Allen Lane.

Gray, J. (2009) *Gray's Anatomy: John Gray's Selected Writings*. London: Allen Lane.

Green, A. and Mostafa, T. (2011) *Preschool Education and Care: A Win-Win Policy? LLAKES Research Paper 32*. London: Institute of Education, University of London.

Guattari, F. (2000) *The Three Ecologies*. London: Athlone Press.

Hacker, J.S. and Pierson, P. (2011) *Winner-Take-All Politics: How Washington Made the Rich Richer – and Turned Its Back on the Middle Class*. New York: Simon and Schuster.

Hall, S., Massey, D. and Rustin, M. (2013) 'After neoliberalism: Analysing the present', in *After Neoliberalism? The Kilburn Manifesto*. London: Soundings. (www.lwbooks.co.uk/journals/soundings/pdfs/manifestoframingstatement.pdf).

Halpin, D. (2003) *Hope and Education*. London: Routledge.

Hammersley, M. (2013) *The Myth of Research-Based Policy and Practice*. London: Sage.

Hardt, M. and Negri, A. (2005) *Multitude: War and Democracy in the Age of Empire*. London: Penguin Books.

Häring, N. and Douglas, N. (2012) *Economists and the Powerful: Convenient Theories, Distorted Facts, Ample Awards*. London: Anthem Press.

Harvey, D. (2000) *Spaces of Hope*. Edinburgh: Edinburgh University Press.

Harvey, D. (2005) *A Brief History of Neoliberalism*. Oxford: Oxford University Press.

Harvey, D. (2010) *The Enigma of Capital and the Crisis of Capitalism*. London: Profile Books.

Hatcher, R. (2012) 'Democracy and participation in the governance of local school systems', *Journal of Educational Administration and History*, 44 (1), 21–42.

Heckman, J. and Masterov, D. (2007) 'The productivity argument for investing in young children'. T.W. Schultz Award Lecture given at the Allied Social Sciences Association annual meeting, Chicago, 5–7 January 2007 (http://jenni.uchicago.edu/human-inequality/papers/Heckman_final_all_wp_2007-03-22c_jsb.pdf).

Held, V. (2002) 'Care and the extension of markets', *Hypatia*, 17 (2), 19–33.

Henry, J.S. (2012) *The Price of Offshore Revisited: New Estimates for 'Missing' Global Private Wealth, Income, Inequality and Lost Taxes*. (www.taxjustice.net/cms/upload/pdf/Price_of_Offshore_Revisited_120722.pdf).

Hill, A. (2012) 'Millions of working families one push from penury, Guardian research finds', *The Guardian*, 18 June 2012. (www.guardian.co.uk/society/2012/jun/18/working-britons-one-push-from-penury).

House of Commons Children, Schools and Families Committee (2010) *Sure Start Children's Centres*, Fifth Report of Session 2009–10, Volumes I and II, HC 130-I and HCO 130-II. London: The Stationery Office.

Hoyuelos, A. (2004) 'A pedagogy of transgression', *Children in Europe*, 6, 6–7.

Hoyuelos, A. (2013) *The Ethics in Loris Malaguzzi's Philosophy*. Reykjavik: Isalda.

Hutton, W. and Schneider, P. (2008) *The Failure of Market Failure: Towards a 21st Century Keynesianism*. London: NESTA.

Hyslop-Margison, E.J. and Sears, A.M. (2006) *Neo-Liberalism, Globalization and Human Capital Learning: Reclaiming Education for Democratic Citizenship*. Dordrecht: Springer.

Institute of Medicine of the National Academies (2013) *U.S. Health in International Perspective: Shorter Lives, Poorer Health: Report Brief*. (www.iom.edu/~/media/Files/Report%20Files/2013/US-Health-International-Perspective/USHealth_Intl_PerspectiveRB.pdf).

International Panel on Climate Change (2013) *Working Group I Contribution to the IPCC Fifth Assessment Report Climate Change 2013: The Physical Science Basis Summary for Policymakers*. (www.climatechange2013.org/images/uploads/WGIAR5-SPM_Approved27Sep2013.pdf).

Jackson, T. (2009) *Prosperity without Growth*. (www.sd-commission.org.uk/data/files/publications/prosperity_without_growth_report.pdf).

Jeffreys, T. (2011) 'Payment by results for Sure Start Children's Centres'. Letter sent on 9 June 2011 from Department of Education. (http://media.education.gov.uk/assets/files/pdf/t/tom%20jeffery%20letter%20to%20dcss%209%20june%202011.pdf).

Judt, T. (2009) 'What is living and what is dead in Social Democracy?', *New York Review of Books*, 56 (20), 86–97.

Judt, T. (2010) *Ill Fares the Land*. London: Allen Lane.

Kaga, Y., Bennett, J. and Moss, P. (2010) *Caring and Learning Together: Cross-National Research on the Integration of ECCE within Education*. Paris: UNESCO. (unesdoc. unesco.org/images/0018/001878/187818E.pdf).

Kagan, J. (2000) *Three Seductive Ideas*. Cambridge, MA: Harvard University Press.

Kant, I. (1784) *Was ist Äufklarung?* [What is Enlightenment?] (www.fordham.edu/ halsall/mod/kant-whatis.asp).

Kenway, P. (2008) *Addressing in-Work Poverty*. York: Joseph Rowntree Foundation. (www.jrf.org.uk/sites/files/jrf/2269-poverty-employment-income.pdf).

Kumhof, M. and Rancière, R. (2010) *Inequality, Leverage and Crises*. IMF Working Paper 10/268. Washington, DC: International Monetary Fund. (www.imf.org/ external/pubs/ft/wp/2010/wp10268.pdf).

Laing & Buisson (2010) *Children's Nurseries UK Market Report*. London: Laing & Buisson Ltd.

Langsted, O. (1994) 'Looking at quality from the child's perspective', in P. Moss and A. Pence (eds) *Valuing Quality in Early Childhood Services: New Approaches to Defining Quality*. London: Paul Chapman Publishing.

Lather, P. (2006) 'Foucauldian scientificity: Rethinking the nexus of qualitative research and education policy analysis', *International Journal of Qualitative Studies in Education*, 19 (6), 782–91.

Lazzarato, M. (2009) 'Neoliberalism in action: Inequality, insecurity and the reconstitution of the social', *Theory, Culture and Society*, 26 (6), 109–33.

Lazzari, A. (2011) 'Reconceptualising professional development in early childhood: A study on teachers' professionalism carried out in Bologna province'. PhD thesis, University of Bologna.

Leadbeater, C. (2008) *What's Next? 21 Ideas for 21st Century Learning*. London: The Innovations Unit. (www.innovationunit.org/sites/default/files/What's%20Next%20-%2 021%20ideas%20for%2021st%20century%20learning.pdf).

Lenz Taguchi, H. (1997) *Varför pedagogisk documentation* [why pedagogical documentation]. Stockholm: HLS Förlag.

Lenz Taguchi, H. (2010a) 'Rethinking pedagogical practices in early childhood education: A multidimensional approach to learning and inclusion', in N. Yelland (ed.) *Contemporary Perspectives on Early Childhood Education*. Maidenhead: Open University Press.

Lenz Taguchi, H. (2010b) *Going Beyond the Theory/Practice Divide in Early Childhood Education: Introducing an Intra-active Pedagogy*. London: Routledge.

Lenz Taguchi, H. and Munkammar, I. (2003) *Consolidating Governmental Early Childhood Education and Care Services under the Ministry of Education and Science: A Swedish Case Study*. Paris: UNESCO. (http://unesdoc.unesco.org/images/0013/001301/130135e.pdf).

Levitas, R. (2003) 'Introduction: The elusive idea of utopia', *History of the Human Sciences*, 16 (1), 1–10.

Levitas, R. (2008) 'Be realistic: Demand the impossible', *New Formations*, 65, Autumn, 78–93.

Levitas, R. (2010) 'Secularism and Post-secularism in Roberto Unger and Ernst Bloch: Towards a Utopian Ontology'. *Journal of Contemporary Thought*, Summer issue.

Li, T.M. (2007) *The Will to Improve: Governmentality, Developmnt and the Practice of Politics*. Durham, NC: Duke University Press.

Lloyd, E. (2012) 'Childcare markets: An introduction', in E. Lloyd and H. Penn (eds) *Childcare Markets: Can They Deliver an Equitable Service?* Bristol: Policy Press.

Lloyd, E. and Penn, H. (eds) (2012) *Childcare Markets: Can They Deliver an Equitable Service?* Bristol: Policy Press.

Luth, C. (1998) 'On Wilhelm von Humboldt's theory of *Bildung*. Dedicated to Wolfgang Klafki for his 70th birthday', *Journal of Curriculum Studies*, 30 (1), 43–60.

MacNaughton, G. (2005) *Doing Foucault in Early Childhood Studies: Applying Poststructural Ideas*. London: Routledge.

Malaguzzi, L. (1995) 'La storia, le idee, la cultura', in C. Edwards, L. Gandini and G. Forman (eds) *I cento linguaggi dei bambini*. Bergamo: Edizioni Junior.

Marangos, A. and Plantenga, J. (2006) 'Introducing market forces', *Children in Europe*, 11, 18–19.

Maroney, H.J. (nd) Review of *The End of Capitalism (As We Knew It): A Feminist Critique of Political Economy* (http://clogic.eserver.org/2–1/maroney.html)

Marquand, D. (2004) *The Decline of the Public*. Cambridge: Polity Press.

Meagher, G. (2004) 'Do Australians want a private welfare state? Are they getting one anyway?' *The Drawing Board: An Australian Review of Public Affairs*, 3 May 2004. Sydney: School of Economics and Political Science, University of Sydney. (www.australianreview.net/digest/2004/05/meagher.html).

Meleady, C. and Broadhead, P. (2002) '"The norm not the exception": Putting diversity in its place', *Children in Europe*, 2, 14–16.

Miller, P. and Rose, N. (1993) 'Governing economic life', in M. Gane and T. Johnston (eds) *Foucault's New Domains*. London: Routledge.

Ministry of Education (New Zealand) (2013) Centres of Innovation (COI) Programme Ngā Kauhanga Whakarehu. (www.educate.ece.govt.nz/Programmes/CentresOfInnovation.aspx).

Mirowski, P. (2013a) *Never Let a Serious Crisis Go to Waste: How Neoliberalism Survived the Financial Meltdown*. London: Verso.

Mirowski, P. (2013b) *The Thirteen Commandments of Neoliberalism*. (www.the-utopian.org/post/ . . . /the-thirteen-commandments-of-neoliberalis).

Mitchell, L. (2011) 'Enquiring teachers and democratic politics: Transformation of New Zealand's early childhood education landscape', *Early Years*, DOI:10.1080/09575146.2011.588787.

Morel, N., Palier, B. and Palme, J. (eds) (2012) *Towards a Social Investment Welfare State? Ideas, Policies and Challenges*. Bristol: Policy Press.

Morin, E. (1999) *Homeland Earth: A Manifesto for the New Millennium*. Cresskill, NJ: Hampton Press.

Morin, E. (2001) *Seven Complex Lessons in Education for the Future*. Paris: UNESCO.

Morton, K. (2013) 'Bright Horizons adds 64 settings in £45m deal', *Nursery World*, 22 April–5 May 2013, 6–7 (http://www.nurseryworld.co.uk/nursery-world/news/1106719/bright-horizons-acquires-kidsunlimited).

Moss, P. (2009) *There Are Alternatives! Markets and Democratic Experimentalism in Early Childhood Education and Care*. The Hague: Bernard van leer Foundation. (www.bernardvanleer.org/publications_results?SearchableText=B-WOP-053).

Moss, P. (2013) 'The relationship between early childhood and compulsory education: A properly political question', in P. Moss (ed.) *Early Childhood and Compulsory Education: Reconceptualising the Relationship*. London: Routledge.

Mouffe, C. (2000) *The Democratic Paradox*. London: Verso.

Mouffe, C. (2007) 'Artistic activism and agonistic spaces', *Art and Research*, 1 (2), Summer.

Musatti, T., Giovannini, D., Mayer, S. and Group Nido LagoMago (2014) 'How to construct a curriculum in an Italian nido', in C. Cameron and L. Miller (eds) *International Perspectives in the Early Years*. London: Sage.

National Scientific Council on the Developing Child (2007) *The Timing and Quality of Early Experiences Combine to Shape Brain Architecture: Working Paper #5*. (http://developingchild.harvard.edu/index.php/download_file/-/view/74/?).

NESSE (2009) *Early Childhood Education and Care: Key Lessons from Research for Policy Makers*. (www.nesse.fr/nesse/activities/reports/ecec-report-pdf).

Nussbaum, M. (2010) *Not for Profit: Why Democracy Needs the Humanities*. Princeton, NJ: Princeton University Press.

Nxumalo, F., Pacini-Ketchabaw, V. and Rowan, M.C. (2011) 'Lunch time in the child care center: Neoliberal assemblages in early childhood education', *Journal of Pedagogy*, 2 (2), 195–223.

Obama, B. (2013) *State of the Union Address, 12 February 2013*. (www.whitehouse. gov/the-press-office/2013/02/12/remarks-president-state-union-address).

Oberhuemer, P. (2005) 'Conceptualising the early childhood professional'. Paper given at the *15th Annual EECERA Conference*, Malta, 3 September 2005.

OECD (Organisation for Economic Cooperation and Development) (2001). *Starting Strong I*. Paris: OECD.

OECD (2006) *Starting Strong II*. Paris: OECD.

OECD (2011a) *Investing in High-Quality Early Childhood Education and Care (ECEC)* (www.oecd.org/education/preschoolandschool/48980282.pdf).

OECD (2011b) *Does Participation in Pre-Primary Education Translate into Better Learning Outcomes at School? PISA in Focus 1*. (http://www.oecd-ilibrary.org/education/does-participation-in-pre-primary-education-translate-into-better-learning-outcomes-at-school_5k9h362tpvxp-en).

OECD (2011c) *Divided We Stand: Why Inequality Keeps Rising. US Country Note*. (www. oecd.org/unitedstates/49170253.pdf).

OECD (2012) *Starting Strong III: A Quality Toolbox for Early Childhood Education and Care. Executive Summary*. Paris: OECD. (www.oecd.org/edu/school/49325825.pdf).

OECD (2013) 'Size of GDP', in *OECD Factbook 2013: Economic, Environmental and Social Statistics*. (http://dx.doi.org/10.1787/factbook-2013–10-en).

Olssen, M. and Peters, M. (2005) 'Neoliberalism, Higher Education and the Knowledge Economy: From the free market to knowledge capitalism', *Journal of Education Policy*, 20 (3), 313–47.

Olsson, L.M. (2009) *Movement and Experimentation in Young Children's Learning: Deleuze and Guattari in Early Childhood Education*. London: Routledge.

Olsson, L.M. (2012) 'Eventicizing curriculum learning to read and write through becoming a citizen of the world', *Journal of Curriculum Theorizing*, 28 (1), 88–107.

Olsson, L.M. (2013) 'Taking children's questions seriously: The need for creative thought', *Global Studies of Childhood*, 3 (3), 230–53.

Osberg, D. and Biesta, G. (2007) 'Beyond presence: Epistemological and pedagogical implications of "strong"emergence', *Interchange*, 38(1), 31–51.

Osgood, J. (2004) 'Time to get down to business? The responses of early years practitioners to entrepreneurial approaches to professionalism', *Journal of Early Childhood Research*, 2 (1), 5–24.

Otto, D. (1999) 'Everything is dangerous: Some poststructural tools for human rights law', *Australian Journal of Human Rights*, 5 (1), 17–47.

Parijs, P. van (2004) 'A basic income for all: A brief defence to secure real freedom, grant everyone a subsistence income', in L.F.M. Groot (ed) *Basic Income, Unemployment and Compensatory Justice*. Dordrecht: Springer.

Pawson, R. (2006) *Evidence-Based Policy: A Realist Perspective*. London: Sage.

Penn, H. (2010) 'Shaping the future: How human capital arguments about investment in early childhood are being (mis)used in poor countries', in N. Yelland (ed.) *Contemporary Perspectives on Early Childhood Education*. Maidenhead: Open University Press.

Penn, H. (2011) *Quality in Early Childhood Services: An International Perspective*. Maidenhead: Open University Press.

Penn, H., Burton, V., Lloyd, E., Mugford, M., Potter, S. and Sayeed, Z. (2006a) *Early Years: What Is Known about the Long-Term Economic Impact of Centre-Based Early Childhood Interventions? Technical Report*. London: EPPI-centre, Institute of Education University of London. (http://eppi.ioe.ac.uk/cms/LinkClick.aspx?fileticket=l5do4A7UCSo%3D&tabid=676&mid=1572).

Penn, H., Burton, V., Lloyd, E., Mugford, M., Potter, S. and Sayeed, Z. (2006b) *Early Years: What Is Known about the Long-Term Economic Impact of Centre-Based Early Childhood Interventions? Summary*. London: EPPI-centre, Institute of Education University of London. (http://eppi.ioe.ac.uk/cms/LinkClick. aspx?fileticket=LrZZFRxoUr4%3d&tabid=676&mid=1572).

Pinder, D. (2002) 'In defence of utopian urbanism: Imagining cities after "the end of utopia"', *Geografisker Annaler*, Series B 84, B: 3–4, 229–41.

Plantenga, J. (2012) 'Local providers and loyal parents: Competition and consumer choice in the Dutch childcare market', in E. Lloyd and H. Penn (eds) *Childcare Markets: Can They Deliver Equitable Service?* Bristol: Policy Press.

Power Inquiry (2006) *The Report of Power: An Independent Inquiry into Britain's Democracy*. London: The Power Inquiry.

Pring, R. (2007) *John Dewey*. London: Continuum.

Puma, M., Bell, S., Cook, R., Heid, C., Broene, P., Jenkins, F. Mashburn, A. and Downer, J. (2012) *Third Grade Follow-Up to the Head Start Impact Study Final Report. OPRE Report # 2012–45*. Washington, DC: Office of Planning, Research and Evaluation, Administration for Children and Families, U.S. Department of Health and Human Services. (www.acf.hhs.gov/sites/default/files/opre/head_start_report.pdf).

Radin, N.J. (1996) *Contested Commodities: The Trouble with Trade in Sex, Children, Body Parts, and Other Things*. Cambridge, MA: Harvard University Press.

Ransom, S. (2003) 'Public accountability in the age of neoliberal governance', *Journal of Educational Policy*, 18 (5), 459–80.

Read, J. (2009) 'A Genealogy of homo-economicus: Neoliberalism and the production of subjectivity', *Foucault Studies*, 6, 25–36.

Readings, B. (1996) *The University in Ruins*. Cambridge, MA: Harvard University Press.

Reggio Children (2012) *One City, Many Children: Reggio Emilia, a History of the Present*. Reggio Emilia: Reggio Children.

Rinaldi, C. (1993) 'The emergent curriculum and social constructivism', in C. Edwards, L. Gandini and G. Forman (eds) *The Hundred Languages of Children: The Reggio Emilia Approach to Early Childhood Education*. Norwood, NJ: Ablex.

Rinaldi, C. (2005) 'Is a curriculum necessary?' *Children in Europe*, 9, 15.

Rinaldi, C. (2006) *In Dialogue with Reggio Emilia: Listening, Researching and Learning*. London: Routledge.

Rose, H. and Rose, S. (2012) *Genes, Cells and Brains: The Promethean Promises of the New Biology*. London: Verso.

Rose, N. (1999) *Powers of Freedom: Reframing Political Thought*. Cambridge: Cambridge University Press.

Rossi, M. (2013) 'Consider Jack and Oskar', *London Review of Books*, 35 (3), 7 February 2013, 27–8.

Rowbotham, S. (1979) 'The women's movement and organizing for socialism', in S. Rowbotham, L. Segal and H. Wainwright (eds) *Beyond the Fragments: Feminism and the Making of Socialism*. London: Merlin Press.

Roy, K. (2004) 'Overcoming nihilism: From communication to Deleuzian expression', *Educational Philosophy and Theory*, 36 (3), 297–312.

Ruhm, C. and Waldfogel, J. (2011) *Long-Term Effects of Early Childhood Care and Education*, IZA DP. No.6149. (http://ftp.iza.org/dp6149.pdf).

Santos, B. de S. (1995). *Towards a New Common Sense: Law, Science and Politics in the Paradigmatic Transition*. London: Routledge.

Santos, B. de S. (2004) 'Interview with Boaventura de Sousa Santos', *Globalisation, Societies and Education*, 2 (2), 147–60.

Schostak, J. and Goodson, I. (2012) 'What's wrong with democracy at the moment and why it matters for research and education', *Power and Education*, 4 (3), 257–76.

Sellers, M. (2013) *Young Children becoming Curriculum: Deleuze, Te Whāriki and Curricular Understandings*. London: Routledge.

Shah, H. and Goss, S. (eds) (2007) *Democracy and the Public Realm*. London: Compass and Lawrence Wishart.

Skidmore, P. and Bound, K. (2008) *The Everyday Democracy Index*. London: Demos.

Skolverket (2010) *Curriculum for the Preschool Lpfö 98 Revised 2010*. Stockholm: Skolverket. (www.skolverket.se/publikationer?id=2704).

Skolverket (2012) *Facts and Figures 2011. Preschool Activities, School-Age Childcare, Schools and Adult Education in Sweden. Summary of Report 363*. Stockholm: Skolverket. (www.skolverket.se/publikationer?id=2768).

Sosinsky, L.S. (2012) 'Childcare markets in the US: Supply and demand, quality and cost, and public policy', in E. Lloyd and H. Penn (eds) *Childcare Markets: Can They Deliver Equitable Service?* Bristol: Policy Press.

Stern, J. (2013) 'Surprise in schools: Martin Buber and dialogic schooling', *FORUM*, 55 (1), 45–58.

Stiglitz, J.E. (2013a) 'The end of neo-liberalism?', *Project Syndicate Commentary*, July. (www.project-syndicate.org/commentary/the-end-of-neo-liberalism-).

Stiglitz, J.E. (2013b) *The Price of Inequality*. London: Penguin Books.

Sumsion, J. (2006) 'The corporatization of Australian childcare: Towards an ethical audit and research agenda', *Journal of Early Childhood Research*, 4 (2), 99–120.

Sylva, K., Melhuish, E., Sammons, P., Siraj-Blatchford, I. and Taggart, B. (2008) *Final Report from the Primary Phase: Preschool, School and Family Influences on Children's Development during Key Stage 2*. (http://eppe.ioe.ac.uk/eppe3–11/eppe3–11%20pdfs/eppepapers/Final%203–11%20report%20DfE-RR061%2027nov08.pdf).

Tallis, R. (2011) *Aping Mankind: Neuromania, Darwinitis and the Misrepresentation of Humanity*. Durham: Acumen.

Tallis, R. (2013) 'Think brain scans can reveal our innermost thoughts? Think again', *The Observer*, 2 June 2013. (www.guardian.co.uk/commentisfree/2013/jun/02brain-scans-innermost-thoughts).

Taylor, A. (2013) *Reconfiguring the Natures of Childhood*. London: Routledge.

Taylor, C. (1995) 'Overcoming epistemology', in *Philosophical Arguments*. Cambridge, MA: Harvard University Press.

Thatcher, M. (1981) 'Economics are the method: The object is to change the soul', *The Sunday Times*, 3 May 1981. (www.margaretthatcher.org/document/104475).

Thomas, L. (2011) 'Decentralisation for schools, but not for knowledge: The RSA area based curriculum and the limits of localism in coalition education policy', *FORUM*, 53 (2), 293–304.

Thomson, P. Lingard, B. and Wrigley, T. (2012) *Reimagining Social Change in Changing Schools: Alternative Ways to Make a World of Difference*. London: Routledge.

Tizard, J., Moss, P. and Perry, J. (1976) *All Our Children: Preschool Services in a Changing Society*. London: Temple-Smith/New Society.

Tobin, J. (2007) 'Rôle de la théorie dans le movement Reconceptualiser l'éducation de la petite enfance', in G. Brougère and M. Vandenbroeck (eds) *Repenser l'éducation des jeunes enfants*. Brussels: P.I.E. Peter Lang.

Tronto, J. (1993) *Moral Boundaries: A Political Argument for the Ethics of Care*. London: Routledge.

Truss, E. (2013) 'More great childcare'. Speech to a *Policy Exchange meeting*, London, 29 January 2013. (www.policyexchange.org.uk/modevents/item/elizabeth-truss-mp-more-great-childcare).

Ulmer, G.L. (1985) *Applied Grammatology: Post(e)-pedagogy from Jacques Derrida to Joseph Beuys*. Baltimore, MD: Johns Hopkins University Press.

UNESCO (2012) *Youth and Skills: Putting Education to Work*. Paris: UNESCO (http://unesdoc.unesco.org/images/0021/002180/218003e.pdf).

Unger, R. (1998) *Democracy Realized: The Progressive Alternative*. London: Verso

Unger, R. (2004, 2nd edn) *False Necessity: Anti-Necessitarian Social Theory in the Service of Radical Democracy*. London: Verso.

Unger, R.M. (2005a) *What Should the Left Propose?* London: Verso.

Unger, R.M. (2005b) 'The future of the Left: James Crabtree interviews Roberto Unger', *Renewal*, 13 (2/3), 173–84.

UNICEF (2010) *The Children Left Behind: A League Table of Inequality in Child Well-Being in the World's Rich Countries. Innocenti Report Card 9*. Florence: UNICEF Office of Research – Innocenti. (www.unicef-irc.org/publications/pdf/rc9_eng.pdf).

UNICEF (2012) *Measuring Child Poverty: New League Tables of Child Poverty in the World's Rich Countries. Innocenti Report Card 11*. Florence: UNICEF Office of Research – Innocenti. (www.unicef-irc.org/publications/pdf/rc10_eng.pdf).

UNICEF (2013) *Child Well-Being in Rich Countries: A Comparative Overview. Innocenti Report Card 11*. Florence: UNICEF Office of Research – Innocenti. (www.unicef.org.uk/Images/Campaigns/FINAL_RC11-ENG-LORES-fnl2.pdf).

Vecchi, V. (1996) 'Birth of two horses', in *The Hundred Languages of Children (Catalogue of the Hundred Languages of Children exhibition)*. Reggio Emilia: Reggio Children.

Vecchi, V. (2004) 'The multiple fonts of knowledge', *Children in Europe*, 6, 18–21.

Vecchi, V. (2010) *Art and Creativity in Reggio Emilia: Exploring the Role and Potentiality of Ateliers in Early Childhood Education*. London: Routledge.

Wagner, J.T. (2006) 'An outsider's perspective: Childhoods and early education in the Nordic countries', in J. Einarsdottir and J.T. Wagner (eds) *Nordic Childhoods and Early Education: Philosophy, Research, Policy and Practice in Denmark, Finland, Iceland, Norway, and Sweden*. Greenwich, CT: Information Age Publishing.

Waldfogel, J. (2004) *Social Mobility, Life Chances and the Early Years*. Case Paper 88. London: Centre for the Analysis of Social Inclusion.

Waslander, S., Pater, C. and Weide, M. van der (2010) *Markets in Education: An Analytical Review of Empirical Research on Market Mechanisms in Education*. OECD Education Working Papers, No. 52. Paris: OECD. (www.oecd.org/edu/ceri/47229500.pdf).

Wave Trust (2013) *Conception to Age 2: The Age of Opportunity*. London: Wave Trust. (www.wavetrust.org/key-publications/reports/conception-to-age-2).

White, J. (2005) *The Curriculum and the Child: The Selected Writings of John White*. London: RoutledgeFalmer.

White, S. (2008) 'Markets, time and citizenship', in S. White and D. Leighton (eds) *Building a Citizen Society: The Emerging Politics of Republican Democracy*. London: Lawrence and Wishart.

White House (2013) *Fact Sheet President Obama's Plan for Early Education for All Americans*. (www.whitehouse.gov/the-press-office/2013 /02/13/fact-sheet-president-obama-s-plan-early education-all-americans).

Whitty, G., Power, S. and Halpin, D. (1998) *Devolution and Choice in Schools*. Buckingham: Open University Press.

Wilkinson, R. and Pickett, K. (2009) *The Spirit Level: Why More Equal Societies Almost Always Do Better*. London: Allen Lane.

World Economic Forum (2013) *Table 3: The Global Competitiveness Index 2012–2013 Rankings and 2011–2012 Comparisons*. (www3.weforum.org/docs/CSI/2012–13/GCR_Rankings_2012–13.pdf).

Wright, E.O. (2006) 'Compass points: Towards a socialist alternative', *New Left Review*, 41 (September–October), 93–124.

Wright, E.O. (2007) 'Guidelines for envisioning real utopias', *Soundings*, 36 (Summer), 26–39.

Wright, E.O. (2010) *Envisioning Real Utopias*. London: Verso.

Wright, E.O. (2012) 'Envisioning real utopias: Alternatives within and beyond capitalism'. David Glass Memorial lecture, London School of Economics, 22 May 2012. (www2.lse.ac.uk/assets/richmedia/channels/publicLecturesAndEvents/slides/20120522_1830_EnvisioningRealUtopias_sl.pdf).

Wright, E.O. (2013) *Prospectus for Winter School*. University of Wisconsin-Madison. (issr.uq.edu.au/system/storage/serve/20380/WinterSchoolFlyer.pdf?).

Yeatman, A. (1994) *Postmodern Revisionings of the Political*. London: Routledge.

Young, R. (1990) *White Mythologies: Writing History and the West*. London: Routledge.

Zigler, E. (2003) 'Forty years of believing in magic is enough', *Social Policy Report*, 17 (1), 10.

Index